BROWS 4/18 £17.99 (R)

Social Policy for Social Work

Social Policy for Social Work

Placing Social Work in its Wider Context

LORRAINE GREEN AND KAREN CLARKE

polity

First published in 2016 by Polity Press

Polity Press
65 Bridge Street
Cambridge CB2 1UR, UK

Polity Press
350 Main Street
Malden, MA 02148, USA

ISBN-13: 978-0-7456-6082-0
ISBN-13: 978-0-7456-6083-7 (pb)

A catalogue record for this book is available from the British Library.

Library of Congress Cataloging-in-Publication Data
Green, Lorraine Carol, author.
    Social policy for social work : placing social work in its wider context / Lorraine Green, Karen Clarke.
      pages cm
    Includes bibliographical references and index.
    ISBN 978-0-7456-6082-0 (hardcover : alk. paper) -- ISBN 0-7456-6082-7 (hardcover : alk. paper) -- ISBN 978-0-7456-6083-7 (pbk. : alk. paper) -- ISBN 0-7456-6083-5 (pbk. : alk. paper) 1. Social service--Great Britain. 2. Social policy. 3. Public welfare--Great Britain. 4. Great Britain--Social policy. I. Clarke, Karen, author. II. Title.
    HV245.G864 2016
    361.6'10941--dc23
                                                                              2015024620

Typeset in 9.5 on 12 pt Utopia
by Servis Filmsetting Ltd, Stockport, Cheshire
Printed and bound in the UK by Clays Ltd. St Ives PLC.

For further information on Polity, visit our website: politybooks.com

Contents

Acknowledgements

A number of people have helped us by commenting on draft chapters of this book. We would like to thank John Churcher, Ros Day, Sue Ferris, Caroline Glendinning and Nick Turnbull. Anna Churcher Clarke and Kirstein Rummery gave advice on specific issues. Thanks are due to the anonymous academic referees who reviewed the book for Polity and made some useful suggestions, and to Guy Davies, a Social Work MA student at Manchester University, who read the manuscript and gave us valuable feedback from a student perspective. Jonathan Skerrett, our editor at Polity Press, was both patient and encouraging, and Leigh Mueller was a meticulous and speedy copy-editor.

Acronyms and abbreviations

ADASS	Association of Directors of Adult Social Services
ADP	anti-discriminatory practice
AMHP	Approved Mental Health Professional
AOP	anti-oppressive practice
APPG	All Party Parliamentary Group
APSW	Association of Professors of Social Work
ASBO	anti-social behaviour order
ASYE	Assessed and Supported Year in Employment
BASW	British Association of Social Workers
CAF	Common Assessment Framework
Cafcass	Child and Family Court Advisory and Support Service
CAMHS	Child and Adolescent Mental Health Services
CCETSW	Central Council for Education and Training in Social Work
COS	Charity Organization Society
CPD	Continuing Professional Development
CQC	Care Quality Commission
CQSW	Certificate of Qualification in Social Work
CTO	community treatment order
DCLG	Department for Communities and Local Government
DCSF	Department of Children, Schools and Families
DfE	Department for Education
DFES	Department for Education and Skills
DH	Department of Health
DP	direct payment
DV	domestic violence
DVLA	Driver and Vehicle Licensing Authority
EBP	evidence-based practice
EC	European Community
ECHR	European Convention on Human Rights
ECtHR	European Court of Human Rights
ECJ	European Court of Justice
ECOSOC	Economic and Social Council of the United Nations
EHRC	Equality and Human Rights Commission
ESPN	European Social Policy Network
EU	European Union
FGM	Female Genital Mutilation
GDP	Gross Domestic Product
GP	General Practitioner

GSCC	General Social Care Council
HCPC	Health and Care Professions Council
HR	Human Resources
IASSW	International Association of Schools of Social Work
ICS	Integrated Children's System
ICSW	International Council on Social Welfare
IFSW	International Federation of Social Workers
IGO	International Government Organization
INGO	international non-governmental organization
JUCSWEC	Joint University Council Social Work Education Committee
LA	local authority
LCSB	Local Children's Safeguarding Board
MP	Member of Parliament
NGO	non-governmental organization
NHS	National Health Service
NICE	National Institute for Health and Care Excellence
NPM	new public management
OECD	Organisation for Economic Co-operation and Development
Ofsted	Office for Standards in Education
ONS	Office of National Statistics
OU	Open University
PA	personal assistant
PCF	Professional Capabilities Framework
PFI	Private Finance Initiative
RCT	randomized controlled trial
SCIE	Social Care Institute for Excellence
SCR	Serious Case Review
SES	socio-economic status
SEU	Social Exclusion Unit
SOP	Standards of Proficiency
SWTF	Social Work Task Force
TCSW	The College of Social Work
UDHR	Universal Declaration of Human Rights
UK	United Kingdom
UN	United Nations
UNCRC	United Nations Convention on the Rights of the Child
UNHCR	United Nations High Commissioner for Refugees
UNICEF	United Nations Children's Fund
USA	United States of America
VAT	Value-added Tax
WHO	World Health Organization
WTO	World Trade Organization

Introduction

The role of social workers and the kinds of problems they work with are shaped by the broader policy context they work within. This policy context is in turn the product of political decisions based on competing ideas about the nature of society and what role the state should play in meeting the needs of its citizens. The context for social work practice is, however, not confined to the nation state, as developments at a supranational level also affect the social policies of individual nations. Globalization has undermined the control which individual governments can exercise over the economy, with implications for employment, for how need is categorized and met, and for the resources available to be spent on welfare services. International treaties and conventions – such as the European Convention on Human Rights, or the United Nations (UN) Convention on the Rights of the Child – and the requirements of EU membership – such as equality legislation – create new rights for citizens and obligations for governments, which are also relevant to social work practice. This book aims to give social work and social policy students, practitioners and educators a critical understanding of social work in the UK and the issues which it currently faces, by placing it within this broader political, economic and social policy context.

The first section of this introduction briefly examines what social work is and how it has changed over time in terms of its role, professional status and location. The second section examines social policy, its permeable and contested boundaries and its relevance for social work. The final section explains the structure of the book and briefly summarizes the different chapters and their contents.

What is social work?

Social work in the UK originated in nineteenth-century philanthropic and state responses to the increasingly visible social problems associated with working-class poverty in the context of accelerated industrialization and urbanization. These responses took a number of different forms. From the 1870s, in a precursor to case-work, the Charity Organization Society (COS) worked with individual families to support them to help themselves out of poverty. A different kind of philanthropic activity, exemplified by the Settlement Movement, which began at around the same time, emphasized the potential of social action and a collective response to social problems that foreshadowed a community work approach within social work. Finally, the administration of the Poor Law by local government involved the assessment of individuals and families in terms of their eligibility for state support and the management of institutions such as the workhouse which catered for destitute people.

Professional social work in the twentieth century developed out of these antecedents in tandem with the evolution of the British welfare state in the period following the Second World War when social workers became state employees, mainly employed by local authorities. However, social workers also continued to work in the voluntary (third) sector, which has in recent times once again come to play a more significant role in delivering social work services, as has the private, for-profit sector. Social workers today are routinely found in a variety of voluntary, charitable and community organizations, and also in private residential care homes for the elderly and commercial fostering and adoption agencies. The great majority are, however, still state employees, employed primarily by local authorities and healthcare trusts.

While social work has always been concerned with meeting the needs of individuals and families, it has always also had a controlling function. The work of the COS was concerned with differentiating the 'deserving' from the 'undeserving' poor, in order to ensure that support was only provided to the 'deserving', and in this way was involved in disciplining the 'undeserving'. Contemporary social workers may have to control or police parents in order to ensure the well-being of children, or restrict the freedom of people with serious mental illness in order to protect them or other people. In exercising these dual roles of care and control, social workers have to balance the needs and interests of different individuals in relation to one another in ways that require careful professional judgement and draw on a range of disciplines and theoretical perspectives.

Social workers work with many different groups – children and young people, older adults, physically disabled people, people with learning disabilities, mentally ill people, refugees and asylum seekers – and also with a wide range of different kinds of problems – abuse and neglect, poor parenting, alcohol and other substance misuse, mental illness and disabilities of various kinds. The kinds of circumstances that require social worker involvement and the interventions that they make depend on a whole range of factors, including:

- what is identified as a social problem (for example, when does the unhappiness of an individual child become a public 'problem' of child neglect, requiring intervention by social workers?)
- how the social problem is understood (for example, is it seen as a problem arising from an individual or from a social deficit?)
- what other forms of informal social support are available (for example, social care services for frail elderly people will be less necessary in cultures where multigeneration households are the norm, older people are respected and women's role is primarily domestic)
- what other kinds of formal state or voluntary-organization services are provided and how they are funded. These services may complement social work intervention or reduce the need for it (such as services offering parenting support, or support for those affected by domestic violence, or providing respite care for disabled family members to help their carers).

The way in which social workers intervene depends both on the model of change that is dominant within the profession at a particular historical time, and on the broader political and policy climate within which social work is practised. Payne (1996) identified three alternative orientations to social work practice: (i) *individual-reformist*, in which social work forms part of welfare services and is concerned with meeting need and improving services; (ii) *reflexive–therapeutic*, in which social work tries to promote individual psychological growth, self-development and self-realization; and (iii) *socialist–collective*, in which the focus is on empowering oppressed peoples and challenging structural inequalities. British understandings and practice have mostly allied themselves with individual–reformist and reflexive-therapeutic perspectives, although these three perspectives are not necessarily incompatible (Lymbery 2005).

Changes in the economic situation and in prevailing ideologies and political agendas have led to changes in ideas about the roles social workers should perform and the tasks they should undertake, and what kinds of knowledge social workers require, and how this should be applied to practice. The emphasis on individual casework that focused on need, which characterized social work from the 1950s to the 1980s, has given way to a concern with risk management, which has seen local authority social workers, particularly in adult social care, increasingly concerned with care management and brokering services for clients, rather than directly delivering services themselves.

There have also been important changes in how the recipients of social work interventions are conceptualized. The families and individuals whom social workers engaged with were once seen as relatively passive clients who were expected to defer to social workers. Service users nowadays are seen as consumers who should be given choices about the services they receive and whose views should be fully taken into account. Clearly, there are limits to this, engendered by both resource constraints and social work's 'control' role – for example, where child protection or serious mental illness are concerned.

Placing these changes in social workers' roles and in their relationships with service users in the broader context of the developments in social policy over the same period helps to explain why the changes occurred, and offers social workers the intellectual tools to question and challenge current policy and practice, when these appear to conflict with the profession's ethical commitment to social justice.

What is social policy?

'Social policy' refers broadly to those government policies designed to address a range of human needs, such as housing, education, subsistence and health. Which needs and problems are the responsibility of the state and how best to address them are questions that have been, and continue to be, the subject of intense political debate. Furthermore, the boundaries of what constitutes 'social policy' are hard to define. Many different aspects of social organization affect well-being and needs – for example, measures to reduce crime or address problems such as obesity, domestic violence or relationship breakdown. Policies on income redistribution through direct and indirect taxation – the rates of income tax which individuals should pay, and the level of VAT (Value-added Tax) and the range of goods and services on which it should be levied are also important in determining the number of people living in poverty, for example. Should they be regarded as economic or social policies?

Wilson et al. (2011: 41) argue it is imperative for social workers to be aware of how social policies impact upon their work, the organizational contexts in which they are placed and their relationship to other professions. Social workers need to be able to evaluate both the potential impact of social policies on practice and the evidence put forward to support particular policies and then decide how to respond. For example, changes in policy relating to child protection practice and social work education from the 1980s onwards have been strongly influenced by highly publicized cases of children dying at the hands of their parents or carers. These cases have often resulted in crude, dichotomized media representations, followed by public inquiries which have scapegoated social workers. The public sentiment that such cases evoke, whether inadvertently or deliberately generated, has led to policies that are based on a small number of atypical tragic cases (sometimes just one), rather than an informed evaluation of standard and/or more successful practice. Child deaths have been repeatedly linked to the same kind of problems, such as insufficient communication between different professionals and organizations, which suggests that changing social policy or practice responses to this have not been successful (and perhaps could never be wholly successful in eliminating all risk).

Since the 1990s there has been a strong policy emphasis on performance measurement, leading to the introduction of standardized procedures and rigid timescales, using information systems as a way of introducing greater control and accountability of services. Standardization in this way was also intended to be a way of ensuring greater equity of service across different geographical areas. These measures have contributed to social workers sometimes taking dangerous short cuts – for example, by conducting superficial assessments that are heavily dependent on evaluation by other professionals, in order to conform to policies and regulations (Broadhurst et al. 2010b).

Front-line practitioners may also respond to social policies in ways that aim to thwart policy goals. However, such subversion can sometimes, paradoxically, have the opposite effect. The extent to which social workers are able to resist centrally prescribed policies has, however, been constrained by the imposition of these new managerial practices adapted from business models, and an associated audit culture. Nevertheless, neither the need nor the opportunity to exercise individual discretion can ever be totally eliminated. Social workers therefore need to understand that social policies have both intended and unintended consequences, may be ambiguous and are often filtered through many different organizational layers, each with different interpretations of and responses to the same policy.

There have been suggestions from some authors since the 1980s that social workers do not need to study wider social theory and social policy, discrediting these as biased 'idealistic left-wing dogma' (Brewer and Lait 1980; Lavalette 2014). The commentators responsible for such claims often present social work as a purely practical profession. At the same time, they stress the need for high entry requirements and resilient practitioners, implicitly acknowledging that social workers operate in complex, dynamic and high-risk situations which require multidisciplinary knowledge, competent inter-agency working and excellent communication and analytical skills. These confused statements present contradictions which perhaps can only be understood and dealt with by having a broader understanding of social policy.

The structure and logic of the book

This book aims to provide social workers and social work students with the knowledge and skills to be able to understand social policy critically, as well as how it shapes the form and direction of social work. It adopts a critical, analytical approach, exploring different political and philosophical positions and ways of viewing important concepts, such as equality and social justice, to give students and practitioners some options about what they take from this book and how they might use this knowledge to inform their practice. Although the individual chapters can be read and understood on their own, each chapter also builds on the preceding chapters. The questions for discussion at the end of each chapter can be used by individual students to reflect on and consolidate what they have learnt, or utilized by seminar leaders or lecturers to structure small or large group discussion. Students can also be directed to the additional reading material listed or invited to link the questions to specific case studies to enhance the discussion further.

Chapter 1 locates social work in its wider historical context. It looks at the socio-political conditions which shaped the beginnings of the state's involvement in welfare provision in the UK and traces how professional social work developed in tandem with the expansion of the welfare state from the 1950s to the 1970s. It examines the consequences for the welfare state and for social work of the changes brought about by Thatcherism, New Labour's Third Way and the 2010–15 Coalition government.

Chapter 2 focuses on the different political and philosophical perspectives, or welfare ideologies, that shaped ideas about the welfare state, such as Marxism, conservatism and neoliberalism. Longstanding cultural and ideological differences have resulted in different ways of organizing welfare states across the industrialized and post-industrialized world, dividing them into distinctive kinds of welfare regimes. These produce rather different outcomes – for example, in terms of socio-economic disparities, gender equality and wider population health and well-being. Different welfare regimes have different conceptions of citizens' entitlements, and of the role that social work and other associated social professions can play in helping people to reach their potential. Comparisons with welfare regimes in other countries offer a useful perspective on the organization of social welfare and social work in the UK. These comparisons therefore not only illuminate the current situation in the UK but show the potential for positive change, how that might be achieved and structured, and its potential effects.

Chapter 3 addresses how particular issues come to be identified as social problems and illustrates how different understandings of social problems and their causes lead to different ideas about the appropriate solutions. Social change may result in the disappearance of a social problem – for example, 'illegitimate children' – or the appearance of new problems, such as the care of an ageing population. Other problems, such as child abuse, have become much more broadly defined; others may disappear and then re-emerge, but be represented differently each time – for example, the 'deviant' potential of young working-class men. The chapter shows how what might be taken to be an objective social problem may actually not be one, while other issues may remain unrecognized as social problems. Although a number of perspectives on social problems are described and explored, social constructionism is presented as offering the most helpful approach to understanding social problems.

Chapter 4 examines a number of concepts central to social work, such as citizenship, rights, equality, diversity and social justice, and traces the links between them as well as disputes surrounding their meaning and appropriate deployment. It evaluates how these concepts are used by social workers in the context of anti-discriminatory or anti-oppressive practice, using case examples to illustrate the knowledge and skills required to work effectively with difficult and highly sensitive social work situations.

Chapter 5 focuses on the changing institutional location of social work and the systems in place to manage it, within and across organizations. It examines the impact of the marketization of many services and the implications of this for inter-agency partnership and inter-professional working, which have become important policy priorities. The effects of current service quality and performance management techniques are considered, as is the impact of the financial crash in 2008 and of the 2010–15 Coalition government's austerity policies which followed. All of these developments have had important implications for social work as a profession, and we discuss their impact on professional education, training and regulation.

Chapter 6 examines social work in practice in terms of the interface between the state and the individual. It traces the shift from responding to need, which characterized much early social work and welfare state provision, to an emphasis on risk, which currently determines eligibility for access to many social work services. We examine the rationale for and ascendance of evidence-based practice in social work, and the types of research methodologies and knowledge favoured by policy makers. Following this, concepts and practices associated with service user empowerment are discussed, exemplified by the personalization agenda in adult social care. We consider the consequences of the dual emphasis on risk and empowerment for the relationship between service users and social workers.

Chapter 7 positions UK social work within an international context and explains the impact of globalization – technologically, culturally, socially, politically and economically – on social work both internationally and in respect of individual countries. It examines how globalization has given rise to new problems in which social workers have a role to play – such as migration and the position of legal and illegal immigrants, asylum seekers and refugees – as well as highlighting the contribution of migrants to different countries' social work and social care workforces and the global chains of care which migration creates. We show how global capital investment in care services as profitable businesses creates new kinds of local problems in a marketized system of care. The chapter discusses the importance of supranational organizations such as the European Union (EU), the International Monetary Fund (IMF) and the UN, and their role in shaping the social policies of individual nations. It shows how the attempt to build a global profession has to address differences in knowledge and cultures both within and between nations, and differences in power and resources, particularly between the Global North and South.

The concluding chapter summarizes the key issues addressed in the book and makes some suggestions about how social workers individually, and as a profession, can use the analysis presented here to support them in defending social work and continuing to pursue its goals of responding to need and promoting social justice, equality and human rights.

1 Tracing the Roots of Welfare and the Evolution of Social Policy and Social Work

1.1 Introduction

As the Introduction showed, there are important links between social work, social policy and the welfare state. The welfare state was established in the period immediately after the Second World War, but state involvement in meeting need goes back much further. Social work has been an important part of welfare provision since the nineteenth century, although it only came into existence as a recognized profession in the post-war period, as part of the welfare state. This chapter provides a historical analysis of the development of the welfare state and social work's role within it, to show how social work's evolution has been shaped by the broader social policy context in which it is placed.

1.2 Origins of state provision of welfare: from the Elizabethan Poor Laws to the late 1800s

The state has been involved in meeting need, particularly poverty as a consequence of old age, disability or unemployment, for centuries. The 1597 and 1601 Poor Laws provided for individual parishes to levy local taxes and use the money to 'set the poor on work', maintain those unable to work and place pauper children as apprentices (Harris 2004: 113). However, state involvement in addressing a variety of social problems increased rapidly in the nineteenth century in response to the consequences of the industrial revolution, particularly the problems associated with accelerated urbanization. The large-scale migration of people from the countryside to the towns to work in the newly established factories generated new kinds of problems, such as mass disease and poverty, which were increasingly seen as requiring state intervention.

The 1834 Poor Law and increasing state intervention

The system of parish poor relief introduced in the 1600s was inadequate to deal with the scale of poverty that accompanied industrialization and urbanization in the nineteenth century. Poverty was also more visible in urban areas than it had been in more dispersed rural communities, and responses were at least partly linked to middle-class fears of social unrest as well as being a humanitarian reaction to need (Howe 2009). A new Poor Law was introduced in 1834 which instituted a national Commission to establish the rules for the management of the poor throughout England and Wales. One issue of great concern to the Commission, which continues to preoccupy policy makers today, was how to ensure that the provision of support to the poor did not undermine work incentives. The problem was 'solved' in the Poor Law by the principle of 'less eligibility', under which those capable of work should only be offered support 'in kind' by being accommodated in the workhouse, where they would have shelter and food, and be required to undertake productive work, and where conditions meant there was every incentive to leave as soon as possible, so that entering the workhouse would be a last resort.

Underpinning this approach was the view that poverty amongst those capable of work was an indication of personal fault and moral inadequacy (Whiteside 2012: 117). This led to the belief that it was possible to differentiate the 'deserving' poor, who were clearly the victims of misfortune as a consequence of illness, accident or old age, from the 'undeserving' poor. This latter group were seen as having brought their difficulties on themselves by their laziness or immorality. Within the workhouse families were broken up, with men, women and children separated from each other, and, in order to promote desirable characteristics, good behaviour was rewarded with extra food, or greater comfort. This gradually led to the development of more specialist institutions: hospitals for the sick, asylums for the mad, and various kinds of educational institutions for children (Thane 1996: 35–6).

Other problems arising from industrialization and urbanization led to some state regulation of living and working conditions. Factory legislation was introduced from the 1840s onwards, first to restrict women's and children's employment, and later to regulate men's working conditions. The huge influx of population to the cities and the unregulated building of housing to accommodate the working class resulted in periodic epidemics which affected not only the working class, but also the middle class. From the mid nineteenth century onwards, legislation was passed to control building standards and provide sanitation (Harris 2004). The need for a better-educated working class led to the introduction of state funding for education, and, from 1880, compulsory education up to the age of ten.

These state measures were important in seeking to provide certain minimum welfare standards for the population, but private charity and mutual self-help also played an essential role in welfare provision throughout the nineteenth century. The expansion of the middle class as a direct consequence of industrialization, combined with the growth of evangelical Christianity and the existence of large numbers of middle-class women with no opportunity for employment other than in charitable work, resulted in a mushrooming of philanthropic activity. Schools, hospitals, health visiting, housing for the poor, orphanages and many other forms of welfare support were provided through large numbers of local charities. At the end of the nineteenth century, it is estimated that about £8 million a year was dispensed through charities in London alone – an amount which exceeded the total *national* Poor Law expenditure (Thane 1996: 21).

The role of charities and self-help

In 1869, in an effort to impose some kind of order on the proliferation of charitable effort, the COS was set up by a group of philanthropists, drawn from a new professional middle-class elite which included doctors, lawyers, civil servants and their wives. They were concerned that charity was being dispensed in a haphazard way that did not promote moral improvement amongst the poor. They established a system of home visiting to ensure that charitable help only went to those who were capable of becoming self-supporting. Those responsible for administering the Poor Law also enlisted the help of the COS by passing lists of paupers on to them. Charles Loch, the leader of the COS from 1875 to 1913, personally schooled COS workers, known as 'trained social physicians', in assessments, case recording and later in applying psychology to their work (Howe 2009). This 'scientific charity' involved a rigorous analysis of the applicant's lifestyle, habits, morality and character, and produced an action plan with attached recommendations. For those deemed 'deserving', this might include material support and continuing casework which combined friendship and surveillance but was intended to be temporary, individual and reformatory (Woodroffe 1962). This individual casework can be seen as an early form of social work (Seed 1973).

Families who received help from the COS were able to remain living in their local community, rather than entering the workhouse. The COS visitor sought to analyse the families' problems and help them find a lasting solution which would restore their independence (Thane 1996: 21-3). This approach essentially individualized the problem of poverty, rather than seeing it as a structural consequence of the economic cycle. It was also inherently paradoxical as those denied assistance and seen as undeserving might have the greatest need for help, whereas those who received support were seen as more respectable and provident and arguably had less need (Lymbery 2005). The terminology also later changed from 'deserving' and 'undeserving' to 'helpable' and 'unhelpable', and although this change suggested a less moralistic and more objective approach to the poor, it was actually more damaging because it suggested not just that some individuals were not worthy of support but that they could not be helped at all.

Despite the COS' rather discriminatory moral ethos, social work's 'best practice' philanthropic origins embodied a commitment to social inclusion (Forsythe and Jordan 2002), albeit a very conservative one in which the rich had a Christian obligation to help the poor improve themselves, with the 'welfare subject' generally seen as subordinate to the 'welfare provider' (Simpson and Connor 2011: 10). 'Scientific charity' was additionally based on principles of honesty, commitment and empathy (Forsythe and Jordan 2002), still evident in contemporary social work.

The University Settlement Movement was another significant development in late nineteenth-century philanthropy. It represented a different approach to addressing poverty, and pre-figured an alternative approach within contemporary social work – community development. The Settlement Movement took the view that both the state and charity had a role to play in promoting social harmony, and that the relationship between middle-class philanthropists and the working class should be one of mutual respect, rather than middle-class condescension and exploitation. The settlements recruited young university graduates to live and work in poor areas, sharing the benefits of their knowledge and education and using their skills to solve social problems (Thane 1996: 23; Hugman 2009).

Self-help and mutualism were also important sources of welfare provision. Friendly Societies, open mainly to men from the skilled working class, offered insurance against sickness and old age. Trade unions played an important part in providing health, old-age and unemployment benefits for members. The Co-operative movement provided relatively cheap, good-quality food and other necessities. All these forms of assistance, however, failed to provide significant support to the poorest members of the working class, whose employment was intermittent and who therefore did not have the resources to join a trade union or the Co-operative movement (Thane 1996: 25–30).

The inadequacies of the dominant nineteenth-century explanation of poverty, and of self-help, charitable and Poor Law provision as a system for dealing with it, were demonstrated by Rowntree's survey of poverty in York in 1899. This showed that many households whose members were in work nevertheless had insufficient incomes to meet even basic needs. The consequences of this for national well-being were dramatically revealed when it proved impossible to find sufficient 'healthy' numbers of recruits to fight in the Boer War. Of those who volunteered, 40 per cent were found unfit to serve because of poverty-related poor eyesight, rickets and other chronic health problems (Harris 2004: 156). Government anxiety about the implications of this 'national deterioration' for the future of the Empire and for Britain's economic competitiveness relative to other emergent industrial nations, such as Germany and the United States, promoted support for greater direct state involvement in welfare provision. Political pressure also came from the trade union movement and from the newly formed Labour Party.

1.3 From the Poor Law to the welfare state: 1900–1948

The welfare measures introduced by the 1906–14 Liberal government established a much greater role for the state in meeting social needs, and moved away from the principle which dominated the nineteenth-century approach to poverty: that individuals were entirely responsible for their circumstances, and that provision to relieve poverty should be on the basis of its being a stigmatizing last resort (Digby 1989). Anxiety about national deterioration resulted in legislation to allow local authorities to provide school meals, a school medical service and maternal and child welfare clinics in an effort to improve the health of the next generation of working-class children. Other important welfare measures included the introduction of old-age pensions, funded out of taxation, and an insurance system to provide for unemployment and medical care, to which employers, the state and the workers themselves contributed. By the eve of the Second World War in 1939, middle-class self-interest, working-class pressure through the trade union movement, and an increasing voice for the working class through the Labour Party had changed the political and ideological climate, so that problems which had, in the nineteenth century, been seen as the result of individual weakness and failings, came to be understood as originating also in aspects of the social structure. Action by the state to moderate some of these structural effects was increasingly widely accepted by all the political parties, though to differing extents, particularly in the wake of the international consequences of the 1929 Wall Street crash in the USA and the mass unemployment which followed this in the 1930s. As a result, there was limited state provision for some of the contingencies of life: unemployment, illness, old age were all provided for to some extent. Children's health and education were seen as a joint responsibility of parents and the state. Nonetheless, provision was far from universal, and the stigma associated with the Poor Law remained.

Just as the Boer War had precipitated a crisis about 'national deterioration' which, combined with the growing political strength of the working class in Britain, brought about significant changes in the accepted role of the state, so the experiences of the civilian population of Britain in the Second World War and government responses to the crisis which the war precipitated, resulted in a further shift in the role of the state in providing for the needs of its citizens. The extent of poverty in big cities was revealed in new ways to middle-class Britain when children and expectant mothers were evacuated from London and other major cities at the start of the war and billeted with families in the countryside, in anticipation of a possible aerial bombardment campaign.

The anticipation of air raids and civilian casualties required a major reorganization of hospital services, revealing the poor standards in public hospitals and creating pressure for reform after the war. Food shortages led to state intervention through rationing, to ensure that limited resources were fairly distributed, which produced a significant reduction in health inequalities and an improvement in the standard of public health. These wartime experiences demonstrated the necessity and desirability of state intervention to address a variety of social problems, and stimulated demand for change in welfare provision after the war. Underpinning this was an acceptance of the need for collective rather than individual solutions to social problems.

The Beveridge Report

As part of the government's planning for the post-war period, Sir William Beveridge chaired a committee to look at the future provision of social insurance benefits (financial support in the event of unemployment, illness and old age). His report, published in 1942, set out a comprehensive plan for the reform of state welfare provision, to address what he called the five giant evils: Want (poverty), Disease (ill health), Ignorance (educational inequality), Idleness (unemployment) and Squalor (homelessness / poor housing). These were to be addressed through a *comprehensive* and *universal* system, offering protection from poverty and its effects 'from the cradle to the grave'.

The report's recommendations had extensive popular support and were largely implemented by the Labour government elected immediately after the war. The legislation marks the beginning of the modern welfare state in the UK. Other sources of welfare dominant in the nineteenth and early twentieth centuries – philanthropy, trade unions and Friendly Societies – did not disappear, but the state became the principal source of both funding and delivery of welfare support.

The key measures introduced were:

- A comprehensive social insurance system for all (male full-time) workers providing cover against unemployment, industrial injury, sickness and old age, for themselves and for any dependants. Employees, employers and the state all contributed to the scheme. Although the intention was originally that the level of benefits should cover subsistence needs, this aspiration was never realized in practice.
- A 'safety net' means-tested national assistance scheme for those who fell outside the new national insurance scheme. It was anticipated that this would gradually disappear as the proportion of the population covered by the national insurance system grew.

- A universal system of family allowances to contribute to the costs of child-rearing.
- A national health service providing universal healthcare free at the point of delivery, replacing the patchwork of voluntary, charitable and poor law hospitals and private general practitioners which had developed over the preceding 150 years. It was hoped that, as the health of the population improved through the various welfare measures introduced, the demands on the health service would gradually reduce.
- Universal, free secondary education up to the age of fifteen.
- A public programme of house-building. The Labour government promised to build 4–5 million new homes, with local authorities playing a major role.

The Beveridge Report was underpinned by a commitment to maintain full employment through the adoption of Keynesian economic policies. This meant state involvement in managing the demand for labour, spending money on capital projects during periods of economic downturn to create employment and prevent economic recession.

The cost of this increased state expenditure on welfare was met through taxation. The tax threshold had been lowered during the Second World War, and although it was raised again after the war, wage rises and inflation meant that an increasing proportion of the population became tax payers. Whereas, at the start of the twentieth century, someone on the median wage was below the tax threshold, and there was widespread support for income taxation, by the 1970s someone with a wife and two children, earning *less than half* of male full-time average earnings, was liable for tax. As a result, popular attitudes to taxation changed significantly (Harris 2004: 300).

1.4 The post-war welfare consensus: 1948–1979

From the mid-1940s to the mid-1970s there was considerable political consensus (i.e. agreement from all political parties/persuasions) about the need for greater state involvement in welfare provision, and during this period the range and level of services provided by the welfare state gradually expanded. Contrary to the hope and expectation that better and more universal welfare provision would reduce the need for the welfare state, as the health and well-being of the population improved, the welfare budget continued to increase.

In 1965 a survey by Brian Abel-Smith and Peter Townsend revealed that, despite the welfare state, the number of people living in poverty had increased from 600,000 in 1953–4 to 2 million in 1964. There were several reasons for this growth in poverty: the Beveridge national insurance system assumed a 'male breadwinner' family – a male head of household employed full-time over his entire working lifetime, providing for a dependent wife and children. The system did not provide well for single or divorced women, for households where the man had low-paid or intermittent employment, or for people with long-term illness or disability, and it did not allow for the costs of housing. National insurance benefits had not kept pace with inflation during the post-war period. As a consequence, many households were dependent on the 'safety net' national assistance benefits to supplement their national insurance entitlement. This provided only a minimum subsistence-level income and left households in poverty.

The beginnings of state social work

Personal social services were not addressed directly in the Beveridge Report, possibly because Beveridge thought that, if poverty, unemployment and sickness could be controlled by the rational planning of economic production and distribution, the need for social work would wither away (Parry and Parry 1979). To the extent that psychosocial needs remained, these were not seen as having anything to do with the fundamentally economic strategy of the welfare state. Social work therefore appeared more as an afterthought than as a central element in the original welfare state plan, but its importance became more evident after the death in 1945 of a child, Dennis O'Neill, killed by his foster father. This led to a government inquiry, the Curtis Committee, in the following year. The committee concluded that the existing legislation and services catering for deprived children were seriously inadequate and recommended that every local authority should have a Children's Committee overseeing a department consisting of a chief officer and trained social workers who could investigate neglect and abuse and place children in the care of the local authority whenever necessary. The 1948 Children Act gave local authorities responsibility for children whose parents were either 'unfit' or unable to care for them, and for supervising adoption. Policy before this had concentrated on organizing work placements and apprenticeships for orphans and disadvantaged children (Denney 1998). The introduction of direct state responsibility for the protection of children made the needs of children a central concern and represented a major shift in social attitudes to the state's responsibilities towards children (Hughes 1998: 150). The 1947 Younghusband Report also recommended increasing social worker numbers through cultivating a reliable knowledge base and developing university courses that combined practical training and social science knowledge (Davis 2008).

The legislation which established the post-war welfare state distributed responsibility for services that had previously been covered by the Poor Law to different departments within the local authority and to the newly established health service. Three separate local authority departments were created to undertake social work with different groups in the population: (i) children's departments for children who were denied a 'normal' family life; (ii) welfare departments to work with elderly, physically handicapped and homeless people; and (iii) local health departments to deal with mentally ill people and the 'mentally handicapped' (Cree 2008). In addition, local authority education departments developed their own welfare provision to address the educational needs of disabled children, deal with truancy and provide free school meals, clothing and educational maintenance allowances to poor families. These different local authority departments came under the control of different central government ministries, leading to a 'chaotic' national picture (Hall 1976: 6), with three different central government departments responsible for welfare services for different populations, and with overlapping responsibilities within local authorities and local health departments.

The Seebohm Committee

During the 1950s and 1960s, expenditure on services for these different groups grew more rapidly than public expenditure generally. The recommendations of a number of government departmental enquiries into specific service areas during the period converged on a common theme: the importance of early intervention and prevention. In the context of a shift from seeing social problems as the result of individual failure to seeing them as resulting from social and family pressures, much greater emphasis was placed on community work and work with families. This in turn demonstrated the need for much better co-ordination of the various fragmented services that had developed in the post-war period to serve specific client groups such as children, elderly people and those with mental health problems or disabilities. There was concern about the numbers of vulnerable and isolated elderly people in the community (Dickens 2011), and about the fact that families with multiple problems did not know where to go for help. Some therefore ended up receiving support from different professionals situated in different organizations in different locations who did not communicate with each other. A lack of coherence within social work was also evident from the existence of five different bodies that approved or provided both university and non-university social work training which varied in quality and length. Although most courses were supposed to provide generic training, the majority of students were either funded by or recruited for a particular service or client group, meaning that students did not receive a sufficiently broad education (Dickens 2011).

In 1965, the government established a committee under Lord Seebohm to look at local authority and allied personal social services. The Committee recommended the establishment of a single social services department in each local authority to provide a comprehensive family service, with a body of generically trained, professional social workers, to replace the different services delivered by people with varying amounts of professional training in the existing fragmented system. The report envisaged a joined-up community service offering 'one door to knock upon' (Stevenson 1999: 85). The recommendations were implemented in the Local Authority Social Services (England and Wales) Act 1970. Similar measures were introduced in Scotland in the Social Worker (Scotland) Act 1968, following the 1965 Kilbrandon Report. State funding for statutory social services meant they became the principal service providers for all client groups and this arguably marks the beginning of social work as a unified profession. The various professional associations for social workers came together in 1970 to form the British Association of Social Workers (BASW), and in 1971 the Central Council for Education and Training in Social Work (CCETSW) was established, responsible for a new generic social work qualification (Dickens 2011).

This legislation brought social work out of the margins of the welfare state into the mainstream. The 1970s are generally acknowledged as the high point of social work (Rogowski 2010), with the Seebohm Report a seminal moment in its evolution. Politically and professionally, the personal social services became a fully recognized fifth pillar of the welfare state with a legislative base, professional recognition, and functions funded and endorsed by the state. The Seebohm Report additionally dispelled some of social work's lingering associations with stigma, paternalistic charity and the COS. Despite this, the personal social services still occupied an 'odd', indeterminate category within the welfare state as they dealt with heterogeneous needs not easily incorporated into health, education or social security, ranging from protecting children to supporting the vulnerable elderly to remain in their own homes (Spicker 2008: 114).

The Seebohm Report argued for the importance of social services in promoting the capacity of communities to identify solutions to their problems through citizen participation and voluntarism, locating community development within social work. This vision of a community-based service opened the way for community work to achieve greater recognition as an alternative method to casework, echoing the earlier role of the Settlement Movement (Thomas 1983: 19–25). The concern with prevention and early intervention in relation to juvenile crime, which had prompted the setting-up of the Seebohm Committee, also gave a new importance to youth work, whose aim was to provide young people with social education to support them in the transition to adulthood (Jeffs and Smith 1983). Youth and community work, after a brief flourishing in the early 1970s, succumbed to the changes in political ideology and the financial climate during the later part of the decade and in the 1980s. This is discussed in section 1.5. The Barclay Report in 1982, which examined the roles and tasks of social workers, argued for a holistic and community-based approach to social work, alongside counselling and social care planning, but reported at the worst possible time politically and financially, and its recommendations were completely ignored by the Conservative government.

Developments during the 1970s

The 1970s were a period of economic, political and social upheaval in the UK and globally, resulting in an end to the political consensus that had enabled the expansion of the welfare state during the preceding twenty-five years. A four-fold increase in the price of oil led to inflation, and the decline of traditional UK manufacturing industries meant rising male unemployment, while expansion of the service sector of the economy and changing attitudes to gender roles saw women's employment increase. Keynesian economic policy, involving increased government expenditure to counteract high levels of unemployment, did not appear to be able to address the economic problems that the UK faced. In 1976, as a result of the oil crisis, the government was forced to borrow from the IMF. One of the conditions of the loan was that there should be substantial cuts in public expenditure. Welfare expenditure as a proportion of GDP (Gross Domestic Product) fell sharply in 1976–9 (Burchardt and Hills 1999: 29), and the increasing cost of the welfare state, funded by high levels of taxation, began to be called into question.

Demographic change challenged some of the assumptions that underpinned Beveridge's system of national insurance. Long-term male unemployment combined with women's greater economic independence and rising levels of divorce meant that the male breadwinner family that was the basis of the national insurance system no longer corresponded to social reality. Men no longer had the certainty of continuous full-time employment during their working lifetime. Women could no longer rely on a husband to provide for them and their dependent children, or on a husband's contributions to provide them with a pension in their old age, because marriage was increasingly likely to end in divorce. Falling fertility and increased life expectancy meant that rising numbers of elderly people were dependent on welfare services funded from the tax contributions of a shrinking number of people of working age. At the same time, the continuous expansion of the welfare state in the post-war period led to increased expectations. The women's (feminist / sex equality) movement and anti-racism and disability movements in the 1960s and 1970s challenged existing roles and prejudices and gave political voice to oppressed minorities, who demanded recognition and social change.

Political responses from both the left and the right were critical of the welfare state, albeit for different reasons. Right-wing politicians presented the welfare state as inefficient and a drain on the economy, and claimed that state regulation and high taxation were inhibiting economic growth. The welfare state was seen as creating dependency, and discouraging initiative. Collective solutions were rejected in favour of individualism. Critiques from the left identified the welfare state as a bureaucratic and paternalist institution that upheld the professional interests of those who worked in it rather than those of the people whose welfare it was meant to promote. It was seen as a means of social control, through the requirements placed on those using state welfare services. Feminists and disability activists drew attention to the ways in which the welfare state discriminated against and stigmatized certain groups and reinforced patriarchal institutions.

For social work, developments in the 1970s meant that its role and professional status became increasingly aligned with the growth of the British welfare state, but this also constrained it (Bilton 1979). The stigma attached to welfare still lingered, and the individualistic way social workers performed their role obscured the societal causes of many problems. Like other welfare professionals, social workers adopted a paternalist deficit model in which clients were the passive recipients of their professional expertise. The welfare state was assumed to be inherently beneficial and social workers took for granted its continued growth. These attitudes and assumptions came under increasing criticism and challenge from the new social movements emerging in the 1970s.

1.5 Thatcherism and the Conservative governments: 1979–1997

The election in 1979 of a 'New Right' Conservative government under Margaret Thatcher committed to 'rolling back the state' marked the start of a new era in the history of the welfare state. The welfare state was seen as (i) economically damaging because it interfered with the free market and placed an unnecessary financial burden on the state; (ii) socially damaging because it rewarded and perpetuated dependence, undermining individual, family and community responsibility and creating a welfare-dependent underclass; and (iii) politically damaging because it allocated unnecessary roles and responsibility to government.

Keynesian economic policy was abandoned and the government's economic role was identified as controlling inflation rather than maintaining full employment. Unemployment rose to record post-war levels, reaching over 3 million in 1982, as the result of the collapse of old manufacturing industries (Timmins 2001: 386). The government, pursuing neoliberal economic policies (see chapter 2), cut taxes and tried to cut public expenditure. However, unprecedentedly high unemployment, an increasing elderly population and the growth in the number of lone parents (many dependent on social security benefits because of the difficulty of combining paid employment with caring for children) meant that welfare spending constituted a higher percentage of government spending than ever towards the end of the Conservative administration (Burchardt and Hills 1999).

State services were seen as bureaucratic and inefficient, and the government believed that market competition would produce services that were economical, efficient and effective (Thatcher's 'three E's'). In health and education, individual schools and hospitals competed with each other to attract pupils and patients. Those attracting more pupils/patients were allocated commensurately more funding; those that failed to attract sufficient numbers were, in theory at least, to close. Increasing numbers of services were contracted out to the private or voluntary sector through a process of competitive tendering. Thus, although the state remained the principal *funder* of welfare services, these services were *provided* to an increasing extent by a mixture of private and voluntary agencies under contract to the state.

The process of putting services out to tender and managing contracts contributed to a substantial growth in the number of managers within the public sector, and to the introduction of models of management based on the private sector. These increasingly replaced the top-down bureaucratic systems that had hitherto characterized the public sector with systems of performance management instituted through the setting of targets. The Conservative government emphasized individual responsibility, with state support presented as a residual safety net, rather than a citizenship right. Entitlement to national insurance benefits, the centrepiece of the Beveridge system, was eroded, and means-testing for benefits was substantially increased as a way of limiting state support to those who needed it most. As a consequence, welfare provision was no longer represented as a collective response to individual need arising from misfortune, for which individuals could not be held responsible; rather, reliance on social security benefits was seen as a symptom of individual moral failure. Individuals and families were responsible for their own welfare, with state support a last resort when all else failed. This was exemplified in policy on housing. The government saw owner occupation as the solution to housing needs. Public house-building programmes, maintenance programmes and rent subsidies were drastically cut. Tenants in local authority housing were given the right to buy their property at heavily discounted prices to encourage home ownership. The stock of public housing therefore reduced dramatically, becoming a residual service, increasingly only available to those who could not enter the housing market. The implementation of policies which reflected the view that state support should be restricted to the poorest in society and the emphasis on individualism, combined with cuts in taxation and the promotion of 'enterprise', led to an increase in poverty and inequality over the period of Conservative government. The proportion of households in poverty in the UK increased sharply during the 1980s, so that, by 1991/2, 25% of households were below the poverty line (defined as having an income below 50% of average income after housing costs), compared with 9% in 1979. Inequality also increased substantially during this period, with the income of the bottom 10% of households falling by 13%, while the income of the top 10% increased by 65% (Oppenheim 1997).

One consequence of the 'marketization' of services was that those using them were increasingly defined not as passive clients of a paternalist state provider, but consumers whose choices would determine which service providers thrived. The transformation of service users into consumers was used as part of the Thatcher government's strategy for increasing the accountability of the professions and reducing professional power. The growth of the welfare state during the post-war period had been accompanied by a growth in the authority of the various different professions involved in the delivery of state welfare services: doctors, teachers, social workers.

They had extensive discretion to define needs and problems and to allocate resources to meet these. Critiques of this professional power developed during the 1970s from both the political left and the right (Foster and Wilding 2000: 144). From a right-wing perspective, professionals were seen as self-interested and unresponsive to clients or patients, and lacking in accountability. Professionals and bureaucracies, not service users, were seen as the main beneficiaries of the welfare state, with Thatcher condemning public-sector professionals as 'parasites' (Toynbee and Walker 2010). Increased political control, tighter managerial control and consumer empowerment were introduced as mechanisms for reining in the power of welfare professionals.

The impact of Thatcherism on social work

Thatcher's commitment to 'rolling back the state' and to using market competition as a mechanism for containing the costs of the welfare state, as well as her preference for private and voluntary-sector service provision, all had important implications for social work during this period. This was exemplified in a renewed policy emphasis on 'community care' for certain groups. Whereas in the 1970s community care referred to the replacement of long-term institutional care with state support for the mentally ill and the elderly to enable them to live in the community, in the 1980s it came increasingly to mean care *by* the community, that is, 'free' informal care provided by family, friends and neighbours – in practice, women – as a way of cutting the spiralling costs of residential care. The 1990 NHS and Community Care Act resulted in a fundamental change in the role of local authority social services departments, and of social workers working with elderly people and people with disabilities. Social services departments were required to produce a community care plan, identifying the level and extent of need for care services. These services then had to be commissioned from a range of providers in the private and voluntary sectors, with 90 per cent of the 'care' having to come from outside the local authority (Jordan and Drakeford 2012). Putting community care services out to competitive tender was seen as a way of keeping the cost of services down whilst introducing some degree of consumer choice (Johnson 1999). Thus, rather than directly providing care and support services, social services departments became responsible for contracting other organizations to provide them, and social workers became care managers not caseworkers, responsible for assessing care needs and allocating services from within a limited budget, in the form of an individually devised 'care package'. Where individuals had the means to do so, they were required to pay.

There were fewer formal, structural changes in the role of social workers in relation to children and families, but the Conservatives were very critical of social workers' failure to detect or prevent child abuse tragedies, whilst paradoxically promoting the role of voluntary provision and the family *vis-à-vis* an overpowering 'nanny state' (Pinkney 1998). Cuts in public expenditure, combined with a series of high-profile inquiries into the deaths of children at the hands of their parents/carers during the 1970s and 1980s, meant that social work with families became heavily focused on child protection. These inquiries repeatedly identified failures in cooperation and information exchange between different agencies involved with families as a key issue in the failure to protect children, and led to the Department of Health issuing guidance to local authorities, under the title *Working Together* (Department of Health

and Social Security (DHSS) 1988), on inter-agency cooperation and the identification of high-risk cases. Identifying and monitoring 'dangerous families' (Parton and
Parton 1989) took precedence over more general family support, despite the 1989
Children Act placing a duty on local authorities to assess 'children in need', work in
partnership with families and undertake preventative work to promote children's
development (Aldgate and Tunstill 1995). This shift to residualism and a focus on
risk in social work was also evident in adult probation services, which, from the
mid-1990s, were de-coupled from social work, taking the emphasis away from rehabilitation and refocusing on enforcement and public protection. The contribution to
social problems of structural factors such as poverty, inadequate income, substand-
ard housing and isolation was almost totally unacknowledged. On a positive note, but
probably as a way of reducing expenditure, Thatcher's administration diverted large
numbers of young offenders into alternatives to custody (Rogowski 2010).

In the mid- to late 1980s, social work became more politicized and attention turned
to anti-racist or anti-sexist practice. Formal direction on these issues in social work
training came in guidance published by the CCETSW (1989, 1991). This stipulated
that students must demonstrate an awareness of the structural basis of oppression, and challenge race, disability and gender discrimination. The Conservative
government condemned this as 'loony' political correctness. Other right-wing commentators, appalled by emergent Marxist critiques of social work, accused social
workers of being driven by trendy ideological faddism and a dangerous compassion
untempered by objective scientific principles, at the same time contradicting the
appeal to scientific principles by suggesting that lay wisdom and common sense
were the way forward (e.g. Brewer and Lait 1980). Social work was an easy target for
the New Right and proved unable to resist fully the criticisms directed at it. Unlike
the NHS which served the whole population and had strong public support and a
powerful medical power base, social workers tended to work almost exclusively with
the most marginalized and impoverished sections of society. By 1995, the CCETSW
definition of anti-discriminatory practice had become less orientated towards social
justice and more concerned with helping clients to adjust to existing structures
(Denney 1998). Despite some minor disaffection, little substantive political challenge
was forthcoming from the social work profession, which is perhaps unsurprising
given its individualistic origins and *modus operandi*. Social work, therefore, largely
adapted to the prevailing political climate, a pluralist welfare economy and its changing identity, roles and tasks (Denney 1998).

Other policy measures, although not exclusively associated with social work,
had a significant effect on social work. The Thatcher government was committed to
upholding traditional family values. One example of this was Section 28 of the 1988
Local Government Act (eventually repealed in 2003). This prohibited local authorities
from promoting same-sex relationships as 'pretended family relationships'. Research
into residential children's homes elicited many accounts of prejudiced views and
behaviour or reluctance to talk to teenagers about homosexuality on the part of social
workers and residential workers, which was often linked to fear about this Act (Green
1999, 2005; Green and Masson 2002). This contributed to cases of self-harm and suicide, homophobic harassment and children becoming sexually exploited through
prostitution.

Another example was Thatcher's demonization of single mothers, many of whom had multiple problems and were social work clients. Thatcher applied Charles Murray's analysis of the American 'underclass' to Britain, claiming that there was a section of society whose subversion of the work ethic and the heterosexual nuclear family represented a threat to the wider society (Murray 1990). Lone mothers were characterized as amoral and idle 'welfare scroungers' for whom the welfare state created a vicious cycle of dependency (Levitas 1998).

The 1979–97 Conservative governments, however, did not do away with social work practice, although its status and autonomy were reduced. Cuts to social service spending were implemented and, as poverty and need grew (Walker and Walker 1998; Alcock 2006), the role of social workers was pushed increasingly towards rationing and risk assessment.

1.6 The New Labour governments: 1997–2010

The direction of welfare reform pioneered by the Thatcher and Major Conservative governments continued under the Labour government elected in 1997. Despite a political ideology which appeared to diverge from the Thatcherite New Right perspective, the Third Way, espoused by the Prime Minister, Tony Blair, still propounded market mechanisms as a way to promote efficiency in public services, through contracting out services on the basis of competitive tendering, and using consumer choice as the basis for allocating resources to services (see chapter 2 for further discussion of political ideology).

Unlike the Conservatives, New Labour was prepared to expand public expenditure, particularly in health and education. Anxious to promote a 'modern' accountable state, they greatly extended the use of targets as a mechanism for performance management in public services. Following a comprehensive review of public spending by the Treasury in 1998, the government set performance targets for every central government department. These were 'cascaded' down to the agencies responsible for local service delivery. Targets ranged from increasing childcare and the educational qualifications of children in residential care (Department of Health 1998) to reducing teenage pregnancies and improving the punctuality of rail services and the lives of vulnerable older people (Carvel 2007). A Personal Social Services Performance Assessment Framework was introduced, with a 'star system' for rating the quality of social services departments. Social workers argued that simplistic targets and crude performance indicators de-professionalized them, corrupted professional values and failed to recognize that sensitive work with vulnerable and disadvantaged groups required holistic social work knowledge not generic managerial skills (Kitchener et al. 2003; Harris 2007).

The Labour government's approach to social policy was characterized by four central concerns (Powell 1999: 15):

- an active, preventative state;
- the distribution of opportunities rather than income;
- the centrality of paid work;
- the balancing of rights and responsibilities.

Reforms to the social security system stressed welfare benefits as 'a hand up not a hand out', with the aim of the welfare system being to get as many people as possible into paid work, and the role of the state being to promote employability. Social justice was conceptualized in terms of opportunity and social inclusion rather than economic redistribution through reducing wealth and income differentials. The problem of poverty, largely denied by the Conservatives in the 1980s and 1990s, was redefined by Labour as a problem of 'social exclusion' (Levitas 1998). This concept was intended to capture the complex interactions between material deprivation and some of its consequences, such as poor health, educational outcomes and housing, and increased criminality.

In policy areas from health to crime, there was a new emphasis on prevention and early intervention – in health, for example, on preventing coronary heart disease, strokes and cancer by reducing smoking. The Sure Start programme, introduced in 1998, sought to prevent educational failure among poor children, by early intervention with pre-school children, offering services to them and their parents to ensure that they arrived at school 'ready to learn'. State investment was used to redistribute opportunities, so that children would have a more equal chance to achieve within the education system (and then in the labour market).

The government attempted to counter the fragmentation of services which had accompanied marketization under the previous Conservative governments, by promoting partnership working: between private and public sectors to co-finance capital projects such as building schools and hospitals (the Private Finance Initiative (PFI) and Public Private Partnerships), and between agencies and across departments in central and local government to achieve 'joined-up' services. Furthermore, new ways were introduced of actively engaging service users in the shaping of the services, from parent governors in schools to local residents in areas of urban regeneration. There was an attempt to change public services from a 'one size fits all' model, with centralized bureaucratic control, to more personalized services, responsive to the needs and wishes of the individuals they served. This was arguably more difficult to achieve in social work because some service users had limited mental capacity because of mental illness, dementia or learning disability, and others were involuntarily involved with social workers because they presented a substantial risk to themselves or others. Making services responsive to local users could also potentially conflict with centrally prescribed performance targets (Clarke and Newman 1993) since their priorities might differ from the policy priorities of the government.

Contradictions under New Labour

The period of New Labour government (1997–2010) was marked by a number of policy contradictions. In its first term (1997–2001) the government pledged to eradicate child poverty by 2020; increased financial benefits for children; instituted a national minimum wage; made a commitment to reducing health inequalities and to neighbourhood renewal; set up the Disability Rights Commission and drew up National Childcare and Carers' Strategies, as well as acknowledging the need to tackle institutional racism and social exclusion (Williams 2001). However, New Labour's policies towards asylum seekers and their axing of lone parent benefit went against some of these positive policy developments. The target of reducing child poverty by 25 per cent by 2004/5 was not achieved by 2008 (Elliot 2008; Gentleman 2009). In its last term (2005–10), New Labour substantially reduced pensioner and child poverty, but poverty increased among working-age adults without children and there was no overall improvement in social mobility (Hills 2013). The 2004 Children Act emphasized children 'being healthy, staying safe, enjoying and achieving, making a positive contribution and achieving economic well-being'. However, a 2007 UNICEF report placed the UK at the bottom of twenty-one affluent countries in terms of children's overall well-being, with British children amongst the poorest, most neglected and least happy, although indicators of educational attainment, children in temporary accommodation, teenage pregnancies and some aspects of children's health subsequently improved (Bradshaw 2012).

New Labour, unlike the New Right, however, validated forms of intimacy and diversity other than the traditional nuclear family. The 2004 Civil Partnership Act gave gay civil partners the same rights and responsibilities as heterosexual married couples, while the 2004 Gender Recognition Act allowed transgendered people to change their sex legally. The 2002 Adoption and Children Act gave unmarried fathers equal parental responsibility if their name was on the child's birth certificate, and made it easier for stepfathers to adopt. It also gave unmarried and gay couples the right to apply to adopt. The 2010 Equality Act consolidated much of the previous race, sex and disability anti-discrimination legislation and added, as new protected characteristics, religion or belief, gender reassignment, sexual orientation, pregnancy and maternity, civil partnership, and age.

New Labour supported parental employment through tax credits, which helped with the cost of childcare, and through increased employment rights for mothers and the introduction of a modest entitlement to (unpaid) paternity leave (Pascall 2008). Despite these advances, the priority given to paid work meant that New Labour gave much less attention to gender equality in unpaid work (Annesley et al. 2007). As Penna pointed out, 'Tax breaks to employers to encourage provision of nursery care will not help with care of elderly confused people, disabled children, teenagers or sick people' (2003: 48).

Social work and social care reforms

The dismantling of the generic social services departments established after Seebohm, which began under the Conservatives with changes to adult services, was completed under New Labour. The Labour government's concern with 'joined-up' services – for example, adequate co-ordination between health and social care in providing for older or disabled people, or between education, social services and healthcare in working with families and children – led to the separation of adults' and children's services which became answerable to two different central government departments. The 2003 Laming inquiry into the death of Victoria Climbié in 2000 at the hands of her aunt and her aunt's partner identified poor communication between different agencies as the underlying cause of the failure to protect Victoria. The government's response to the Laming inquiry, and to a report by the Social Exclusion Unit on raising the educational attainment of children in care, was *Every Child Matters* (Chief Secretary to the Treasury 2003), a Green Paper setting out a series of policy proposals to reform and improve services for children. The policies looked at child protection within the broader context of universal and early intervention services to promote children's well-being. The proposals were implemented in the 2004 Children Act which established Children's Services Departments, bringing social work and education together into a single local authority department, in an attempt to provide better-integrated services for children, together with a whole range of IT and administrative arrangements intended to improve inter-professional communication. The success of these newly integrated services was measured in terms of five outcomes for children: 'be healthy, stay safe, enjoy and achieve, make a positive contribution, achieve economic well-being'. In the wake of this legislation the government issued a further revision to *Working Together* (HM Government 2006), which was concerned with 'safeguarding' and promoting well-being, in contrast to the narrower focus of earlier guidance on child protection.

The consumerism which characterized the Conservative conceptualization of the relationship between service users and providers was adopted, and to some extent transformed, under New Labour, with a fresh emphasis on 'empowerment' and personalization. In relation to adult social care services, this involved individualizing services by providing increasing numbers of service users with their own budget and allowing them to purchase their own care services (see chapter 6).

Not all service users were treated as agentic consumers though, nor were policy decisions always based on sound research evidence or social justice principles. Mental health social workers predominantly assumed the Approved Mental Health Professional (AMHP) role under the reformed Mental Health Act (1983, 2007). This role involves them, if they have the requisite medical recommendations, in making an application for a person deemed to be at significant risk of harm to self or others to be detained against their will in hospital. The 2007 Act also allowed social work involvement in community treatment orders (CTOs), which can be issued to require patients who are discharged after being compulsorily detained in hospital to take prescribed medication and abide by other conditions. Notwithstanding serious ethical considerations around liberty and 'harm' that have always surrounded the Mental Health Act and sectioning, the new CTOs magnify and exacerbate ethical dilemmas and are not supported by a reliable evidence base (McLaughlin and Cordell 2013).

Social workers were also heavily criticized for their role in relation to asylum seekers, particularly their involvement in the unreliable age assessment of unaccompanied asylum-seeking children (Humphries 2004) and in refusing financial support under Section 20 of the 1989 Children Act to families whose asylum application had been rejected. This in turn could potentially lead to social workers removing children in such families into care because their families could not afford to feed them (Cunningham and Tomlinson 2005).

The 1998 Crime and Disorder Act further criminalized already-marginalized groups through the deployment of curfews, anti-social behaviour orders (ASBOs) and parenting orders and removing homeless people from the streets in some areas (Mooney 2006). The punitive focus of the legislation ignored the fact that many of those placed under curfews or receiving ASBOs were vulnerable adults or 'children in need', some at risk of significant harm, from families experiencing entrenched deprivation and disadvantage (Goldson 2002).

The attitudes of the public and of politicians to social workers throughout New Labour's government were marked by ambivalence and, at times, hostility. Social workers were often pilloried for failing to intervene sufficiently early or decisively in cases where children died, or conversely for intervening too much and too soon in the private lives of families. This was one aspect of a more extensive attack by government and the media on the professions, but social work was less able than other professions to defend itself successfully. The death in 2007 of a young child, Peter Connelly (initially referred to as 'Baby P'), precipitated a further crisis and a new set of inquiries, both into the circumstances leading to his death and more broadly into the profession and its organization (see chapters 5 and 6).

One consequence was the re-organization of services and the disappearance of social services departments, leading to the increasing marginalization of social work within social policy in England (Dickens 2011). Social work was largely excluded from policies to address social exclusion, such as Sure Start. Social workers were also not easily able to advocate and campaign for their clientele, whose significant needs and disabilities meant most could not engage in paid work or easily take up opportunities offered to them. As a result, their rights could not be counterbalanced by their responsibilities, making them a poor fit with New Labour's central preoccupation with social inclusion through paid work.

1.7 The Coalition government, contemporary welfare issues and the place of social work: 2010–2015

The 2008 global financial crash and subsequent world-wide economic recession brought the expansion of government spending to an end. The 2010 general election resulted in a Conservative – Liberal Democrat Coalition government, committed to radical cuts in public spending to deal with the financial deficit. This approach was initially concealed to some extent by the Conservative Party's appeal to 'community' and the 'Big Society' which appeared to depart from Thatcherism's individualist ethos and bore some resemblance to New Labour's conservative communitarianism (see chapter 2). The economic crisis, however, provided a rationale for policies that mirrored Thatcherism ideologically in seeking to reduce the role of the state in providing for citizens' welfare.

The Coalition government used its 'Big Society' rhetoric to justify large public expenditure cuts, advocating autonomous community initiatives as an alternative to monolithic state provision. This both pre-empted criticisms that right-wing governments are individualistic and ignore the social, and absolved the state of responsibility for collective social protection (Corbett and Walker 2013: 457). The government contracted private-sector and voluntary organizations to provide an increasing range of welfare services, such as the rehabilitation of offenders and services for the long-term unemployed, many on a 'payment by results' basis, whereby the contracted organization only got paid if it achieved certain agreed outcomes.

Welfare services were further marketized and privatized under the Coalition. Major reforms implemented in 2013 opened the way for private healthcare companies to play a much greater role in the NHS. In education too, more providers have entered the state-funded education 'market', with Academies and Free Schools established outside local democratic control. The financial and economic crisis resulted in a fall in owner occupation, and an increasingly severe housing shortage. The government's policy was to leave the supply of housing primarily to the market, with intervention limited to attempts to stimulate that market by providing some financial assistance to home buyers.

A major reform of the benefit system was implemented in 2012. This is gradually replacing a range of benefits for working-age claimants with a single benefit, Universal Credit. This was supposed to simplify the benefit system and to increase incentives for the unemployed to work and for part-time workers to work longer hours. There were substantial delays to the introduction of Universal Credit because of problems associated with creating a computer system capable of dealing with the complex and changing circumstances of many claimants. Tax reductions for those at the top of the earnings distribution and below-inflation increases in the value of benefits for people of working age meant increasing income inequality, and a fall in the real incomes of large numbers of poorer households (Hills 2014).

As part of the justification for making benefit cuts, and adopting a punitive approach to the unemployed, the government promoted a discourse of 'shirkers' versus 'strivers', echoing the nineteenth-century division of the poor into the 'deserving' and the 'undeserving'. George Osborne, Chancellor of the Exchequer, in his speech to the Conservative Party Conference in 2012, referred to: 'The shift worker, leaving home in the dark hours of the early morning, who looks up at the closed blinds of their next door neighbour, sleeping off a life on benefits' (Osborne 2012). This ignored the fact that in 2012 there were 4.3 million working families who were benefit claimants because of low incomes (Kenway 2013). More than half of the 13 million people in poverty lived in a household with at least one person in work, but, according to the Living Wage Commission, more than one-fifth of the workforce was paid below a 'living wage' (2014).

In May 2015, the Coalition government was replaced by a Conservative government with a small majority. The Conservatives were elected with a commitment to making further sharp cuts in public expenditure, including a reduction of £12 billion in welfare spending, and not to increase taxes. These policies are likely to have a particularly harsh impact on individuals and families at the bottom of the income distribution.

Social work and social care

The Coalition government's 'austerity programme' meant substantial cuts to local authority budgets, particularly in relation to social care, which was cut by £3.5 billion (26 per cent) in 2010–14 (ADASS (Association of Directors of Adult Social Services) 2014). Although the government repeatedly denied that there were unmet needs, funding shortages (House of Commons 2011) or raised eligibility thresholds (Lewis and West 2014), financial restrictions meant that eligibility thresholds for social care were set at 'critical' or 'substantial' levels by local authorities (Care Quality Commission (CQC) 2012). As a result, it was very difficult to provide anything other than the most basic levels of care to the most needy, although services and social workers worked hard to try to ensure not all service users' social, psychological, cultural and environmental needs were neglected.

In relation to children's services, Hopwood et al. (2012) found reduced support for preventative services, such as youth clubs, family support and Early Years' services. Local authorities' dwindling resources resulted in a focus on crisis management, reflected in an increase in child support plans and admissions of children into residential and foster care. Churchill's (2013) analysis of developments in children's services over the first eighteen months of the Coalition government showed that the reduction in family support had resulted in a narrow focus on the most challenging and disadvantaged families, and young people committing crime. Children with mental health issues were also affected by cuts in community services. This depletion of community resources affected the poorest the most, and exacerbated increasing inequality.

1.8 Conclusion

This chapter has examined the historical evolution of social work in conjunction with the expansion, and, more recently, the retrenchment, of the British welfare state. It showed the importance of politics in shaping social policies which have, in turn, framed the development of social work. It illustrated how depictions of poor and disadvantaged people as either 'deserving' or 'undeserving' have been recycled at different historical points in order to justify cuts to state welfare provision. Social work's origins lie within the COS, an unpaid middle-class philanthropic enterprise, supporting and monitoring the 'deserving' poor in the nineteenth century, and, to a lesser extent, within the more politicized Settlement Movement. After the establishment of the welfare state, social work became a state-validated semi-profession that worked with multiple client groups, based on the recognition that individuals' problems may be linked to wider societal issues and require more collective solutions. Its practitioners were seen as state experts who could assess need and care for, rehabilitate and support a range of vulnerable individuals and groups who were experiencing formidable difficulties.

This positive post-war view of social work was challenged from the 1980s onwards by the Thatcher and Major Conservative governments, which attempted to reduce the role of the state in welfare provision. During this period, social workers were characterized as idealistic yet incompetent left-wing radicals, lacking useful knowledge and skills and unable to detect or prevent child-abuse tragedies. Social work's role became increasingly refocused on immediate child protection concerns rather than preventative and community-orientated work with vulnerable children and families. With vulnerable adults, the focus from the 1990s was on assessment of need and risk and then purchasing and co-ordinating services – 'care management' rather than direct therapeutic or community-orientated work with individuals. Local authority social services such as care homes for the elderly or residential homes for children were replaced by private or non-profit sector provision, justified by the view that a market in care provision would be cheaper and allow more consumer choice. The expertise and power of many professions, including the social work profession, was also reduced by the focus on consumerism, 'individual choice' and the market from the 1980s onwards. Social work with other groups, such as young offenders, mentally ill people and struggling families, became increasingly focused on risk and surveillance.

The New Labour governments of 1997–2010 focused on paid work as the main pathway to social inclusion and citizenship, but social work's service users, because of the nature of their problems, were often unable to engage with work-related initiatives. They therefore ended up being further marginalized, despite New Labour in many ways challenging discrimination and oppression in respect of certain minority groups.

The Conservative–Liberal Coalition government (2010–15) was even more dedicated to cutting back the welfare state than the Conservative governments of the 1980s and 1990s, but this was to some extent camouflaged by their 'Big Society' rhetoric, alongside their denial of growing inequality and poverty in the UK. Major cuts to local authority budgets meant that social work was further limited to directing very restricted resources to the highest-risk cases. This situation appears likely to continue under the Conservative government elected in May 2015.

What therefore began as a philanthropic occupation in the nineteenth century, concerned with both the care and the control of the potentially unruly poor, slowly metamorphosed in the mid-twentieth century into an embryonic state profession concerned with assessing and supporting various disadvantaged groups, who, as citizens, had certain entitlements and rights. Differing views over the last 150 years about whether people's problems, including poverty, are the result of individual misfortune or poor choices and therefore resolvable at an individual level, or are at least partially attributable to societal factors which require a collective response, have impacted upon what social policies are brought in and what role social work is expected to play within the wider welfare state. Social work currently has a strong focus on risk and rationing, with its community, social justice and human rights aspirations challenged on a number of fronts, and key decisions about the direction of social work and social care being disproportionately influenced by both funding cuts and atypical child-protection tragedies. Chapter 2 looks in more detail at the political ideologies which underpinned the welfare policies of the various political administrations discussed in this introductory chapter.

Discussion questions

- Why is it important for social work and social policy students to have an understanding of the historical development of social work? Discuss this in relation to provision both before and after the establishment of the welfare state.
- Is it possible to distinguish between the deserving and the undeserving poor? How might accepting such categories impact on health and welfare professionals' judgements and working practices?
- Why has social work been subject to repeated governmental criticism and frequent organizational change?
- Why did social work become a state-supported activity by the middle of the twentieth century?

Further reading

Fraser, D. (2009) *The Evolution of the British Welfare State: A History of Social Policy since the Industrial Revolution*, 4th edn, Basingstoke: Palgrave Macmillan.

Harris, J. (2008) 'State Social Work: Constructing the Present from Moments in the Past', *British Journal of Social Work*, 38, 662–79.

Hendrick, H. (2003) *Child Welfare: Historical Dimensions, Contemporary Debate*. Bristol: Policy Press.

Pierson, J. (2011) *Understanding Social Work: History and Context*. Maidenhead: Open University Press.

2 Welfare Ideologies, Social Policy and Social Work

2.1 Introduction

The history of the development of the welfare state provided in chapter 1 showed the importance of ideas about the causes of poverty in shaping state and philanthropic responses to the problem. It also showed how the responses of philanthropic organizations such as the COS, and later of professional social work, to poor individuals and families were founded on beliefs about the nature of society and the economy and ideas about human nature and individual psychology. In the course of the development of state responses to the social problems that resulted from industrialization, the prevailing beliefs about the causes of those problems changed, reflecting the changing social and economic theories which underpinned these 'common sense' beliefs. The 1834 Poor Law, for example, was premised on the belief that poverty was the result either of unavoidable misfortune (accident, illness, old age) or of individual failure to find work. Provision for the poor reflected this by seeking to ensure that whatever assistance was given never made recipients better off than if they were employed, in however menial a job. By the mid twentieth century, the dominant explanation for poverty incorporated theories about the effects of the economic structure on individual employment prospects, as well as about the nature of society as more than a collection of individuals, and this had implications for beliefs about the role of the state. The more comprehensive and less stigmatizing provision offered by the post-war welfare state reflected widespread acceptance of a degree of collectivism. Since the late 1970s, there has been a return to some of the earlier beliefs embodying 'blame the victim' perceptions of poverty (Ryan 1976). These have legitimated the return to increasingly conditional and restrictive state welfare provision in the UK.

These sets of beliefs about the nature of society and the individual constitute *ideologies*. They provide the justification for particular actions or visions of social reality. While at any one time one particular ideology tends to dominate the way in which social problems are understood, or framed, competing ideologies offer alternative explanations based on different theoretical premises. Although one ideological perspective tends to be the dominant one at any historical moment, this does not mean that all policies reflect that ideology in a completely consistent and coherent way. Different areas of policy, such as education, crime, child protection, health or social security, are the result of developments over considerable periods of time, with policy change usually building on existing policies and therefore incorporating earlier dominant ideologies. Thus there may be contradictions within a particular policy area, or between different policy areas. These contradictions will be illustrated in the discussion of different ideologies which follows.

Denney (1998) uses Poulantzas' theory to show how ideology (i) *masks*, (ii) *displaces*, (iii) *fragments* and (iv) produces *imaginary coherence* in relation to how policies are presented. Taking a Treasury document *Competing For Quality* (HM Treasury 1991: 1), Denney shows how, through the claim that 'competition is the best guarantor of quality and value for money', the link between competition and these outcomes is presented as self-evident, *masking* and *displacing* dissent and contrary evidence. He also demonstrates how the Thatcher government, by introducing market principles into welfare, *fragmented* the welfare system, by separating users from each other, thereby limiting collective recognition and counter action. The assumption that an invisible hand guides markets disregards the uncertainties and instabilities present in all markets, and implies an *imaginary coherence*. Elston (2014) refers to policy statements where one idea is linked with another to imply a probabilistic effect but without an articulated middle premise (which should contain evidence for the link) as a *truncated syllogism* or *enthymeme* which acts as a form of rhetorical persuasion. For example, the Centre for Social Justice in its analyses of 'Breakdown Britain' (e.g. Centre for Social Justice 2006) put forward the view that cohabitation was a much less stable form of relationship than marriage and that therefore policies, such as a married couples tax allowance, should be introduced to promote and support marriage. The middle premise in this argument is that the lack of any financial advantage from marriage has led to the rise in cohabitation. This overlooks many other factors that have led to the increase in cohabitation and also implicitly assumes that the married couples allowance would be a sufficient incentive to keep married couples together. Underlying this argument is the belief that the married two-parent family is uniquely able to raise healthy, achieving, well-adjusted children.

Public support for dominant ideologies is promoted through the media, using influential figures to validate policies, and through repetition and reiteration (Clarke and Newman 2012). For example, the Channel 4 documentary series *Benefits Street*, broadcast in 2014, focused on a single street in Birmingham where there were large numbers of households dependent on a variety of state benefits. The programme reinforced the ideological position of the Coalition government that unemployment is the result of individual laziness and unwillingness to work which are encouraged by the benefits system (Wiggan 2012), rather than families' situations reflecting low skills, ill health and poor employment opportunities. The role of the media in framing social problems is discussed further in chapter 3.

George and Wilding (1994) identify five issues that distinguish between different ideologies of welfare:

- the level of state involvement in social and economic affairs
- the kinds of positive and negative consequences of state welfare provision for society, the economy and politics
- the desirable organizational forms for state intervention
- the ideal form of society in the future
- the means of attaining this ideal society.

This chapter analyses the principal ideologies that have helped to shape politics and contemporary social policies in the UK, in order to provide social work students with a critical perspective on the policies that they are involved in implementing, and on the methods that they are expected to use. We examine the relationship of these different ideologies to political parties in the UK and look at how ideology is reflected in different political perspectives on the role of the welfare state. The first part of the chapter examines liberalism, conservatism, Marxism, socialism and the Third Way. We then look beyond the UK to examine the contrasting approaches to welfare provision that have developed across different nations in the developed world. The final section of the chapter discusses the implications of ideological difference for social work in Britain and across nations.

2.2 Liberalism and neoliberalism

As the previous chapter showed, the dominant ideology shaping welfare provision during the nineteenth and early twentieth centuries was liberalism. Classic liberals, drawing on the writings of the nineteenth-century political economist Adam Smith and philosophers such as Locke, Bentham and Mill, emphasize the central importance of individual freedom and autonomy, with the role of the state being to protect that freedom, by upholding individual rights, including property rights. Protecting freedom, from a liberal point of view, means a minimal role for the state, because any activity by the state to force individuals to do anything other than respect the freedom of others to act as they choose is seen as restricting those individuals' freedom. John Stuart Mill even believed that intervention was unacceptable if an individual was at serious risk of harming him/herself:

> the only purpose for which power can be rightfully exercised over any member of a civilised community, against his will, is to prevent harm to others. His own good, either physical or moral, is not a sufficient warrant. He cannot rightfully be compelled to do or forbear because it will be better for him to do so, because it will make him happier, because, in the opinions of others, to do so would be wise, or even right. These are good reasons for remonstrating with him, or reasoning with him, or persuading him, or entreating him, but not for compelling him, or visiting him with any evil in case he do otherwise. (Mill [1859] 1989: 13)

Liberal ideology, however, does not always adhere strictly to the doctrine of state non-intervention and *laissez-faire* capitalism. Although Smith believed 'unfettered individualism would lead towards the state of economic equilibrium in which labour, land and capital were combined in the most effective way to satisfy consumer demand' (George and Page 1995: 3), he recognized that some collectively organized 'public goods', such as compulsory education, were sometimes necessary to enhance the commercial order. Other leading liberals in the late nineteenth and early twentieth centuries, such as T. H. Green and Hobhouse, also believed in the concept of *positive* as opposed to *negative* liberty, which required giving all individuals adequate opportunities for self-realization. These liberals saw the state as able to act in a disinterested way that might promote a more humane society. This led to the acknowledgement that limited state intervention concerned with education, employment and public health (organized attempts to prevent disease, promote health and prolong life in the whole population) might be necessary to promote the 'common good' (Hill et al. 1986). Hobhouse, for example, was sympathetic to public services, such as the municipal provision of gas and water, where a constant quality and a regular supply were necessary. He also supported the public provision of hospitals, libraries, transport and parks as long as the private sector was not prevented from offering alternatives, and he viewed state old-age pensions not as a hand-out but as a kind of deferred pay. As the last chapter showed, liberal ideology was therefore modified as the nineteenth century went on, with a gradual acceptance of the need for state intervention in an increasingly wide range of activities, such as public health, employment legislation to restrict the hours of work of women and children, and the introduction of legislation requiring parents to send their children to school.

Neoliberalism represents a contemporary revival of liberal ideology, particularly in relation to the role of the state in the economy. The economic and social problems experienced by the USA and Western Europe in the 1970s led to questions about the viability of the continued expansion of their welfare states because of the levels of taxation and public expenditure required. Neoliberal economists, such as Milton Friedman, who developed the doctrine of monetarism, argued that the role of the state in the economy should be limited to controlling the money supply, and, through that, inflation. Taxes should be kept as low as possible in order not to interfere with the free operation of the market. The state's remit, according to neoliberals, should therefore be limited to providing services, like public health, which the market could not supply (Ellison 2012), with individuals otherwise responsible for purchasing services in the open market. These ideas reflected the political philosophy of writers such as Friedrich Hayek, who, in his 1944 book *The Road to Serfdom*, argued that the greater the role of the state in society, the more it necessarily coerced people and reduced their liberty/freedom.

Pratt (2006) argues that three key assumptions underpin neoliberalism: (i) *methodological individualism*, which asserts everything can be understood as and reduced to the level of the individual – this is encapsulated in Thatcher's widely quoted assertion, 'there is no such thing as society, only individuals and families'; (ii) *rationality*, embodying the belief that individuals always act both rationally and in their own self-interest; and (iii) *market supremacy*, the notion of the market as the ideal location in which calculative, rational and well-informed individuals can engage in exchanges. Neoliberals argued that low taxation and minimal state intervention in the market would generate wealth which would 'trickle down' from the rich to the poor, avoiding the need for any redistribution of income by the state. However, there is convincing research evidence that low, non-progressive taxation (i.e. the same rate of tax at all levels of income) benefits those in the higher social classes and disadvantages those in the lowest social classes.

2.3 Conservatism and neo-conservatism

Conservatism is an ideology that has been seen as difficult to define because there is no single text, or group of texts, that provides its foundation (Bochel 2012: 64), and, indeed, it is characterized by pragmatism, which means that its principles are flexible. Lowe (2005: 25) described traditional conservative philosophy as a commitment to 'conserving what is best in the old while adapting constantly to the new', which raises the question of what things are seen as 'best in the old'. Conservatives conceive of society as an organic whole which has developed according to natural laws, and which is therefore threatened by any sudden, radical change. The heterosexual nuclear family, with its clearly differentiated gender roles, is seen as a universal natural system central to social stability. Social hierarchy and inequality are accepted as part of the natural order, but within an unequal society the wealthy have an obligation to help those who are less fortunate, through charity and through some limited social reform by the state, although this obligation is tempered by the extent to which those deemed less fortunate are prepared to live by and support traditional values. Conservatism, like liberalism, is committed to private property and support for a free-market economy, and views state intervention as inefficient, and state monopoly as damaging to individual freedom. However, because human nature is seen as imperfect, conservatives concede some government intervention is necessary, particularly to control crime and to maintain law and order (Bochel 2012). The importance of Parliament, the monarchy, nationality and retaining and strengthening national pride are also key aspects of British conservatism.

These beliefs are associated with the Conservative Party of the post-war period until the late 1970s, when neoliberal ideology became more influential within the party. The Conservative Party, and conservatism, in the period from 1950 to 1979, was characterized by a pragmatic approach to social policy, sometimes referred to as the Middle Way (George and Wilding 1994), which is exemplified by their qualified support for the welfare state, despite the fact that it represented a fairly radical extension of the role of the state and a shift in the balance of responsibility for some aspects of individual welfare from the family to the state.

Neo-Conservatives seek to revive some social principles that were prevalent in the nineteenth century. Heywood (2012) lists the main concerns of neo-Conservatives as being (i) law and order, (ii) public morality, and (iii) national identity. They hold a pessimistic view of human nature. For example, they do not accept that crime could be linked to structural inequalities and place emphasis on punishment for those who break the law and deterrence of potential criminals, rather than on rehabilitation and prevention by addressing some of the underlying causes. This is summed up in the assertion by Michael Howard when he was Home Secretary in 1993 that:

> Prison works. It ensures that we are protected from murderers, muggers and rapists – and it makes many who are tempted to commit crime think twice ... This may mean that more people will go to prison. I do not flinch from that. We shall no longer judge the success of our system of justice by a fall in our prison population. (Quoted in the *Guardian*, 26 August 2004)

Neo-Conservatives believe, furthermore, that conventional lifestyles prevent a breakdown of the social order. Young people are often characterized as unable to defer gratification, and those who adopt 'alternative' lifestyles, such as single mothers and gay couples, are held responsible for a host of social ills. Similarly, immigrants and asylum seekers who may come to the UK with different ethnic and religious identities are likely to be perceived by neo-Conservatives as threatening 'our' national heritage and identity unless they assimilate fully into 'homogeneous' British society.

The New Right and the welfare state: neoliberalism combined with neo-Conservatism

Neoliberal ideas were taken up enthusiastically in Britain by the 'New Right' Conservative Party in the 1980s and 1990s, under the leadership of Margaret Thatcher and later John Major, and in the USA by the Republican president Ronald Reagan.

The New Right embraced aspects of both neoliberalism and neo-Conservatism despite some of the implicit contradictions between the two ideologies. For example, the Thatcher government's neoliberal economic policy abandoned the commitment to full employment, as an unjustified intervention in the free market, and deliberately allowed unemployment to rise in order to control inflation. This resulted in very high levels of male unemployment which undermined men's breadwinner role within the family and, according to some neo-Conservative writers, led to increasing levels of family breakdown, and, in the absence of male authority in the increasing numbers of lone mother families, to increased levels of crime by young men who lacked an appropriate role model (Morgan 1995).

The political consensus which had prevailed during the post-war period about the need for universal welfare provision broke down. Neoliberals, such as Reagan and Thatcher, advocated the 'rolling back' of the state's involvement in the economy and society, in order to allow the free operation of the market, in which competition was seen to maximize economy, efficiency and effectiveness. Although it was not politically possible to fully implement neoliberal economic policies, there was a policy shift in that direction with important implications for welfare provision generally (see chapter 1) and for social work. Ideas about minimizing state intervention and promoting individual autonomy and enterprise were key tenets.

The New Right's aim was to cut public expenditure, leaving state-provided services as a minimal last-resort 'safety net' for those who were unable to buy the services that they needed in the market. Consumer choice within a market was seen as the mechanism which, through competition, would produce services to meet individual needs and wants in the most efficient and cost-effective way. No consideration was given to the possibility that the private sector might only respond to initiatives promising high profit margins, and could potentially exploit vulnerable people to ensure maximum profits, thereby reducing rather than enhancing choice and quality.

The New Right depicted the provision of services by the state as inefficient and unresponsive to individual needs and preferences, a view captured by the derogatory reference to a 'one size fits all' approach. Under the Thatcher and Major governments, there was an important shift in the balance within the *mixed economy of welfare.* State-provided services, such as social care in the community or residential care services for children, were increasingly replaced by services *provided* by private and third-sector non-profit contractors, but *funded* by the state on the basis of a competitive tendering process. It was argued that this would ensure services that were better matched to individual needs, offered choice and were both cheaper and more innovative.

Some areas, such as education, health and personal social services, remain publicly *provided*, as well as publicly *funded* services, but now operating in *quasi markets.* In these quasi markets, different parts of the public sector compete with each other for funding, with competition seen as the most effective way to ensure the best service for the lowest cost. Services are funded and provided by the state and subject to state regulation – for example, through audits and inspections. The term 'quasi market' was first used by Le Grand in 1991 to refer to the split between purchaser and provider in the NHS. GPs were given the power to 'purchase' hospital services for their patients from competing 'provider' hospitals. The assumption underpinning this policy approach was that the hospitals providing services that offered the best value for money would thrive, gaining contracts from GPs, while less efficient hospitals would have to improve their services or face 'going out of business'. It is important to note that the 'purchaser' in this case is not the individual patient, operating in a healthcare market, but a GP, or GP practice, bulk-purchasing hospital services on behalf of all their patients.

Although this neoliberal perspective was originally identified with the New Right governments of Thatcher and Major, the ideology continued to shape the policies of the succeeding New Labour and Coalition governments. Citizens are conceptualized as individual consumers choosing which welfare services to 'consume', as if these were no different from commodities offered by competing supermarkets. Competition is the principal mechanism determining the cost of the services available, within a state regulatory framework which sets certain minimum quality standards. This competition ensures that services are provided at the lowest cost compatible with achieving the minimum prescribed standard. There is a presumption that consumer demand will ensure that the market responds by offering services that the public want.

John Clarke (2004), in an article on the limits and logic of neoliberalism, shows how it gains legitimacy and obscures other ways of seeing the world. It presents a version of reality which depoliticizes the public realm and draws false boundaries between public and private spheres. In this way, resistances are neutralized and alternative positions demobilized because the view that is projected is that there is no viable alternative. Such an analysis can be linked to Lukes' notion of three dimensions of power (Lukes [1974] 2005). The first dimension is concerned with the exercise of power to determine the outcome where issues are explicitly contested; the second involves the power to exclude issues from consideration by 'agenda setting'; the third dimension concerns the shaping of people's desires and preferences, without their being aware of it. The third dimension of power is the dimension in which ideology operates to produce a particular set of common-sense beliefs which are particularly difficult to question, or to think beyond. Clarke draws on Foucault's notion of discursive power (the power of culturally accepted and reinforced ideas to shape norms and views) which bears some resemblance to Lukes' third dimension of power. Clarke shows how neoliberal ideology, which presents globalized capitalism as an uncontrollable force, makes spending on welfare indefensible because it undermines the capacity of nations to compete successfully in a global market. He also shows how neoliberalism has consistently been hostile to welfare states and collectivism by claiming they were characterized by bureaucratic inefficiency and limited by the selfish interests of professionals. This provided the basis for arguing that competitive markets would open up greater choice, be more efficient economically and more flexible and dynamic. In this way neoliberalism conflates the motives, interests and calculative ability of the most well-informed consumers of commodities with service users looking for services to meet their needs. The needs and welfare of this latter group merit serious societal consideration and expert assessment and they may arguably be poorly met by a state system whose key criterion is efficiency, conceptualized as 'value for money'. By reducing all considerations to issues of the cost-effectiveness of state-funded services, neoliberalism dehumanizes and commodifies both service users and those who deliver services to them. In doing so, it overlooks moral and social principles which may offer an alternative set of rationales for the way in which the state provides welfare services for its citizens.

The neoliberalism of the 2010–15 Coalition government was unrestrained by any countervailing ideology which might have sought to protect the family. There was a further withdrawal of the state from both funding and providing welfare services, with substantial cuts to local authority budgets and major reforms of the social security system, with the aim of maximizing labour market participation. Working-age claimants of welfare benefits have had the value of their benefits cut, and have been stigmatized as 'shirkers' and 'skivers' by government ministers, despite the fact that, in the majority of working-age households that are poor and claiming benefits, at least one member is in paid work.

2.4 Marxism and socialism

Marx, writing in the nineteenth century, at the height of the industrial revolution in Britain, offered an analysis of the economy and society which fundamentally challenged liberalism, and provided the foundations for Marxism and socialism. He argued that the basis for capitalism is private property, and in particular the ownership of the means of production by a small minority – the capitalist class or *bourgeoisie* – which is able to exploit the majority of the population – the working class, referred to by Marx as the *proletariat* – who are forced to sell their labour power to the capitalists in order to survive. Capitalists seek to maximize the profits that they make by exploiting the working class, paying workers the minimum necessary for them to reproduce themselves and their families from day to day, and from generation to generation. The bourgeoisie constitute the ruling class and they exercize power within the state in the interests of capital. The working class, by organizing itself collectively to resist capitalists, seeks to increase wages and improve working conditions. Capitalists in turn resist these demands because they threaten their profits. Capitalist society is characterized, therefore, by exploitation, class conflict, inequality and social injustice. Marxists believe that this situation can only be brought to an end by revolution, resulting in the overthrow of capitalism and its replacement by communism, a system in which private property is abolished, the means of production are collectively owned, and goods are distributed according to need. Within Marxist theory, *socialism* represents a transitional state between capitalism and communism, in which the state controls the means of production and plays a key role in planning the economy.

Marxism is a *materialist* ideology, which means that it is based on the view that the economic system determines the characteristics of society, and it is therefore only by changing the economic system that real social change can be achieved. Marxism is simultaneously descriptive, analytical and prescriptive, in that it not only describes how society is and why it is the way that it is but also suggests a specific course of action which is needed to change it.

From a Marxist point of view, the welfare state is seen as the outcome of class struggle, in which concessions have been made to the working class, in order to ensure the continuation of capitalism and prevent its revolutionary overthrow. Dean (2012) identifies three different strands within Marxist critiques of the welfare state. The *instrumentalist* critique sees the welfare state as operating entirely in the interests of capitalism. The education system and the health service, for example, function to produce workers with the qualities that capitalist employers require. The social security system and labour market policies operate to control and regulate workers who are unemployed or temporarily inactive. The *structural-logical* critique acknowledges that the welfare state is the outcome of political struggle and has brought genuine gains to the working class, but argues that ultimately the economic interests of capital prevail, so that economic growth and the protection of profit limit the expansion of the welfare state. The welfare state functions ideologically to manipulate the working class so that they are unaware of the fact that they continue to be exploited. Finally, *neo-Marxists* argue that the welfare state contains inherent contradictions. While it genuinely benefits the working class, at the same time it functions to discipline working-class people and maintain their exploitation. So, for example, compulsory education or the conditions attached to social security benefits act as a form of social control. Marxist critiques of social work argue that, at the same time as social workers help to alleviate suffering, their work is part of the surveillance and containment of the working class by the state in the interests of the ruling class.

The term *socialism* is used in a broad sense to refer to an ideology whose central premise is a commitment to social ownership of the means of production and to equality, in contrast to liberalism's central commitment to private property and individual liberty (Dean 2012). It has many variants but it is founded largely on Marxist ideas, although it also has its origins in religious and ethical utopian thinking that predates Marx's writings. Socialism starts from a very different conception of human nature and the nature of society from neoliberalism or conservatism. Whereas neoliberalism and conservatism are premised on a view of human nature as fundamentally selfish and society as composed of individuals in a permanent state of competition for resources, socialism has a more optimistic view of human nature and society.

Socialists, drawing on Marx, believe that the working class is exploited by and through capitalism. Socialism is directly critical of capitalism because of its dehumanizing effects, its individualistic competitive ethos and its willing exacerbation of social inequality (Dean 2012). The solution put forward by socialists has been to abolish capitalism by taking the means of production into collective ownership, controlled by the state on behalf of society as a whole rather than being in the hands of private entrepreneurs and investors. Socialists are divided in their ideas about how a transition from a capitalist economy to a socialist one can be achieved, and in whether they see socialism as the end goal or a means to achieving communism (Dean 2012).

Revolutionary socialists envisage the overthrow of capitalism and its replacement with a socialist system, under which the state would gradually 'wither away', leading to a truly communist state. Early *democratic socialists*, such as Tawney, Titmuss, Plant and Harrington, believed a socialist society could be successfully achieved through a process of incremental reform, or that market socialism was possible, whereby cooperative, private and state forms of ownership, with substantial worker control, could coexist within a largely socialist society.

Social Democracy, the Labour Party and the welfare state

Socialist ideology found political expression in the nineteenth-century trade union movement, representing the interests of the working class, and in the early twentieth century in the founding of the Labour Party. The ideals of the Labour Party, at least until the early 1990s, were broadly socialist, in the sense that the party sought a reduction in inequality through state intervention in the economy to redistribute resources, both directly in the form of financial redistribution and through the provision of services. The aim, however, was not to replace capitalism with socialism but rather to moderate the effects of capitalism and to achieve a greater degree of social justice. This political approach is referred to as *social democracy*. The National Health Service, in its provision of a universal service free at the point of delivery, reflected social democratic ideology, as did state intervention in the economy to maintain full employment. Other aspects of the post-war welfare state, such as the contributory national insurance system, with a national assistance 'safety net' for those who did not qualify for national insurance benefits, arguably reflected a continuation of liberal political ideology.

The vision which underpinned the Seebohm Report's proposal for a generic social work service (see chapter 1 and chapter 5 for further discussion) arguably reflects a social democratic perspective on the role of social work. Its vision of a community service for all families, in which a universal service would be offered to families on the basis of need – had it been fully implemented – would have provided a social equivalent to the NHS. Similarly the community development movement in social work in the 1970s represented an attempt to move away from the liberal paternalism that characterized social work in the post-war period, and towards providing communities with the necessary resources to devise their own solutions to problems.

2.5 The Third Way

The Third Way emerged as a political ideology during the 1990s, in the wake of a series of global economic crises and the demise of the Eastern-bloc communist regimes. The key architects of Third Way ideology were the sociologist Anthony Giddens, and Tony Blair, then leader of the Labour Party. The Third Way was a response to the economic and political challenges posed by changes in capitalism in the latter part of the twentieth century. Capitalism increasingly operated at a supranational level, with multinational corporations operating in a rapidly changing global economy (see chapter 7). As a result, the power of nation states to control national economies was greatly reduced, and this undermined the basis of Keynesian economics, which was an important part of the post-war welfare settlement, and which was based on state intervention in the economy to maintain full employment.

Third Way ideology represented a pragmatic response to the problems created for nation states by globalization, neither advocating a strong, omnipresent state nor an all-embracing market. It emphasized 'modernization', which meant combining centralized state planning with the adoption of the managerialist techniques associated with the private sector. Third Way ideology was committed, on the one hand, to promoting social justice and democracy – for example, by tackling child and pensioner poverty and by strengthening the voice of service users – while, on the other hand, it was preoccupied with preventing welfare dependency and promoting economic competitiveness. Its vision of welfare was intrinsically linked with obligation, responsibility and work, and its conception of social justice was equality of *opportunity* rather than equality of *outcome*. The role of the state within Third Way thinking was to ensure the competitiveness of the UK in the global economy. Blair described the Third Way as 'a way of marrying together an open, competitive and successful economy with a just, decent and humane society' (Driver and Martell 2000: 148). Giddens (1998) argued that his ideological position transcended traditional left-wing politics (linked with the old Labour Party and socialism) and right-wing politics (linked with the Conservative Party and neoliberalism), while still allowing Britain to be competitive within a global market.

While stressing equality, in the form of equal opportunity (see chapter 4 for discussion about the different forms and understandings of equality), the Third Way rejected income redistribution as a means to achieve social justice and embraced neoliberal economic policies, attempting to synthesize them with more left-wing social policies. The Third Way has been strongly criticized by both social democrats and socialists, and by some neoliberals who argue the impossibility of combining these apparently contradictory ideologies. By accepting neoliberal economic policies and rejecting Keynesianism, Third Way philosophy embraced the dominance of the market and left the effects of global capitalism largely unchallenged. Within a system that gave a major role to the market, the state's function was to provide a regulatory framework for welfare services and to 'steer' them by using the performance management methods of the private sector, such as setting performance or output targets to achieve policy goals, leaving the means of achieving them to be decided at a more local level.

The role of the state was to promote national economic competitiveness by making a 'social investment' in human capital (people's skills), and thereby to 'enable' people to provide for themselves through employment. Paid work was seen as the basis of citizenship for everyone, and there was therefore a commitment to gender equality, which emphasized women's position in the labour market, to a greater extent than men's rights and obligations in relation to unpaid work in the home (Lewis and Campbell 2007). Because of the centrality of paid work for the Third Way conception of citizenship, state support was conditional on recipients showing themselves to be responsible, diligent and willing to help themselves.

This emphasis on individuals' responsibilities rather than their rights in relation to the state reflects the incorporation of *Communitarian* ideas into Third Way ideology. Communitarianism is a school of thought exemplified by the work of Etzioni (1998). It attempts to moderate what its advocates see as the extreme individualism of neoliberalism through a focus on communities and the common good. It sees families, schools and other social institutions as inculcating moral and community values into individuals and therefore sees individual rights as needing to be matched with, and dependent upon, an individual's social responsibilities.

The Third Way, New Labour and the welfare state

Third Way ideology was given expression in the Labour Party, which, under Blair's leadership, was transformed into 'New Labour'. New Labour represented a very different set of political beliefs from 'old' Labour. The links between the Labour Party and the trade unions were weakened and the party opted not to re-nationalize the many services and industries that the New Right Conservative governments had previously privatized. They also battled against and expelled many of the party's traditionalists, eventually doing away with the highly symbolic, socialist, Clause IV of the Labour Party's constitution, which called for the 'common ownership of the means of production'.

Implementation of the Third Way vision of the 'enabling' state meant that the New Labour government focused on social policies that would reduce dependence on state support and promote labour market participation, so that as many adults as possible were able to support themselves through paid work. New Labour's slogan in the 1997 election was 'Education, education, education', underlining the commitment to invest in skills which would put the UK in a strong position to compete in the 'knowledge economy'. 'Enabling' also involved thinking about long-term social investment to ensure equality of opportunity. New Labour replaced the vocabulary of poverty with the concept of social exclusion, a concept which was intended to convey the complex interaction between a whole host of factors, such as poverty, poor housing, crime and educational underachievement, which led to the intergenerational transmission of social and economic disadvantage. Their solution to social exclusion was early intervention to prevent the repetition of social exclusion in the next generation. The Sure Start programme described in chapter 1 is one example of this social investment strategy, intended to deliver long-term benefits. State support for people of working age who were not in employment, under New Labour as under the New Right, became more limited, means-tested and often conditional upon labour market activity, hence the 'welfare to work' strategy which was one of New Labour's hallmarks ('a hand up not a hand out' was one of the slogans for New Labour's welfare reforms introduced in 1998). Some commentators therefore argue that such a position is merely neoliberalism under another name (Clarke and Newman 1997; Newman 2004).

2.6 Welfare states in context: comparing welfare regimes

> Social work . . . cannot be understood simply as an evolving humanitarian reflex action, nor . . . stemming neatly from the professional projects of social work . . . What has become clear is that context matters and welfare regimes are extremely important. (Harris 2008: 676)

The preceding discussion has examined some of the key political ideologies that have had a significant influence on welfare policies in the UK over the last century. All Western European nations have developed state welfare policies that provide income replacement for unemployment, sickness and retirement; education and health services; entitlements to leave for maternity and paternity; and the provision of social care services. However, the ideologies that inform those policies differ. The specific political and economic histories and the cultural traditions of different countries affect the way in which welfare regimes have developed in these nation states. This in turn leads to alternative models for providing services and to significantly different outcomes in terms of issues such as the distribution of poverty and wealth, employment rates, the position of women in the labour market, and the relative situations of one-parent and two-parent families. Despite most Western countries experiencing economic problems in the decades from the 1970s onwards, and despite the global dominance of neoliberal ideology, the choices made by some governments have resulted in fewer internal fiscal crises and the continuation of more generous and universal welfare provision in those countries.

Esping-Andersen (1990) tried to explain these national differences through an analysis of how differences in political ethos, activism and institutions influenced the development of welfare regimes in industrialized countries. The principal focus of his analysis was on how different welfare regimes structure income replacement when this is necessary because of illness, unemployment and retirement. He divided welfare states into three 'ideal types', differentiated both by levels of state spending on welfare and by the logic underpinning their division of different welfare functions between the family, the state and the market.

Liberal welfare regimes, exemplified by the UK and the USA, are identified as having less generous and more conditional and means-tested benefits, and are highly allied with the private market. The role of the state is 'residual', i.e. state provision is a last resort when an individual's needs cannot be met by the family and the market. This tends to result in the recipients of state support being stigmatized for failing to provide for themselves.

Conservative welfare regimes, typical of much of continental Europe, have much less extensive market involvement in welfare provision. They are more concerned with preserving status, hierarchy and traditional family structures, with care often being undertaken by the family and third-sector organizations. They therefore focus on the needs of the male breadwinner, with less support for female employment and children's rights. Esping-Andersen noted their more generous overall social spending when compared with liberal welfare regimes.

Social democratic welfare regimes, characteristic of the Scandinavian countries, have the most generous state welfare provision and greater income equality (Esping-Andersen and Myles 2011). They also rely less on direct cash transfers and assistance and more on generous expenditure on education, social care and health services. Consequently, most citizens express high interpersonal and inter-group trust and a commitment to voluntary work and supporting the 'common good' (Kvist et al. 2012). These social-democratic regimes promote equality based on citizenship (for further discussion of citizenship, see chapter 4) and offer considerable support to women, children and ethnic minorities. They accord the private market a minimal role and are committed to redistribution. They use high taxation levels to create more comprehensive and universal welfare provision and social protection. This ensures higher levels of income and general well-being, even for those who are retired, unemployed or unable to work. Although both conservative and social democratic welfare states spend a lot on welfare provision, this is organized differently, has different underpinning ideologies and results in different social outcomes – for example, in terms of income inequalities and gender equality.

From the mid-1970s, Western democracies all experienced slow economic growth, intermittent fiscal crises, rising deficits and higher unemployment, albeit to different degrees. At the same time, demographic change – ageing populations and a more extended transition to adulthood – led to rising costs for higher education, pensions and health and social care. Arguments have consequently emerged that all Western nations now need to accept the need for cuts in welfare spending (Pierson 2001) and that welfare state contraction is inevitable, reflecting the dominance at a global level of neoliberal ideology which sees welfare states as a threat to the functioning of the market. Cousins (2005: 36) argues Pierson's terminology of 'austerity' and 'retrench- ment' is not easily consistent with the fact that most European countries, more affluent than ever before, were at the time spending approximately 20 per cent or more of GDP on social protection. Pierson (2001: 410) was, however, arguing that welfare states were being reshaped under the auspices of austerity rather than being completely obliterated. Welfare cutbacks have occurred in all Western welfare regimes, though to a much lesser extent in the Nordic social democratic ones. This suggests the effects of neoliberal ideology are not uniform and its impact must be understood in relation to its interaction with longer-term national political histories and ideologies.

Comparative research has shown that the continuing commitment to more uni- versal and generous welfare state provision in the Scandinavian states is based on trade union power and the solidarity and political mobilization of the working class, combined with middle-class support because of the benefit to them as well as others of collectivist provision (Kvist et al. 2012). These social democratic welfare regimes make generous provision for both young and old, whereas in countries where neolib- eral ideology has been more influential cross-generational divisions and competition are increasing (Willetts 2010).

Esping-Andersen's typology has been criticized as descriptive rather than explana- tory (e.g. Arts and Gelissen 2002), and as offering too static an account of welfare states, which in practice are not as consistent and coherent as his account appears to imply. The countries grouped together as 'Conservative' welfare regimes differ from each other in important ways. The characteristics of welfare states of Southern European countries (Spain, Portugal, Greece) are not systematically included in his typology, though a fourth grouping has subsequently been proposed to cover these countries (Arts and Gelissen 2002). Feminists have been critical of Esping-Andersen's failure to consider gender in his analysis, his exclusive focus on formal employment and the paid labour market, and his lack of attention to the role of women's unpaid caring work (see, for example, Lewis 1992, 1997). A number of alternative categoriza- tions have been proposed, which capture some aspects of welfare provision across different countries more effectively (e.g., the study of child benefit packages by Bradshaw et al. 1993). Nevertheless, despite its limitations, Esping-Andersen's typol- ogy remains a useful framework for cross-national comparisons and is still widely used.

Welfare regimes and well-being

There is a considerable body of research evidence showing that there is a link between various measures of social 'well-being' and the levels of provision and type of state welfare (Castles et al. 2010; Wilkinson and Pickett 2010; Kvist et al. 2012). Deeming and Haye's (2012: 811) comparative multi-level analysis of the *World Values Survey* data, using a modified version of Esping-Andersen's welfare regime model (see Castles et al. 2010), found that people in conservative and liberal countries reported 'at least twice the odds of unhappiness of those living in social democracies'. This finding may be explained by the fact that, although conservative countries spend large amounts on welfare, they are less egalitarian than social democratic countries, particularly in relation to women and the family. Wilkinson and Pickett (2009) have shown that there is a strong association between income inequality and a whole range of indicators of social malaise, such as crime, ill-health, poor mental health and child abuse, across Western nations. These effects are substantial. For example:

> Mental illness is more than three times as common in more unequal countries compared to more equal ones. In more equal societies people are four or five times as likely to feel they can trust each other. The proportion of the population in prison may be eight times as high, obesity twice as common, and the teenage birth rate six or seven times higher in more unequal societies. (Wilkinson and Pickett 2010: 14)

These findings are supported by other studies that show close links between more egalitarian welfare regimes and life satisfaction (Flavin et al. 2011), and between egalitarian regimes and health (Bambra et al. 2010). It is particularly striking that effects of inequality on health and life expectancy, for example, apply not only to the poor in unequal societies but also to the wealthy in those societies, leading Subramanian and Kawachi to describe inequality as a 'social pollutant' (2006: 149).

One important consequence of the association between levels of trust and equality, with implications for social work, is the negative impact of inequality on *social capital*. Social capital refers to the social networks that individuals are able to draw upon to solve problems. Where trust is low, this makes it harder for the social networks, which are the basis of social capital, to flourish. Studies have shown that social capital is linked with a range of indicators of quality of life, such as improved health outcomes, safer communities and access to a range of human and material resources which in turn affect life chances (Healy and Hampshire 2002). Social capital is a contested concept, which has been developed in different ways in the work of a number of authors (e.g. Bourdieu 1986; Coleman 1988; Putnam 2001). Despite the theoretical differences between these authors, it is an important concept because it draws attention to the significance of the social sphere and challenges the priority given to economic capital. As Healy and Hampshire argue:

> By drawing attention to the productivity of the social sphere, social capital can be used to challenge some of the neoliberal beliefs that currently dominate public policy, particularly those ideas that privilege the economic sphere over all others . . . Rather than seeing some spheres, such as the economic, as vastly more important than others, social capital draws attention to the spheres as complexly intertwined. This recognition is important for acknowledging the worth of local, as well as structural, change activity in enhancing individual and community well-being. (2002: 231–2)

A number of studies have shown that levels of social capital are higher in Scandinavian countries than in other European countries, and that this is explained by the characteristics of their welfare regimes, which provide universal services, are redistributive, and result in high levels of equality (Saltkjel and Malmberg-Heimonen 2014). This growing body of research suggests that more generous state welfare provision benefits all citizens rather than just the poor and needy.

2.7 Evaluating the impact of politics and welfare ideologies on social work

The preceding discussion makes it clear that ideologies play a very important role in shaping social policy, and thereby in determining the role of social workers. The final section of this chapter examines how ideological shifts in the UK in the post-war period have impinged on social work. A more detailed account of developments in social work governance and practice is provided in chapters 5 and 6. At the end of this section, UK social work is examined in a broader context, by briefly looking at alternative conceptualizations of the role of social work in conservative and social democratic welfare regimes in Europe.

Ideologies and social work in the UK in the post-war period

The development of social work in the period from 1945 to the 1970s reflects the dominance of liberal ideology in ideas about the roles of the family, the market and the state. Social work did not emerge as a clearly identified profession, or semi-profession, until the Seebohm Report's recommendations in 1968 for a generic service to replace the various specialist services providing for different 'problem' groups within the population. These specialist services were premised on the view that individuals should be free to conduct their affairs without state intervention except where they or others might come to some kind of harm. Most families would not expect to come into contact with welfare services, and social work was therefore a residual form of provision, dealing almost exclusively with poor people and using casework methods which assumed that individuals were responsible for their circumstances, and that with the right guidance to change their behaviour their problems could be overcome.

The Seebohm Committee's brief, when it was set up by the Labour government in 1965, may be seen as offering a more social democratic perspective on the role of the state relative to families. The Committee was asked to 'consider what changes are desirable to secure an effective family service' (Dickens 2011: 24). The Committee recommended the setting up of a new local authority department: 'providing a community based and family oriented service which will be available to all. This department will reach far beyond the discovery and rescue of social casualties; it will enable the greatest number of individuals to act reciprocally, giving and receiving service for the well-being of the whole community' (Seebohm 1968: 11). This recommendation proposed a very different type of provision from the collection of unco-ordinated services aimed at a small minority of the population which had existed hitherto. It was to be a universal service ('available to all', and not just for 'social casualties') and its aim was to promote 'the well-being of the whole community', through reciprocal action, rather than to work in a paternalistic way to reform individuals. It can therefore be seen as based on a rather different ideology from the liberal ideas which had underpinned social work previously.

Although the recommendation for a single local authority social services department was accepted and implemented in 1970, the social democratic vision of a universal service aimed at community well-being was never realized. In part this may be because of the economic crisis that struck in the 1970s, which meant that the resources necessary to establish such a service were not made available. The 1970 general election brought in a Conservative government, which was ideologically opposed to the expansion of the role of the state in relation to the family. The Labour government, elected in 1975, faced continuing economic problems which precluded significant spending on a new, greatly extended social service. The late 1970s and 1980s saw the rise of neoliberal ideology and the attacks from the political right on the state as unaffordable, inefficient and damaging to the economy and to enterprise. At the same time, Marxists and feminists were critical of state power as oppressive, and of social work as serving the interests of the ruling class by individualizing problems and thereby controlling and containing dissent and resistance.

The Thatcher and Major governments of the 1980s and 1990s combined neoliberalism with conservatism, as the discussion of the New Right in section 2.3 has indicated. Conservative ideology, which emphasized the centrality of the heterosexual nuclear family, with clearly differentiated gender roles, underpinned the introduction of community care policies for disabled adults and older people. Care by the family, which effectively meant care by women, was the default arrangement, with social workers responsible for allocating limited resources to provide substitute care only where the family was unable to meet an individual's needs. Social care services were therefore a last resort when the family and the market could not provide.

In relation to families with children, there was a similar residualization, with social work intervention restricted to families where there was a risk of harm to the child. This is consistent with conservatism, which differentiates sharply between the private and the public spheres and sees the privacy of the family as needing protection from state interference.

The influence of neoliberal ideology on social work during this period is evident in a number of ways. The pre-eminence of the market, and the conceptualization of recipients of welfare services, or at least some recipients, as consumers, positioned social workers as brokers, assisting consumers to access services in the 'care market'. At the same time, in the context of the neoliberal attempt to 'roll back the state', cuts to spending on social services meant that the role of social workers was increasingly to ration limited provision to those whose needs were greatest.

The 'Third Way' approach of the 1997 New Labour government sought to synthesize elements of neoliberal economic policy with social democratic social policy. Many of the policies which had been introduced by the Thatcher and Major governments were continued under New Labour. For social work, this involved a continuing commitment to and extension of service user choice as the mechanism for both empowering service users and driving up the quality of services.

Private-sector management methods were seen as the way to modernize public services, and this resulted in the introduction of a multiplicity of performance targets against which the quality of public services was to be measured. One of the consequences of this for social workers was an increasing requirement to record their activities on information systems. These policies were highly centralized, with central government specifying the targets that local services were to meet, and requiring the submission of regular returns to the central government department responsible.

However, the government also devolved tasks to local authorities in relation to social care provision and encouraged them to promote inter-professional and inter-agency working. Local authorities were charged with overseeing and organizing social care, working in partnership with the health service, private and third-sector providers, and with service users. Consumer voice and choice were key discourses in policy documents, but so was 'value for money' linked to increasingly restricted budgets, tightening eligibility criteria and greater means-testing and charging for services. The diversion of adult social care services away from those with moderate levels of need resulted in only services for 'survival' being allocated public resources (Tanner 2003), essentially 'a social trade-off between the majority and the minority' (Humphrey 2003: 19).

New Labour's ideological commitment to 'social investment' resulted in substantial spending on a range of early intervention and prevention initiatives intended to promote social inclusion. However, social work was largely excluded from these community initiatives and from direct support roles. Social workers were denied the opportunity to do supportive and preventative work which might have utilized their relationship-building and therapeutic knowledge and skills, and were increasingly restricted to control and surveillance functions in relation to safeguarding children, and to assessing need and rationing social care services. Social workers were encouraged to persuade service users to take over the wholesale responsibility for their care packages via direct payments and personal budgets (see chapter 6). All these developments imply a residual role for social work, with policies focused on an individualized rather than a social conception of need.

The Coalition government brought together the Conservative and Liberal Democrat parties, both of which were committed to the implementation of 'austerity' as a way of responding to the economic crisis precipitated by the collapse of the banks in 2008. This involved the continuation of neoliberal economic policy privileging the market, and reversion to neoliberal social policies with substantial cuts to public spending and therefore a residual role for the welfare state. For social work, this has meant an emphasis on risk management and on targeting resources on those who constitute the highest risk, to themselves or others.

Welfare regimes and the role of social work

How is the nature of social work affected by the characteristics of the welfare regime in which it operates? One of the difficulties in answering this question is that the conception of what social work is and how it is organized professionally differ significantly between different countries. This makes comparisons between them difficult. As Lorenz (2006: 8) points out, '[i]t is simply impossible to speak of social work in Europe as a coherent, let alone integrated, entity'. A whole range of different titles are associated with what he refers to as 'the social professions' – social assistant, social pedagogue, social educator, youth worker, community worker, care worker, social advisor – and the combination and balance between these different kinds of workers, their level of education and their status, the nature of the work they do, and with whom, mean that it is difficult to delineate what constitutes social work and how it relates to the rest of the welfare system across different countries. The difficulty of making such comparisons across welfare states is in itself informative, and indicates that different welfare states have different conceptions of what social work is and who needs social work services, which may be related to underlying ideological differences between welfare regimes.

To illustrate some of the differences and the difficulties in making these comparisons, we look at the findings of a cross-national study of family support services. This compared English policy – a liberal welfare regime – with policies in five European countries that exemplify conservative (Italy, France, Germany, the Netherlands) and social democratic (Denmark) regimes (Boddy and Statham 2009; Boddy 2013). In France, Germany and Italy, the family has a protected status within the constitution. Denmark, in common with other Scandinavian countries, emphasizes the rights of children as citizens, and stipulates that all citizens have the right to support from the state. This leads to the provision of family support in both types of welfare regime as a universal service, rather than a targeted one, or, in a distinction formulated by Katz and Hetherington (2006), a *holistic* system, in which child protection is just one element of a system that is focused on family support as a universal service. By contrast, the UK and most other English-speaking countries, which are liberal welfare regimes, have a *dualistic* system, which is primarily focused on child protection and rescue, with family support as a separate and subsidiary activity. This is consistent with liberal welfare regimes' reluctance to intervene in the family, and the residual role of the state.

In social democratic regimes, family support is provided primarily by the state, whereas in most of the conservative welfare regimes voluntary organizations and the churches, operating locally, are seen as the most appropriate to provide these services (Katz and Hetherington 2006: 432). In both types of regime, however, services are universal, with more specialist support provided as part of a continuum rather than there being a sharp distinction between universal and targeted services. Specialist services are provided by professionals (psychologists, pedagogues, social workers or healthcare professionals) within the same setting as the universal service, with access to some services available through self-referral as well as through referral by professionals (Boddy 2013). Although Children's Centres in England under the Labour government were briefly intended to be a universal service, bringing together a range of health and welfare professionals offering support to families, specialist services remained relatively inaccessible because of very high eligibility thresholds, (Parton 2009) and under the Coalition government, because of cuts to local authority budgets, Children's Centres have once again become a service targeted on the poorest families. Katz and Hetherington (2006) found that child welfare services in England were more poorly resourced and gave less attention to prevention than in most other European countries. In social democratic welfare regimes, where family support services are provided by the state, they are well integrated with other services, and often co-located in schools. Integration and co-ordination are less easy in conservative welfare states, such as Germany, where services are provided by the voluntary sector and where it is harder to establish a common institutional basis.

The roles and status of 'the social professions' involved in providing services in different welfare regimes are also interesting indicators of ideological differences about the relative roles of state, market and family. In both conservative and social democratic welfare regimes, there is a category of highly trained professionals, known as social pedagogues, who play an important role alongside social workers in working with children and families. Their qualification involves 3–4 years' study at university level. Moss and Petrie (2002: 138) describe pedagogy as 'refer[ring] to the whole domain of social responsibility for children, for their well-being, learning and competence. It can encompass many types of provision such as childcare, youth work, family support, youth justice services, residential care, play work and study support – provision that, to English eyes, appears somewhat disparate.' It is distinguished from social work by not being primarily deficit-oriented, but instead focused on supporting children to develop their potential fully. Its aims are the social integration of children and promoting their participation as citizens: 'Theory and practice are focused on participants' everyday lives, working through relationships, and emphasising individual rights and participation in decision-making, and the development of the *whole* child: body, mind, feelings, spirit and creativity. Crucially the child is seen as a social being, connected to others and with their own distinctive experiences and knowledge' (Boddy and Statham 2009: 6).

The fact that there is no equivalent to this profession in the Anglophone liberal welfare regimes, and that the role is difficult to explain and fit into our conceptual map of social professions, reveals how powerfully ideology shapes the ways in which the relationship between families and the state or wider society are thought about. In the UK it is families that have the primary responsibility for socializing children, with the education system playing an instrumental role in equipping children with the formal qualifications they need to enter the labour market, and social work limited to intervening in families which are in some way placing their children at risk through some form of failure. By contrast, both social democratic and conservative welfare regimes, albeit in different ways, conceptualize the care and upbringing of all children as a task shared between families and the wider community, as represented either by the state or by the church or third-sector organizations.

Analysis of welfare services at a much more generic level across fifteen countries confirms that the organization and delivery of welfare services is consistent with Esping-Andersen's welfare regime typology and their differing underpinning ideologies. In liberal regimes, the family is the default provider of care both for children and for older and disabled adults, with modest levels of means-tested funding of social care by the state, and provision mainly by for-profit organizations. In conservative regimes, social care is funded by social insurance bodies, rather than the state, and services are delivered by for-profit and non-profit organizations. In contrast with both of these, in social democratic welfare states, the state provides high-quality care services for a high proportion of its citizens (Stoy 2014).

However, the global dominance of neoliberal ideology has led to the introduction of market principles into a range of care services in traditionally social democratic welfare states, with service users increasingly offered a choice of care services or cash to buy their own services, and choices for older adults between services provided by for-profit, non-profit or state organizations (Pfau-Effinger and Rostgaard 2011). These changes in turn throw up tensions and contradictions within welfare systems, whose resolution is not yet clear, underlining that globalization subjects welfare regimes to new kinds of external pressures. The implications of globalization for social work are discussed in chapter 7.

2.8 Conclusion

This chapter has outlined the principal ideological influences on the development of state welfare provision in the UK, and their implications for social work. Liberal ideas which emphasized individual liberty and proposed a minimal role for the state were dominant in the UK in the nineteenth century. These ideas were moderated, but not swept away, by social democratic ideology which played an important role in shaping the post-war welfare settlement. The influence of liberal ideology is apparent in some of the provisions of the post-war social security system, as is conservative ideology which gives a central role to the traditional nuclear family. Social work in the period from 1945 until the early 1970s reflected liberal ideology in its individualized approach to social problems and its targeted and residual role, working only with a small and relatively stigmatized section of society. Social workers were professional experts who supported and rehabilitated individuals and families who had significant needs or were experiencing multiple problems.

Although there was a brief flourishing of a conception of social work founded on social democratic ideas, exemplified by the recommendations of the Seebohm Report in 1968 for a universal community-based social work service and by the introduction of a small number of community development projects in the early 1970s, these did not survive the revival of liberal ideology, in the form of neoliberal economic policy in the late 1970s, which sought to reduce the role of the state. This led to a return to increasingly targeted and rationed social services. The pre-eminence given to the market in neoliberal ideology positioned those using care services as consumers, whose choices would influence the nature and quality of services available. Social work's role in adult care was thereby transformed from a broad remit incorporating support, rehabilitation and relationship into a narrow assessment, rationing and brokerage 'care management' incarnation. In relation to children and families, its role was increasingly focused on surveillance in order to protect children from deviant parents.

The New Labour government elected in 1997 gave expression to Third Way ideology, which combined aspects of neoliberal economic policy, and the belief in market mechanisms as producing efficient and effective services, with a commitment to a concept of social justice which stressed equality of opportunity. The care management role in adult social care was retained and strengthened through New Labour's modernization process, which sought to replace centralized bureaucratic hierarchical control in the public sector with systems of performance management modelled on the private sector to achieve a more 'hands-off' method of controlling public services. The focus of child and family social work on a minority of high-risk child protection cases remained the same. Although New Labour brought in some policies around social inclusion and initiated community-based services for children and young people, such as Connexions and Sure Start, social work was largely excluded from these.

The 2010–15 Coalition government's policies were neoliberal, without the commitment to social inclusion and social investment which characterized the Third Way. Government spending was cut very substantially and the provision of welfare benefits and services reduced as a result. Poverty rose both for those unable to work and for many of those in employment. The poorest people in society, on whom social workers primarily focus, were significantly disadvantaged financially and in terms of other rights under the Coalition government, and there was a consistent attempt to stigmatize those claiming welfare benefits as 'scroungers', in contrast to 'hard-working tax-payers'.

Esping-Andersen's (1990) analysis of European welfare regimes, despite criticisms and later modifications to his typology, provides models for welfare provision which are helpful in thinking about the implications of alternatives to current provision in the UK. Comparative analysis helps to highlight and call into question the 'common sense' assumptions of the UK system, and to demonstrate how things can be done differently, even if cultural and political differences mean that policies cannot be transferred wholesale from one national context to another. Both conservative and social democratic regimes provide social services that are more universal and less stigmatizing to their users. They are underpinned by important ideological differences which mean that they have different social goals in terms of issues such as income inequalities, the role of the family in providing welfare, or gender equality in the home and in the labour market. Social democratic welfare regimes which exist in the Nordic countries consistently come out as superior to other welfare regimes in terms of the distribution of wealth, gender equality and a wide range of measures of well-being (Goodin et al. 1999; Kvist et al. 2012). Although neoliberalism has had an impact on all developed welfare states, the lesson from cross-national analysis is that neoliberalism is not inevitable, that social action can change outcomes and that high welfare spending does not necessarily culminate in a weak economy.

Discussion questions

- What are the main arguments for and against the state's involvement in providing for citizens' welfare?
- Discuss the implications of neoliberalism for social work and social care.
- Choose an area of social work (e.g. learning disabilities, frail elderly people or child protection) and identify how Esping-Andersen's different welfare regimes would respond, in terms of the type and extent of social provision to meet need.
- What kinds of lessons can social workers learn from looking at welfare policy and practice in other countries?

Further reading

Alcock, P., May. M. and Wright, S. (eds.) (2012) *The Students' Companion to Social Policy*, 4th edn, Oxford: Wiley-Blackwell. Chapters by Ellison ('Neoliberalism'), Page ('Social Democracy'), Bochel ('The Conservative Tradition').

George, V. and Wilding, P. (1994) *Welfare and Ideology*, Hemel Hempstead: Harvester Wheatsheaf.

Katz, I. and Hetherington, R. (2006) 'Co-operating and communicating: a European perspective on integrating services for children', *Child Abuse Review*, 15 (6), 429–39.

Lister, R. (2010) *Understanding Theories and Concepts in Social Policy*, Bristol: Policy Press, ch. 1, 'Dominant Post-war Ideological Perspectives: From "Middle Way" to "Third Way" and Beyond'.

3 Social Problems and Social Work

3.1 Introduction

As we saw from chapter 1, state social work emerged as a response to the residual problems that were left unresolved by the universal welfare services established by the welfare state. The nature and definition of the social problems which social workers deal with have changed in important ways over the post-war period. 'Cruelty to children' and children being 'sinned against' have been replaced by child abuse; the social care of older people and that of people with disabilities have emerged as new problems in recent years, in terms both of their scale and of the kinds of solutions identified; the 'problem of unmarried mothers' has disappeared, replaced perhaps for a period by the 'problem of teenage pregnancy'. These examples raise questions about how something comes to be defined as a social problem and under what circumstances. This chapter will explore these questions, in order to offer social workers a critical approach to the social problems that they are asked to address, and to enable them to assess for themselves the claims made by experts and by politicians about social problems, which are channelled through the mass media and embedded in social policies.

The chapter begins with a brief summary of debates about knowledge and explains two contrasting views about how society functions to provide a context for understanding the contested nature of social problems. We examine the general process by which some issues become labelled as social problems and others do not, and show how the identification of the source of the problem may change, as the way the problem is understood or 'constructed' changes. We have already seen in chapter 1 how, in the nineteenth century, the problem of poverty was seen as the consequence of individuals' misfortune or idleness, but came to be seen in the immediate post-war period as the product of the economic cycle. These different understandings of the problem are important because they imply very different kinds of solutions and, as the previous two chapters have shown, such understandings are significantly shaped by different ideological perspectives. We outline a number of alternative theoretical perspectives on social problems to show how the adoption of a particular perspective carries with it specific implications for what the appropriate response is. The final section of the chapter offers a detailed analysis of social problems relevant to social work, starting with an examination of the emergence of child abuse as a social problem, and the ways in which its definition has changed and expanded over time. We then look at wealth (as opposed to poverty) as an issue which is generally invisible as a social problem. Looking at wealth as a social problem demonstrates how the interests of the powerful successfully promote certain issues as social problems whilst preventing others from entering our consciousness (Lukes [1974] 2005). Finally we argue that social workers have largely failed to recognize both domestic violence and the abuse of vulnerable adults as widespread social problems or to understand fully their causes and consequences, and discuss some of the possible reasons for this.

3.2 Epistemological debates

This section introduces the rest of the chapter by discussing two contrasting approaches to knowledge and research. These two approaches are founded on conflicting assumptions about the nature of the social world and therefore lead to very different proposals about the best ways to study and understand it. Philosophers have long been concerned with questions about the nature of reality, what exists (*ontology*) and the basis of our knowledge about the world (*epistemology*). How do we know what we know and can we ascertain whether what we think we know is actually true or real? These questions, which are difficult to answer in relation to the physical world, are perhaps even more difficult to answer, and more controversial, in relation to the social world. Are there different ways of understanding the world and are they all equally valid? Can we be impartial, disinterested 'truth' seekers when assessing contested knowledge claims or will we always be unavoidably influenced by our previous experiences and values? Such questions are not only of interest to philosophers, but also important for social workers as they intervene in social situations which have been identified as problematic in some way, in order to ameliorate them. What is the basis for identifying a situation as a problem? And what theories about the nature of individuals, the family and society underpin the intervention being made? How were those theories developed? How can we know what kinds of intervention are appropriate and are likely to produce an effective outcome? What kinds of material constitute evidence? Different theories of knowledge (epistemologies) provide different answers to these questions and lead to different kinds of actions. Here we provide a brief summary of some of the principal epistemological positions before examining their implications for understanding social problems.

A *positivist, objectivist* or *realist epistemology* asserts there is a single reality or truth 'out there' waiting to be discovered through empirical investigation. From within this perspective, impartial research and rigorous hypothesis testing (often using quantitative, ideally experimental methods) will reveal indisputable facts about the world and provide explanations for them. The social world is seen as no different in principle from the natural world, in terms of how it is to be investigated and understood. Within such a framework, randomized controlled trials (RCTs) have privileged status in terms of the quality of the evidence they are seen to produce (see chapter 6 for more in-depth discussion of RCTs in relation to social work research). These methods tend to focus on processes and explanations at the level of the individual, and to overlook or rule out social structural factors. The types and forms of knowledge generated by other kinds of research methods are seen as less objective and therefore less valuable than the kinds of quantitative evidence which experimental and quasi-experimental methods produce. Although there are fierce debates within social work about what forms of knowledge should be prioritized, this kind of positivist epistemology is currently in ascendance. Explanations of social problems suggesting apolitical, often behavioural, ways of dealing with either the individual 'causes' or 'casualties' of social problems correspondingly take precedence.

An *interpretivist, subjectivist* or *social constructionist epistemology*, conversely, asserts there are many different ways of understanding the world, all potentially equally valid. This approach focuses on the meanings of events, practices and relationships and our interpretations of what is real or unreal, true and false, right or wrong, and tends to use qualitative methods of research. Constructionists reject claims that there is one definitive answer to every question or one objective reality 'out there'. They assert that even universally accepted facts are channelled through a simplified common-sense framework (or set of assumptions) influenced by our past and present understandings and experiences. This framework only becomes apparent when it is disrupted or challenged in some way. Garfinkel (1967), an ethnomethodologist, for example, asked his students to disrupt convention and behave in their parents' homes as if they were paying lodgers and barter for goods at supermarket checkouts and then to note the bewildered, hostile responses they had evoked in order to demonstrate just how important shared interpretations and norms are.

Both positivist and constructionist epistemologies are, however, 'ideal types', in that they are rarely adopted in their purest forms. Most positivists today concur with Popper's notion of 'uncertain' or revisable truth in that all theories have the potential to be falsified, although those surviving over long periods of time may be more plausible. Most constructionists would also accept that pure versions of social constructionism or total relativity are problematic. Few people would jump out of an aeroplane to test out the 'socially constructed' law of gravity. The general public, however, probably still believe, it is possible to discover irrefutable truths, although many remain bemused that expert scientific exhortations in relation to what we should eat, drink or do to attain optimum health are constantly revised as new studies gain media attention.

3.3 Consensus and conflict theories of society

To understand this chapter fully, it is necessary not only to comprehend different views about epistemology but also to be aware that sociologists hold different beliefs about the nature of society, how it operates and whom it benefits. A consensus perspective assumes a generally optimistic view of society as functioning harmoniously for the most part and able rapidly to restore equilibrium when problems occur. From the opposing perspective, society is characterized by ongoing inequality and differential interests which lead to conflict and competition.

Consensus or order theories of society are best exemplified by the *structural-functionalist* approach dominant in sociology in the mid twentieth century. This uses metaphors of society as an organism or a machine comprised of various inter-related organs or parts, each of which contributes to its smooth running, with little acknowledgement of conflicts between the different parts that make up the whole. However, it attempts to account for the development of social institutions solely by referring to their effects, which constitutes a circular argument. Even 'deviant' behaviour is deemed functional because social exclusion, stigmatization or imprisonment act as a warning to potential future transgressors. Consensus theories therefore have difficulty in accounting for social change. If institutions all contribute in an organic way to the smooth running of society, how and why does change occur?

By contrast, *conflict theories* see society as characterized by conflicting interests, with elite groups having the power, knowledge and resources to reproduce their own privilege and control subordinate groups through ideology (influencing their desires, thoughts and feelings) and, if necessary, through coercion. From a Marxist perspective, for example, the ruling class uses its power to perpetuate its privileged position within capitalist society through the labour of the working class, who have to sell their labour power in order to survive. Feminists argue that we live in a patriarchal society where men have more power and receive the lion's share of resources, including earning more by doing jobs that are more socially valued than women's and doing less domestic and childcare work.

These contrasting theoretical perspectives on the nature of society have rather different implications for how social problems are understood. Differences in epistemological perspectives mean that there are also conflicting ideas on how social problems can be investigated and on what constitutes evidence. It is clear therefore that there is scope for considerable disagreement about what constitutes a social problem and what kinds of policies are likely to be effective in addressing them. Social workers who are called upon to intervene in a wide range of social problems need to have some understanding of these debates in order to be able to exercise their own critical judgement.

3.4 What are social problems?

It may seem obvious what a social problem is. Many examples spring to mind – violent crime, child abuse, homelessness, the war on drugs, asylum seekers, or the care of an ageing population. But in trying to explain why these are social problems, define them more closely and identify whom they affect and what their causes and solutions might be, it becomes clear that agreement about social problems is not so straightforward. We might even start vehemently disagreeing with each other. We might argue about whether spanking children is child abuse or just necessary discipline for the good of the child, how widespread it is and therefore whether it is a social problem; or perhaps whether asylum seekers are deserving victims fleeing oppressive regimes or, alternatively, duplicitous economic migrants swamping our country and stealing our jobs. Such arguments hinge upon our understanding of society and how we evaluate the information that we are presented with by politicians, the mass media and other sources.

At a basic level, an issue becomes labelled as a social problem when: (i) it attracts the attention of a particular society during a specific time period; (ii) it potentially impacts negatively on significant numbers of people (or smaller numbers of powerful people); and (iii) there is an acceptance that something needs to be and can be done about it. However, what is perceived as a social problem may change as society and social attitudes change. Unmarried motherhood was seen as a significant social problem in the nineteenth and most of the twentieth century but no longer is, because of changes both in behaviour (many more women choosing to have a child without marrying) and in social attitudes (a decline in the power of the Church and in the practice of Christianity). Few in Western societies view witchcraft as a social problem anymore, although it was seen as such in the sixteenth and seventeenth centuries. However, with increasing numbers of people coming to live in England from societies where there is a belief in witchcraft, it has re-emerged as an issue in child abuse cases, with some children in some minority communities at particular risk of being labelled as witches and maltreated. Furthermore, what is included within the scope of a particular social problem may change. Child abuse and domestic violence or abuse are two contemporary social problems whose definitions have broadened considerably over time. Some social problems, such as 'the problem of youth', may disappear and then re-emerge at a different time period but be presented differently on each occasion: from Teddy Boys in the 1950s, Mods and Rockers in the 1960s, Punks in the 1970s through to Chavs and Hoodies in the 2000s. The common element is the depiction of working-class young men as a threat to the accepted social order, despite changes in the ways in which they present themselves (Pearson 1975).

Some social problems come to be identified as such because people 'have' problems, but another route involves certain people themselves being *constituted* as the problem, although the distinction is not always clear-cut. Mentally ill people might, for example, be seen as a social problem because of individual misfortune and represented as requiring help and support. Alternatively, in the rare cases where a mentally ill person kills someone, they often become reconstructed as a threatening social problem, requiring greater surveillance and compulsory treatment. Homeless people too might be constructed as the victims of poverty, mental illness, misfortune and inadequate housing provision, or alternatively seen as culpable because of feckless behaviour or drug addiction and represented as menacing eyesores on our streets. Hence, the same people might be seen as victims, villains or perhaps nuisances at different times, or even simultaneously. When people, such as abused children or elderly or disabled people, are seen as having problems not of their making, the appeal is often to a sense of social justice. Conversely, where people such as drug users or teenage gang members are seen to be the problem because they contravene social norms, the issue often becomes reconstructed as one of social (dis)order, whether social order is achieved through rehabilitation or criminalization and incarceration.

The policies proposed to address social problems will depend on how those problems are explained. The abuse and neglect of vulnerable people in residential institutions or hospitals, for example, tends to be explained as the result of the incompetence or negligence of individual 'bad apples' (Stanley et al. 1999); an alternative explanation might look at the consequences, for staff training, pay and conditions, of services being delivered by private providers motivated by profit. These alternative explanations have rather different policy implications. Contemporary understandings of social problems are often informed by earlier perspectives. The next section provides a historical outline of different perspectives on social problems, showing how they complement or conflict, build upon or mutually influence, each other.

3.5 Early perspectives on social problems

Pathology, disorganization and value conflict

The social pathology perspective was the dominant view on social problems from the 1890s to the 1940s and located social problems mostly within defective individuals, who were seen as containable through re-education and re-socialization or through selective restriction of fertility (eugenics). Welshman (1999), for example, shows how ideas about specific families as 'social problems' in England in the 1920s and 1930s centred around claims about inherited mental deficiency, laziness and immorality caused by inbreeding, with solutions such as enforced sterilization advocated. The association of eugenics with Nazism meant that this became increasingly unacceptable as a policy approach in Britain in the post-war period. As social work emerged as an embryonic profession in the late 1940s, it pioneered casework for problem families. This emphasized re-educating families and providing them with financial and practical support, but this more humane approach remained based on a view of such families as deficient in some way. An alternative perspective, the *social disorganization* approach, emerged after the First World War. This attributed increasing alcoholism, crime and mental illness to the stresses and tensions individuals suffered during a period of significant social change. Both these perspectives were based on a realist epistemology and consensus view of society, with the proposed remedies focused on changing the individual rather than society (Manning 1987).

In the 1950s a contrasting *value conflict* perspective emerged, based on the work of the sociologist C. Wright Mills. He argued that certain groups or alliances – for example the 'power elite' consisting of 'big business', military leaders and politicians – had much greater resources not only for defining certain issues as social problems but for suggesting causes and pursuing solutions. Mills proposed a conflict view of society and challenged positivism by arguing that certain groups had more power than others to represent 'the truth'. In opposition to this conflict perspective, the social pathology/disorganization hypotheses re-emerged, albeit in a different form: the *deviant* perspective. Based on a consensus view of society, it suggested that certain subversions of socially accepted norms and rules (such as homosexuality, drug taking or theft) threatened overall societal unity. Transgressors therefore needed to be identified and neutralized before they constituted a real social problem (Rubington and Weinberg 2003).

Labelling theory, moral panics and critical perspectives

From the 1960s the value conflict perspective was used in *labelling or societal reaction theory* which proposed that deviance was not inherent in what people did, but was based on reactions to their behaviour, with those in positions of greatest power able to exert most influence in determining what was labelled a social problem (Becker 1963; Lemert 1972). People in powerful and privileged institutional positions, such as professional experts or politicians, are able to attach negative labels to relatively powerless groups, and are assisted in this by the media, which reproduce the definitions of those who have power and access to journalists. An interesting study by Chambliss (cited in Hechter and Horne 2003) illustrates the power of labelling.

In his study in Chicago, Chambliss identified two groups of high school students, both of which had a tendency to drink, steal, break curfews and vandalize property. The 'Saints' were boys who overall had good grades, came from stable middle-class households, and were careful not to be caught by the police. The 'Roughnecks' were boys from poorer and less stable households. They were more likely to be hostile in confrontations with the police and were not as careful to avoid being caught. The boys in the 'Roughneck' group were labelled as deviants. The 'Saints', even though they committed similar crimes, were not labelled because they were polite when caught and were from a higher social class. The police consistently took legal action when dealing with the 'Roughnecks'. The 'Saints' were treated far more leniently and were never prosecuted.

The credibility of the labeller and of the labelled persuades the audience of the seriousness of the behaviour and appropriate responses. The labelling school also distinguished between *primary deviance*, based on the initial labelling of a behaviour as deviant, and *secondary deviance*, when a person starts to behave and identify with the label attached to them by society. For example, someone labelled as a criminal for a minor infringement of the law such as shoplifting, may be driven to increasingly serious crimes – burglary or robbery – because of the consequences of being labelled a criminal, such as difficulties in getting a job.

The concept of a *moral panic* also emerged in the UK from the labelling perspective (Young 1971; Cohen 1972, 2002). Cohen showed how the threat posed by a normally powerless group could be artificially intensified, resulting in them being represented as a social problem. He summarized the process in this way:

> A condition, episode, person or group of persons emerges to become defined as a threat to societal values and interests; its nature is presented in a stylized and stereo-typical fashion by the mass media; the moral barricades are manned by bishops, politicians and other right-thinking people; socially accredited experts pronounce their diagnoses or solutions; ways of coping are evolved or (more often) resorted to; the condition then disappears, submerges or deteriorates or becomes more visible.
> (Cohen 1972: 9)

Cohen's study of Mods and Rockers (working-class youth cultures with divergent and distinctive dress styles and musical tastes) in the 1960s showed how, through media amplification of the threat they represented (if, indeed, there was any – the two groups had a few minor scuffles in seaside towns), they became labelled as *folk devils*, symbolizing a wider underlying social malaise or problem, i.e. degenerate youth and family breakdown. Cohen argues that, because the Mods and Rockers were portrayed as violent feuding gangs, they might have felt obliged to play out their roles, and that, as the police presence increased in response to media concern, this might also have triggered violence or uncovered minor feuding which otherwise would have gone unnoticed. Cohen therefore argues that a moral panic of this kind may actually create or aggravate a social problem, rather than simply reporting an existing one.

Gove (1975) criticized the labelling perspective, arguing that people were gener-ally categorized as mentally ill, for example, because of enduring, seriously disturbed behaviour, not because of the 'sticky' application of a mere label. However, Rosenhan (1973) demonstrated the power of labelling when he and seven associates got them-selves admitted to psychiatric hospitals in the USA without difficulty, on the pretext they were hearing voices (a symptom associated with a diagnosis of schizophrenia) despite displaying no other symptoms. After admission, all the pseudo-patients claimed they were no longer hearing voices and behaved 'normally', but had great difficulty in getting themselves discharged and shedding their 'label'. All their 'normal' actions were pathologized by the staff because of their diagnosis of schizo-phrenia, although other inpatients paradoxically discerned that they were not 'mad'. The labelling perspective, unlike the moral panic thesis linked to it, focuses primar-ily on the process and consequences of labelling rather than being concerned with the bigger question of how social problems are constructed. Therefore, although the theory illuminates how labelling can lead to a self-fulfilling prophecy and highlights the differential influence of those in positions of power, it does not offer a full theoretical account of social problems.

A *critical perspective* emerged in the 1960s and 1970s. This built on the value conflict and labelling / moral panic perspectives from a Marxist viewpoint, influenced also by the social movements of the period. The British criminologists Taylor et al. (1973) argued that much crime is caused by the material inequalities created and sustained by capitalism, and that some criminal activity represents active resistance to capitalism. Stuart Hall et al. (1978) drew on Cohen's ideas about moral panics to look at street crime and argued that capitalism used such moral panics as the basis for repression. Hall showed how the term 'mugging' was imported from America, expressing wider anxieties about working-class Black youth. The media reported that muggings had increased by 129 per cent between August 1972 and August 1973. This statistic had no valid basis because mugging was not a category in the recorded crime statistics, but it led to the identification of 'muggers' as sinister young Black men. This reinforced racist fears and prejudices and influenced calls for predominantly Black neighbourhoods to be more vigilantly policed. Folk devils and their supporters do sometimes fight back today, using social media and the internet, but their depiction as 'unambiguously unfavourable symbols' (Cohen 1972: 46) means their resistances are often neutralized and moral panic becomes linked to moral regulation in terms of reinforcing dominant societal discourses (Hier 2011). The perceived proximity of the threat (whether people feel it is likely to happen to them) and discourses of risk also appear to be important preconditions for a successful moral panic.

The six perspectives discussed illustrate how understandings of social problems have evolved and how they draw on different epistemological and political perspectives. Table 3.1, adapted from Rubington and Weinberg (2003), summarizes these different perspectives and some of the key authors associated with each.

These different analyses of social problems are founded on different approaches to knowledge and society, briefly explained at the beginning of this chapter. The early social pathology, disorganization and deviance approaches were unequivocally positivist and 'apolitical' in the sense that they assumed that the identification of social problems was uncontroversial, reflecting a consensus view of society. They saw the problems as located in 'individuals', whether this was because of inherited defects, faulty socialization or rapidly changing socio-economic conditions. The solution lay in controlling or reforming the individual. For biological determinists there was no real cure for those born bad, aside from genetic engineering. More humanitarian individuals argued individual correction was possible for both environmental and genetic causes, so that juvenile delinquents, for example, had to be 'saved' from pursuing a criminal career (Platt 1969). The value conflict perspective recognized differential interests and more powerful groups' ability to get their definitions of and solutions to social problems legitimated. The labelling perspective paid specific attention to: (i) the processes through which people become labelled as deviants or members of 'social problem groups'; (ii) who had the power to attach such labels successfully; and (iii) what the potential consequences might be. Labelling and value conflict perspectives flagged up, but did not fully develop, the significance of different interest groups in society and did not advocate an overtly political solution. Critical

Table 3.1 Alternative theoretical perspectives on social problems

Perspective	Epistemological position	Location of problem	Examples	Solution
Social pathology (e.g. Lombroso and Ferrero 1895; Platt 1969)	Positivist	Defective individuals	Criminals, juvenile delinquents, disability, mental illness	Selective breeding / eugenics or re-education/resocialization
Social disorganization (e.g. Thomas and Znaniecki 1927; Park et al. 1967)	Positivist	Social change and disruption, urbanization, immigration, industrialization	Crime, mental illness, alcoholism, cultural conflict, family breakdown	Work with individuals to counter effects of disorganization and restore equilibrium in systems, e.g. slow down the pace of technological change
Value conflict (e.g. Fuller and Myers 1941; Gusfield 1967)	Broadly interpretivist with some positivist elements	Power and value differences between groups with divergent interests	Child labour, low wages, rising divorce rates, abortion, single parents	Groups must find higher value to agree on or trade values. If this fails, groups with more power retain control to decide on solution
Deviant (e.g. Sutherland and Cressey 1966; Clinard and Quinney 1967)	Positivist	Disruptive or defective individuals	Drug abusers, criminals, homosexuals	Identify and control those transgressing social norms, ideally through rehabilitation or coercion
Labelling / Moral panic (e.g. Becker 1963; Chambliss 1973)	Broadly interpretivist with some positivist elements	Elites and media	Gangs, muggers, drug users	Changing definitions and reducing labelling
Critical (e.g. Taylor et al. 1973; Quinney 1977)	Broadly interpretivist with some positivist elements	Ruling class and privileged elite	Crime, mental illness, poverty, economic exploitation	Reform or revolution which abolishes capitalism, establishing a classless society

Source: adapted from Rubington and Weinberg (2003).

perspectives, although unequivocally allied with a conflict, often Marxist, view of society, were mixed in terms of their epistemological position. On the one hand, they presented an objectivist viewpoint in claiming their Marxist interpretation of society was correct, but they also argued a transition was possible, from an ideologically conditioned acceptance of the status quo to the proletariat recognizing and questioning their oppressed position and envisaging the possibilities for a different society.

Changes in how poverty has been understood as a social problem illustrate the shift from the individualized explanations of the nineteenth and early twentieth centuries, to explanations in the mid twentieth century that give a role to economic and social structures. Recent policies have returned to viewing poverty as the result of individual failings, with the solution lying in greater individual efforts to engage in paid work. This brings us on to the most recent perspective on social problems, the social constructionist perspective, which in modified form offers social workers a framework for deconstructing and understanding social problems.

3.6 A social constructionist approach to social problems

Social constructionism is a perspective which argues that our interpretation of issues and events, and the meanings that we attach to them, shape our actions and beliefs. We might assume a man, bending seemingly intimately over a partially clothed supine woman, is the precursor for a heterosexual couple about to engage in sexual intercourse, but it could be a doctor examining a pregnant woman. However, an interpretation only becomes a solidified social construction when it is 'bought into' by many people, accepted as a self-evident fact and incorporated into institutional and social practices (Berger and Luckmann 1967). Social constructionism is often presented as the counterpoint to essentialist or reductionist viewpoints which tend to explain individual or group characteristics by reference to biology or nature ('men are naturally more logical than women', 'she's less confident because she's a girl') with little acknowledgement of the interactions between biology and culture. Widespread acceptance of the belief that gender differences are based in biology, and that women and men are therefore 'naturally' very different in their personalities and abilities, with male attributes being more socially valued (Lorber 2010), has supported women's economic and social subordination. A social constructionist approach to social problems suggests that the extent to which a particular issue is perceived as problematic, as well as the kind of problem it is understood to be, is a function of social interaction, understanding and interpretation. This runs counter to early social pathology perspectives which often offered purely biological explanations of people's behaviour: 'Social problems are [therefore] ambiguous situations that can be viewed in different ways by different people and that are defined as troubling by some people' (Best and Harris 2012: 3). *Social constructionism* builds on the value conflict and labelling perspectives of the late 1970s but goes further, ultimately arguing 'subjective definitions not objective conditions [are] the "source" of social problems and the proper object of study' (Rubington and Weinberg 2003: 283).

This does not mean that all social problems 'claims' should be given equal weight. Joel Best (1995) advocates *contextual social constructionism*, suggesting both the claims-making processes and claims about the 'objective' situation should be critically analysed within their socio-historical context. Loseke (2010: 7) asserts that social problems are about both '*objective* conditions and people (things and people that exist in the physical world) *and* they are about *subjective* definitions (how we understand the world and the people in it)'. She shows that 'objective' indicators do not necessarily lead to an issue being recognized as a social problem, and conversely something may be identified as a social problem when that has little basis in reality. 'Stranger danger', the risk strangers pose to children in terms of sexual abuse and other harm, was repeatedly flagged up as a 'real' social problem between the 1960s and the new millennium but, according to Loseke, has never 'objectively' constituted one, as most children are harmed by those they know. Similarly, teenage pregnancy has repeatedly been identified by politicians and others as a social problem in the UK. Policy has consequently focused on reducing conceptions among under-eighteens, on the assumption that teenage pregnancies occur because of ignorance and lead to economic dependence and poor outcomes for children. However, research has shown that many pregnancies, if not actively chosen, are certainly not unwanted, can be empowering and do not inevitably lead to poor outcomes (Duncan 2007; Middleton 2011). Although social workers may be involved disproportionately with young people, such as those formerly in care, who struggle with their pregnancies and their children, refusing to see teenage pregnancy as unequivocally problematic could help social workers re-evaluate and respond to it in a more positive way.

Loseke's framework shows not only how social problems are constructed but also which claims are most likely to be successful. Her framework therefore helps the social work practitioner to evaluate the validity of the claims and proposed solutions. Like earlier theorists, Loseke proposes a *hierarchy of credibility of claims makers*, with scientists and other experts, politicians and members of elite groups having maximum credibility, while powerless groups such as children and elderly people have the least credibility, if they manage to publicize their views at all. If the *target audience* is an elite group, fewer people need to be persuaded than if it is the general public. Loseke argues we are persuaded – or not – that something is credible, important and a real social problem by a *package of claims*. *Verbal claims* might involve statistics, personal accounts or research findings. *Visual claims* involve a pictorial depiction, such as a starving child or injured elderly person, and evoke horror, fear, sympathy or even hatred. *Behavioural claims* generally involve activism, such as Black people in the USA protesting against racial segregation in the 1950s by sitting in White-designated areas on public transport.

Packages of claims are most successful when they convey a simple message and focus on the suffering of victims rather than on villains. Many service users, however, are difficult to categorize as 'pure' victims – for example, abused and neglected adolescent boys who commit crimes, or parents who abuse their children. The 'subjects of social suffering may not easily elicit compassion if they do not present themselves as innocent victims, but as aggressive, resentful or suspicious people whose hurt and loss is directed at others' (Frost and Hoggett 2008: 453). If villains are to be effectively presented as social problems they must be pathologized in some way that suggests possible rehabilitation. Alternatively, they need to be represented as dangerous 'outsiders'. Hence the public reluctance to accept that sexual abuse of children is most frequently perpetrated by immediate family members – ordinary 'family men' – rather than by strangers, who are more easily seen as 'other'.

Messages about social problems must also be comprehensible to their audience.

Domain expansion is one strategy adopted to keep a problem in the public eye and aid understanding by including a new issue under an already familiar and publicly understood label. New social problems are 'piggybacked' onto old problems which are thereby broadened. Child abuse, for example, now includes parental smoking. Post-traumatic stress disorder (PTSD) has been extended from being a specific short-term disorder suffered by psychologically shell-shocked war veterans to include a much wider range of circumstances (Loseke 2010). It is now seen as potentially induced by situations varying from witnessing a single road traffic accident to the experience of serial abuse in childhood. Social problem claims are often particularly effective when issues are personalized and the audience can identify with the victims and see how they themselves could be affected. When people evaluate social problem claims, they also draw on their own experiences as 'practical actors', and on commonly accepted cultural themes, such as the fear of crime.

In her book, Loseke devotes an entire chapter to what she calls the 'troubled person industry'. This refers to the various organizations and professionals who support, rehabilitate or punish the victims or villains who are the subjects of most social problem claims. Their existence suggests the success of the claims-making process, at least to some extent. Some of these professionals (including social workers) possess considerable power to deprive individuals of their liberty, or give them access to important services or resources. Victim status leads to diminished power, and victims are expected to behave in a passive way to retain sympathy and support, while those offering sympathy or support, such as professionals, gain status. We will return to these *cultural feeling rules* later in this chapter in the context of a discussion of adult safeguarding, which involves the protection of vulnerable adults.

3.7 Social work and social problems

Although little is known about how social workers understand social problems, they have historically tended to perceive service users in two main ways: (i) as deviant or damaged threats to society requiring control; or (ii) as casualties of a 'sick' society or struggling individuals who require support and therapy. A minority of social workers adopt a third, more radical position, which locates the root cause of many clients' problems within an unjust social order and advocates substantial social change (Pearson 1975; Payne 1996). The first two positions reflect the early pathology, deviance and social disorganization approaches, with only the third showing some awareness of value conflicts and inequalities. There is some indirect evidence of the persistence of the deviance and pathology perspectives. A small-scale study in one English university found that most social work applicants, who wrote about social problems and their possible causes and solutions as part of a literacy entry test, attributed them predominantly to individuals' anti-social behaviour (Gilligan 2007). Although these were social work *applicants*, not students or trained practitioners, this study underlines the importance of adopting a more critical perspective in order not to compound the significant disadvantage most social work clients already experience as a result of prejudice, inequality or misinformation.

Many contemporary social workers, whilst acknowledging the importance of the care and control elements of their occupation, may hold more nuanced views about their service users and be able to work sensitively with tensions and contradictions/

ambiguities. However, as we demonstrate in the examples that follow, there remain problems with how social workers understand and respond to social problems and the social policies linked to them. We offer a critical perspective on four issues directly relevant to social workers' engagement with social problems:

- the emergence of child abuse as a social problem and its changing definition
- wealth as an example of an issue which has not been recognized as a social problem
- the limitations of social work responses to domestic abuse when children and child abuse are involved
- the lack of recognition that the abuse of vulnerable adults is a widespread social problem requiring a collective societal response.

Child abuse as a changing social problem

Child abuse emerged as 'the battered child syndrome' in the 1960s when some paediatricians successfully attracted media attention to the fact that the X-rays of many children who suffered head injuries revealed healed or healing limb fractures (Kempe 1968). Because 'the battered child' was a new concept (like mugging), it was not possible to ascertain whether the number or severity of parents beating their children had increased and therefore a new social problem had come into existence, or whether X-rays had merely revealed something which had been occurring for a long time (Hacking 1991). Since the 'discovery' of the problem in the 1960s, the term 'child abuse' has increasingly been used to refer to a much wider range of practices than physical abuse, illustrating domain expansion (Loseke 2010).

The contemporary definition of child abuse encompasses a wide variety of contexts, perpetrators and types of behaviour towards children. Child abuse can be perpetrated by adults or children, acting as individuals or in groups. It may occur as organizational or institutional abuse, for example in schools or residential children's homes, and involve physical, psychological or sexual abuse by individuals or groups. Alternatively, abuse may be the result of the organization's procedures or *modus operandi* which are directly disrespectful and abusive to children or have unintended abusive consequences. The boundaries of what constitutes child abuse are hard to define. Is physical punishment child abuse at every level, including one 'mild' smack, even if the law says otherwise, or only if it results in severe injuries or is repeated? Is a fourteen-year-old having consensual and non-pressurized sexual intercourse with a seventeen-year-old child abuse? Could allowing children to live in crime-ravaged and poverty-stricken areas be constituted as societal child abuse in an affluent nation? Are parents who 'hothouse' their children academically or systematically groom them to be child 'stars' or sporting champions abusers?

Multiple definitions, different political agendas and professional interests mean that there is a lack of agreement about both causes and solutions (e.g. Green 2006). The interests of the medical profession are apparent in the 1960s 'discovery' of physical child abuse, as are those of religious institutions in their denial of widespread sexual abuse of children within their care. Social workers and doctors are frequently vilified for being insufficiently vigilant (as occurred in the cases of Victoria Climbié and Peter Connelly), or alternatively overzealous, as occurred in Cleveland, England, in 1987, when over 100 children were taken into care due to concerns about sexual abuse. The doctors and social workers had very serious concerns that these children had been sexually abused and deployed a 'new' diagnostic procedure – anal dilation (previously used to investigate adult anal rape) – to try and confirm or dismiss these concerns. Some of the men accused of abuse, with the support of a very vocal MP, orchestrated media coverage which was more concerned with fighting state intervention into the private sphere of the patriarchal family (arguing that ordinary fathers could not possibly have committed such heinous crimes in such large numbers), than with the protection of the children involved (Campbell 1988; Hacking 1991). The social workers and doctors were publicly demonized and the needs of the children became lost in the media coverage of the 'scandal', many being returned home. Here we clearly see how social problem claims are less successful (Loseke 2010) when the 'villains' cannot be categorized as marginalized outsiders, and that responses to child abuse as a social problem are not always benevolent.

When child abuse was first 'discovered' in the 1960s, there was disagreement about whether it should be understood as a criminal act or a medical disorder. Paediatricians tended to see it as the expression of individual pathology and this medicalization served their professional interests, as demand for their work declined with the advent of vaccination and improved environmental conditions. The gradual acceptance that child sexual abuse is common and predominantly perpetrated by known males – often family members, friends or neighbours – rather than demonic strangers, calls for a different explanation from 'individual pathology'. Beckett's (1996) analysis of media accounts of child abuse in the USA over four different five-year periods revealed different social problem claimants with contradictory views about causes and potential solutions at different times. Between 1980 and 1984, professionals working in child abuse dominated the discussion, arguing child abuse was a widespread problem that society could no longer deny, focusing on the suffering children endured. Between 1985 and 1990 a backlash occurred, with the assertion that many allegations were false, that children could fabricate abuse, misinterpret situations or be manipulated into lying – for example, in relation to child custody cases. Doubt was also cast upon professionals' ability to diagnose and treat abuse and there were suggestions their techniques were leading and unreliable. Between 1991 and 1994, the plight of adult abuse survivors, often celebrities, dominated news reporting, echoing the early 1980–4 period. However, this focus was short-lived and there was again a backlash which focused upon potentially false allegations, including *false memory syndrome* – a synonym for professionals implanting false abuse memories in the minds of suggestible, vulnerable individuals.

Some commentators suggest social problem claims about child abuse and its causes and solutions are less about the child and more about state power and controlling 'deviant' and threatening families (Donzelot 1980; Dingwall et al. 1984) whilst simultaneously denying sufficient financial support to poor families and discouraging them from protesting by inducing fear: 'A mild version of this observation is that the child abuse movement serves to conceal the decline in social support for children. The strong version says that child abuse legislation is a cheaper and more effective form of control of deviant families than welfare (Hacking 1991: 262). This comment may help us to understand the current situation in the UK. Rising inequality, compounded by a narrow focus on high-risk child protection social work with mostly poor families, undermines social workers' ability to build strong partnerships with children and families, which are humane, preventative and community-orientated (Featherstone et al. 2012, 2013). Child and family social work has been influenced by recurrent moral panics about children killed by their carers, and some argue that most child protection policy does more harm than good (Lonne et al. 2009). Clapton et al. (2013: 213) argue, echoing Cohen (2002: xxxv), that one important consequence of moral panics is that we have been 'taking some things too seriously and others not seriously enough'. Perhaps this is this case with the concern about high-risk families taking precedence over adequate financial support and long-term preventive work with families. The current narrow social work emphasis on detecting child abuse may have adverse consequences for poor families, particularly female-headed families, who tend to be placed under surveillance and demonized (Wrennall 2010), whilst little attention is paid to the injustices and multiple disadvantages they routinely suffer (Equality and Human Rights Commission (EHRC) 2012). Horwath's (2011) small-scale study involving sixty-two social work practitioners and managers iden- tified an over-riding preoccupation with risk management, strict timescales and a form-filling culture. This encouraged a siege mentality, separated 'need' from risk of harm, and marginalized adolescents, disabled, asylum-seeker and refugee children, and those from different faiths and higher socio-economic groups. Parton's (2011) analysis of child protection and safeguarding work from the 1980s to 2008 also found that moral panics, alongside bureaucracy, managerialism and time-consuming elec- tronic (ICT) systems (examined further in chapter 5), led to forensic forms of social work concerned only with identifying and intervening in 'high-risk' cases. Although the *Every Child Matters* reforms from 2004 onwards superficially offered a broader emphasis on safeguarding, which promoted the general health and well-being of all children, not just those deemed to be 'in need' or 'at risk', in 2008, after the murder of 17-month-old Peter Connelly, social workers, managers and doctors associated with the case were vilified and the pendulum swung fully back to focusing on the heavy end of 'at-risk' cases. Wrennall (2010: 1477) goes further than most in arguing that the rhetoric of child protection enables hard-won civil and human rights to be bypassed, disguises surveillance and disarms opposition, thereby allowing social workers to penetrate 'where orthodox policing can no longer go', whilst simultaneously conceal- ing wider economic and political interests.

The Rotherham grooming scandal, examined by the Jay Report (2014), showed how 1,400 vulnerable children, predominantly girls, often from care backgrounds, had been groomed and repeatedly sexually assaulted by mostly Asian gangs in Rotherham between 1987 and 2013. Little effective action was taken by police and the council, who often viewed these abused children as errant teenagers and were fearful of being accused of racism or religious prejudice. Since the media scandal, a number of high-ranking professionals have been dismissed or pressured into resigning, but few of the men reported to the police by victims have been arrested, and support services and help with compensation were limited (Ahmed 2014). The absence of a more comprehensive response to the problems revealed raises questions about how seriously the issue has been taken by central and local government.

So what might social workers take from an in-depth understanding of the differing ways child abuse has been constructed as a social problem and the changing policy responses to it? They should understand that child abuse is not a fixed category and media or governmental representations of it are not always 'neutral' or concerned with the child's needs or well-being. Social workers therefore need to evaluate social problem claims about child abuse critically and decide how they might respond as individuals or groups of social workers. Although the boundaries of what constitutes child abuse have changed and are contested, and responses to it have been variable and have not always benefited the children concerned, it is generally accepted as something that is wrong and should not occur. However, the next social problem to be examined, wealth, has rarely been conceptualized as such, presumably because this would be to the detriment of wealthy elites who have considerable power to influence what is defined as a social problem.

Wealth as a social problem?

Social workers deal predominantly with people who are poor and who are often depicted as causing social problems (the social pathology approach), intervening in the lives of people who are presented *both* as requiring support *and* as possessing the potential to cause problems to others – such as juvenile delinquents or poor mentally ill people in the community. Poor families and individuals have been referred to in different ways over time ('the residuum' in the nineteenth century, 'the underclass' in the 1990s, 'troubled families' in the present century), but these different labels conceal a common perception of the problem as located in these individuals rather than there being some other cause. Questions about the causes of poverty and whose responsibility it is to resolve it therefore become diverted into a discussion about how to 'save' abused or 'at-risk' children or control deviant or threatening groups.

A number of recent studies have put the problem of poverty in a new perspective by examining whether the rich deserve their wealth and whether the same standards are applied to rich and poor (Rowlingson and Connor 2011; Rowlingson and McKay 2012). It is hard to see how the enormous salaries of bankers and financiers across Western nations are justified when their actions in the last decade have bankrupted financial institutions and threatened the stability of capitalism. The cost to the state of rescuing these institutions has been met, in the UK, by cuts to other areas of government spending, affecting the poorest most. Even disregarding difficult debates about what constitutes desert in terms of hard work, productivity or value to society, many of the rich acquire their wealth not through work, effort or merit (however defined) but through inheritance.

Social class and power have a significant impact on how social problems are defined and understood. For example, in the late 1980s and early 1990s, negative equity – houses selling for significantly less than their purchase price – was identified as a social problem affecting significant numbers of home owners (Open University 2011). At the same time, rising rents and poor-quality rented housing affecting similar numbers of people were not recognized as a social problem that required some kind of government response; rather, the difficulties faced by those in rented accommodation were seen as private, individual troubles. The repercussions of the withdrawal of the state from housing provision, and the sale of council housing, were even more apparent three decades later (Hodkinson et al. 2013). The Coalition government continued to put resources into helping people into home ownership, through a variety of mortgage assistance schemes, but did little to support the building of more social housing or to control rents in the private sector. Landlord repossessions rose, and in 2012 there were over 5 million people on waiting lists for social housing (Hodkinson et al. 2013), yet because these issues affected those on lower incomes, who did not constitute a social threat at the time, and could not be depicted as pitiful victims, this crisis was not represented as a social problem.

The final two sections examine two social work issues where arguably there has been a *mis*recognition of a social problem: domestic violence and mother blaming in the context of child protection, and the abuse of vulnerable adults.

Domestic violence and 'mother blaming'

Domestic violence (DV) or domestic abuse involves one partner or ex-partner, or other family member, subjecting another to physical, psychological, sexual or financial abuse or humiliation or combined forms of these (Home Office 2013). It is intermittently recognized as a social problem and has been subject to domain expansion because it originally referred only to physical interpersonal violence but now incorporates other forms of violence and subjugation. DV is now defined in England as a child protection/safeguarding issue. The Adoption and Children Act 2002 extended the term 'child abuse' to include the harm children may suffer from witnessing others being abused, another example of domain expansion. Although the situation of children witnessing abuse (but not having abuse directly perpetrated upon them) is now constituted as a form of indirect child abuse, children themselves are additionally at greater risk of being directly abused or neglected in families where one adult is subjecting another to violence. This section is principally concerned with children who witness a father or father figure subjecting their mother to domestic abuse and are simultaneously directly at risk from or subject to harm from the same perpetrator. Domestic abuse is not confined to heterosexual relationships and women are not always the victims. However, its frequency and severity are much greater in relation to heterosexual relationships where men are the perpetrators and women the victims. Here we examine how adequately DV has been recognized as a gendered social problem by social workers.

The British Crime Survey, a nationally representative survey of over 23,000 men and women, revealed DV as a widespread, gendered social problem. Men are the principal perpetrators, if living in fear, frequency of assaults and physical harm are taken as the key indicators (Walby and Allen 2004). Humphreys and Absler's (2011) content analysis of thirteen publications from the USA, Australia, Ireland and England found that there was little support for women experiencing DV whose children were also being harmed, or at risk of being harmed, by the perpetrator. They argued implicit 'mother blaming' had been prominent in child protection discourse for decades, principally because DV had been individualized rather than its gendered dynamics and patterning being understood and acted upon. This position is also likely to have been exacerbated by social work's often uncritical reliance upon traditional developmental psychology which concentrates the professional gaze on, above all, *the mother's shortcomings* (Andenaes 2005). Humphreys and Absler identified three cross-national themes from 1900 to 2010 in relation to child protection: (i) the absence of male perpetrators from child protection assessments or interventions; (ii) the exclusion of DV from standard assessments or formal meetings and, if recorded in case notes, its being reinterpreted as 'marital arguments'; and (iii) the representation of DV as a private problem with the onus on the woman to resolve the issues. Interventions, for more than a century and across different countries, have focused upon the responsibility of the mother to protect children but have paid little attention to her support needs or the man's responsibilities. Consequently, those working outside child protection, such as refuge workers, still report women being too frightened to seek help from social services for fear their children will be removed (Humphreys and Absler 2011; Keeling and van Wormer 2012). This concern is now so entrenched within the minds of poor families that many are deterred from even approaching health services for other kinds of help (Canvin et al. 2007).

Other recent UK studies also confirm Humphreys and Absler's findings that mothers who are themselves the victims of DV are judged negatively and expected to resolve the situation singlehandedly in child protection cases, while men are overlooked and excused despite being the source of the problem (Hester 2011; Roskill 2011; Baynes and Holland 2012; Featherstone and Fraser 2012; Charles and Mackay 2013). Scourfield's (2006) study of a child protection team found that, although social workers acknowledged many mothers' economic oppression, their empathy diminished if the mothers failed to protect the children from violent partners. The social construction of gender which positions women as 'naturally' tied to childcare through social norms and policy (Daniel et al. 2005), together with insufficient support networks and services, helps explain why practitioners do not see gendered DV as the central social problem. This lack of recognition has far-reaching consequences for mothers' ability to protect themselves or their children.

In cases of DV there is both a child and an adult victim, but child protection work focuses on the child, rarely invoking broader-based interventions (Featherstone, White and Morris 2014). The benefits of a broader focus are demonstrated by a recent study with 2,500 women, which found that intensive case management, which also focused on maternal support, greatly improved children's safety, and also reduced parent–child contact conflicts (Horwath et al. 2009). Many studies recommend inter-professional training which co-ordinates inter-agency goals and leads to cooperative working, but, without adequate recourse to effective family-based treatment alongside an understanding of gendered violence, this is unlikely to be effective (Humphreys and Absler 2011). This does not, however, mean social workers are powerless, and, although they work with individuals, collective responses and pressure groups can change and have changed policy. However, to be sufficiently willing and adequately informed to consider these strategies social workers need to understand the social construction of gender, gender inequalities and gendered violence, and to be able to conceive of DV in these terms. Abused women are rarely seen as vulnerable unless they have physical or learning disabilities, or are elderly or mentally ill (Humphreys and Absler 2011), but, as the next section on adult safeguarding shows, even those deemed vulnerable do not necessarily receive sufficient protection from social workers.

Adult protection/safeguarding issues

A number of studies on abuse of adults have shown that knowledge of policy among practitioners, including social work professionals, is variable, and that they work with a number of different definitions of adult abuse. Their working definitions are often narrower than those enshrined in policy, some excluding abuse by other service users or inadvertent neglect, or vary according to resource availability (Brown and Stein 1998; Johnson 2012). A study in Scotland looked at how professionals constructed adult protection issues and implemented inter-agency practice (Johnson 2011). It examined the cases of twenty-three 'at-risk' adults in four local authorities, covering adults living alone, in families or staffed settings, and including individuals with learning and physical disabilities, physical and mental health issues, and older adults. Johnson identified four main issues: (i) professionals interpreted protection issues and policy in different ways; (ii) organizations and over-loaded carers were rarely held culpable for failing to protect; (iii) service users were only seen as victims if they were submissive, passive and deserving; and (iv) safeguarding issues were not linked with more macro social inequalities (such as ageism, inadequate care budgets and the low social status and political priority of vulnerable adults). As a result, the abuse of vulnerable adults was not recognized as a social problem.

In Johnson's research, in relation to (i) *differential interpretation*, a young woman, with probable but undiagnosed learning disabilities, often had sex with strangers when inebriated, and later married a man suspected of assaulting her. She was considered vulnerable by social workers but not by her former therapist or the police. They deemed her to have capacity because she rejected any intervention. One social worker said he would view just one instance of sexual exploitation as a protection issue, but physical assault only if severe and repeated, although others disagreed. Some incidents were labelled as 'poor practice' rather than abuse in some institutions/organizations, although others responded differently to similar instances. Regarding (ii) *organizations and carers not being judged culpable*, in just under one-third of the cases the suspected perpetrator was an institution. Examples included one housing department placing a vulnerable young woman with mental health difficulties in a predominantly male facility that accommodated known sexual predators; police failure to investigate an assault; a medical consultant discharging a man with dementia into a very unsafe environment; and the under-resourcing/ineffectiveness of certain services, which led to direct vulnerability and neglect. In one case, a mother developed dementia and was no longer able to care adequately for her learning-disabled daughter. The case was designated a protection issue and an agency was contracted to provide daily support but was extremely negligent. Despite this, neither the agency, nor the contracting body – Social Services – was held responsible. Policy was also not written in a way that allowed institutional failings to be dealt with, and the institution dealing with complaints was often both the social worker's employer and the organization responsible for providing the person's care, either directly or indirectly.

As regards (iii) *passivity, deservingness and vulnerability* as the basis for deciding whether a situation was one of adult protection, one physically disabled man vocally and repeatedly alleged his father regularly beat him but social workers perceived it as a 'tit for tat' relationship, in which he had capacity, and therefore it did not raise adult protection issues. In contrast, a man with learning disabilities who drank alcohol voluntarily with his cousin, who routinely stole from and humiliated him, was seen to be a vulnerable victim due to diminished mental capacity, despite his not manifesting any distress. Johnson's findings concur with Loseke's assertion that the most successful social problem claims occur when victims are perceived as blameless and passive, with abusers being ignored unless they can be projected as monstrous and qualitatively different from most ordinary people. This suggests a parallel between how lay people perceive social problems and how social workers respond to issues which could be deemed to be social problems. What seemed to influence these professionals' construction of an adult protection issue was their perception of the service user's vulnerability and best interests, and whether they felt intervention with the resources they had would make a difference. For example, they might believe that a vulnerable adult who was being neglected by his main carer because of limited resources did not constitute a protection issue because his treatment at home might still be better than if he was moved into residential care. It is also interesting that when scandals about the care of elderly people erupt they tend mostly to focus on abuse within institutions, which may also influence practitioner and lay perceptions of what constitutes abuse.

Ash (2013), from interview research with thirty-three social workers and managers, found, in the context of limited resources and high caseloads, few workers were able to envisage how difficult it might be for elderly service users to disclose abuse. Many of Ash's findings mirror Johnson's, including practitioners turning a blind eye to abuse in care homes if the homes complied with regulatory procedures, and reframing abuse as poor practice. They also failed to ask persistent questions about the absence of support for elderly people because they were unable to envision alternative possibilities, or contextualize elderly people's position within a wider social and cultural landscape. They implicitly accepted that, due to inadequate societal resources, which they did not believe could be increased, older people were likely to be abused or neglected and there was nothing they could do.

These two examples – child protection in the context of DV and adult safeguarding – illustrate how social workers tend to adopt a narrow individualized approach dictated by organizational policies and resource availability, with little consideration of wider structural issues such as gender inequalities, ageism and poverty. Domestic violence and the abuse of vulnerable adults constitute social problems because of their frequency and effects, and both receive intermittent media coverage, but there has been a reluctance to accept the gendered nature of DV or that the abuse of vulnerable adults may require collective responses and system changes. The fact that society accords victims of DV and vulnerable adults few resources implicitly condones widespread violence. Social workers are professionals who supposedly uphold human rights and social justice; however, these examples show that by failing to challenge the lack of resources they collude with the status quo. Preston-Shoot (2011) exposes the fracture between professional ethics and workers' obeisance to bureaucracy and statute as an 'administrative evil doing'. Arendt (1963), referring to Nazi Germany, argued that 'banal evil' derives not from monstrous people or demonic actions but from unthinking conformity and a dulled conscience. Bauman (1989) coined the term 'distanciation' to describe a situation in which people are separated from the consequences of their actions or perceive their actions as purely technical. This occurred in Nazi Germany when social workers carried out assessments which were later used to justify genocide or enforced sterilizations of certain groups (Waaldijk 2011) but could be argued to occur in contemporary care management where social workers' personal involvement with service users is limited to assessment and most services are then contracted out. The fact that it is frequently undercover journalists, and not trained health and welfare professionals, who expose the abuse of vulnerable adults is of great concern. Social workers could draw on the professional codes of practice, human rights legislation (e.g. Article 3 of the 1998 Human Rights Act – the right not to be subject to inhumane and degrading treatment) and whistleblowing legislation to challenge institutional practices, but seem rarely to do so (Ash 2013). They could work collectively and with other professionals, service users, MPs, activists and pressure groups to have issues such as these recognized as legitimate social problems and to campaign for better understanding and resources, but such mobilization requires an understanding of why it is important to do this. Loseke's work on how certain social problem claims become accepted as legitimate is a useful framework to work within, although clearly it requires some complexity to be sacrificed.

3.8 Conclusion

Social workers work with a variety of social problems, including child abuse, mental illness and the care of older or disabled adults. This chapter has shown how the identification of social problems is a social and political process which is shaped by how the issue in question is understood. For this reason, social workers need to have some understanding of different sociological perspectives on the nature of society and on the processes by which social problems are recognized. We argued that social constructionism is a useful perspective through which to analyse social problems, and it enables social workers to reconstruct and re-present social problems in ways more beneficial to their clients. Child abuse and wealth offer two contrasting examples of the way in which different social interests are deployed, leading in one case to the identification of a new social problem which then became broadened and in the other to a problem being ignored or implicitly denied. The discussions of DV and adult protection illustrate how, even where a social problem is recognized, too narrow a focus on the causes at an individual level may mean that wider structural causes, such as the gendered nature of DV or the under-resourcing of adult services, which require a more political response, are overlooked.

Social workers play a key role in implementing policies directed at a wide range of social problems and groups seen as a problem in society. Many enter social work with laudable aims in relation to supporting vulnerable people, or occasionally with the wider goal of combating social injustice. However, much research shows they frequently work in parochial, depoliticized and individualized ways. This often results in them inadvertently reproducing dominant, inequitable discourses and upholding oppressive stereotypes associated with a social pathology or deviance perspective on social problems. We hope that this chapter will enable social workers to critically analyse how social problems are constructed and the impact of this upon the social policies which inform and direct their work, and provide them with the necessary knowledge and professional confidence to understand service users' problems within a broader context. Through this, they may be able to recognize and challenge oppressive policies and practices both institutionally and politically, as well as working effectively with service users at an individual level.

Discussion questions

- Choose an issue conceived of as a social problem and not examined in depth in this chapter (e.g. obesity, unemployment, substance misuse or immigration). Discuss how it has been socially constructed and the consequences for the kinds of policies proposed to address it.
- How could the issue you chose have been constructed and represented differently, and what effect might this have on how social workers perceive and respond to such issues?
- Take one of the social problems discussed in the final part of this chapter and devise a set of practice guidelines for social workers in the light of the issues identified.
- How might social workers engage productively with the micro context (small-scale interpersonal interactions with individuals and groups), the meso context (the mid-level of organizational practice and policies and communities and neighbourhoods) and the macro context (wider societal attitudes, norms, values and policy and legislation) in respect of one or more social problem groups?

Further reading

Hacking, I. (1991) 'The Making and Molding of Child Abuse', *Critical Inquiry*, 17 (2), 253–88.

Johnson, F. (2012) 'Problems with the Term and Concept of "Abuse": Critical Reflections on the Scottish Adult Support and Protection Study', *British Journal of Social Work*, 42: 833–50.

Lister, R. (2010) *Understanding Theories and Concepts in Social Policy*, Bristol: Policy Press, ch. 3.

Loseke, D. R. (2010) *Thinking about Social Problems: An Introduction to Constructionist Perspectives*, 2nd edn, Aldine: New Jersey.

Weinberg, L. (2015) *Contemporary Social Constructionism: Key Themes*, Philadelphia: Temple University Press.

4 Social Justice, Citizenship and Equality

4.1 Introduction

Social work nationally and internationally presents itself as a human rights and social justice profession, and a commitment to equality and to anti-discriminatory and anti-oppressive practice (ADP/AOP) has been a key professional tenet in the UK since the late 1980s. However, as chapter 2 has shown, what constitutes justice and equality are contested political questions. What is just from one ideological perspective is unjust from another. Solas (2008) argues that social workers have a professional responsibility to promote social justice by challenging discrimination, recognizing diversity, promoting equitable distribution of resources and collaborative working. But some understanding of important underlying philosophical and political debates is necessary in order to translate these principles into practice and deal with the complex issues that they engender.

Many social workers interpret ADP or AOP only at a micro interpersonal level and very literally, understanding it to mean they must act in accordance with the law and not personally discriminate against service users on the basis of 'race'/ethnicity, sexual orientation, sex, age, religion or disability, or alternatively that they have a duty to challenge service users' discriminatory attitudes. Few envisage social work practice as including resistance to laws and organizational policies that may be oppressive, or as involving policy advocacy or wider political campaigning (Cocker and Hafford-Letchfield 2014). Nevertheless, a more critical approach is necessary to help social workers with the real difficulties they face in putting the ideals of the profession into practice. This can help them to deal with the fear of being accused of religious discrimination, racism or homophobia. It can also facilitate an understanding that cultural sensitivity is not the same as an uncritical acceptance of all difference, or that a safeguarding authority role does not automatically entail being oppressive to marginalized groups. Fears of this kind have sometimes resulted in high-risk situations – for example, those involving vulnerable children – being ignored or misinterpreted, with tragic consequences. At the same time, social workers have arguably been complicit in oppressing some children through their legally mandated role – for example, in conducting age assessments on unaccompanied asylum-seeking children (e.g. Humphries 2004). Many social workers understandably find it difficult to articulate what the ethical commitment to social justice means in practice. As Reisch comments: 'The marginalization of macro practice within social work . . . has produced a corruption of the profession's vocabulary. Terms such as social justice, oppression and empowerment are freely used but have been largely drained of their broader political and ideological implications' (2013: 718).

This chapter examines the inter-related concepts of social justice, equality and citizenship in order to give practitioners a deeper understanding of them and illuminate their positive possibilities for social work. Social justice is a broad and political concept, loosely pivoting around 'fairness', but is an issue on which there are many different views. Questions about how to promote social justice involve thinking about what is meant by equality, how to deal with difference, who is entitled to what kinds of provision in a socially just society and whether some rights transcend particular societies and apply to all human beings. When the abstract concepts of social justice and equality are applied in practice, this often occurs within the particular context of nation states where only *citizens* qualify for many of the rights that give them access to justice and equality. This then raises questions about the basis of citizenship, and the nature of the rights associated with it. It is difficult, if not impossible, to disentangle these different but often interlinked concepts from one another fully and discuss them individually. The oldest foundational concept of citizenship is examined first, leading to a discussion of rights, equality and diversity. Wider visions of social justice which often incorporate one or more of these subsidiary concepts are covered towards the end of the theoretical part of the chapter. Their direct relationship to social work is then analysed through an examination of debates about ADP and AOP, which are currently the most obvious manifestations of the profession's practical commitment to social justice and equality. The final section of the chapter discusses case examples which illustrate the difficulties and dilemmas that are raised in implementing the principles examined in this chapter.

4.2 Citizenship and rights

Citizenship is a concept dating back to the Ancient Greek city states of Athens and Sparta, denoting a particular kind of relationship between an individual and a community, involving both obligations and rights. In Ancient Greek society, all free adult males had citizenship status, which brought with it the duty to defend the state and the duty (and the right) to participate in both ruling, and being ruled by, the body of fellow citizens (Dwyer 2010: 18–19). Women, children, strangers and slaves were accorded few rights or opportunities, their servitude releasing time for free males to perform their citizenship duties. From its inception to the present day, citizenship has denoted inclusion and rights for some, but exclusion for others, traditionally depending upon a formal, legal relationship between the individual and the state and an associated 'national' identity (Lister 2010).

T. H. Marshall's book *Citizenship and Social Class*, published in 1950, offers a historical and theoretical analysis of citizenship which is still a key point of reference for contemporary discussion. Marshall subdivided the rights conferred by citizenship into civil (legal), political and social rights. *Civil rights* brought equality under the law, freedom of speech, thought and religion, the right to own property and to enter into contracts. These became significant political issues in the UK from the mid eighteenth century. In the nineteenth and early twentieth centuries, *political rights*, such as the right to vote and stand for election, were gradually extended in most European countries, although women and working-class men gained the vote much later than White upper-class Protestant males (Van Ewijk 2010). *Social rights*, by which Marshall meant 'the whole range from the right to a modicum of economic welfare and security to the right to share to the full in the social heritage and to live the civilised life according to the standards prevailing in society' ([1950] 1992: 8), were not established to any significant extent in the UK until the second half of the twentieth century.

The post-war welfare settlement in the UK (discussed in chapter 1) incorporated the state's acceptance of the rights of all citizens to a certain minimum level of income security, public housing, education, social services and healthcare provision. Marshall's conception of social citizenship, however, was never fully realized (Lockwood 1996). The unemployment benefit rate set by Beveridge in the 1940s fell short of the subsistence rate advocated by Rowntree, and entitlement was conditional on looking for work. From the 1980s onwards, benefits have increasingly been means-tested, with the stigma that brings, and subject to tighter job search requirements. Arguably, the failure to accord adequate social rights to all citizens undermines their civil and political rights (Turner 1997) because exercising those rights becomes difficult or meaningless to someone who is homeless, hungry or economically trapped in a violent crime-ridden area.

Marshall and the pioneers of the welfare state were principally concerned with social rights as a way of addressing class inequalities, and showed little understanding of other sources of inequality such as gender, disability, sexual orientation, 'race' and ethnicity. Access to financial security in the post-war welfare state was premised on a heterosexual male breadwinner, with married women's and children's access to social rights based on their dependence on the husband/father. Citizenship rights were also based on nationality and therefore excluded many immigrants.

In parallel with the development of social rights associated with national citizenship in the UK and many other European countries in the post-war period, the revelations of the atrocities committed by the Nazis during the Second World War resulted in the formalization of a new conception of *universal human rights* that transcended national boundaries. These were set out in the Universal Declaration of Human Rights (UDHR) in 1948, underlining the 'basic rights and fundamental freedoms [which] are inherent to all human beings, inalienable and equally applicable to everyone' (UN website). These rights were hugely important but were aspirational rather than being legally binding on all nation states (Martell 2009). The European Convention on Human Rights (ECHR), drawn up in 1950, set out a series of civil rights that apply to all citizens of the signatory nations. These can be enforced by the European Court of Human Rights (ECtHR), to which individuals from any of the signatory nations can apply if they believe that their rights have been violated by the state in which they live. The rights covered by the ECHR include the right to privacy; the right to family life; the right to freedom of thought, conscience and religion; the right to freedom of expression; and the right to freedom from inhumane and degrading treatment. The UDHR and the ECHR therefore introduced a conception of rights which transcended citizenship of a particular nation and was based on ideas about universal human attributes. 'Human rights' involve an identification between the individual and the human species, without any intermediary source of collective identity (such as gender, social class or ethnicity), and in this way are ultimately individualistic, unlike citizenship rights which are based on common nationality.

Although human rights law has in some limited respects equalized the position of citizens and non-citizens within and between nation states, individuals are dependent on a complex mix of human and citizenship rights applied across different groups and in different countries very unevenly (Nash 2009). There are increasing numbers of people living in the UK who do not have full citizenship rights – for example migrants from inside and outside the EU, whose residence may give them some but not all of the rights of citizens, and asylum seekers, who have no citizenship rights or rights deriving from residence, but have human rights which may provide them with some protection (Calhoun 2003).

Early analysis of social citizenship focused on social class inequalities and poverty as obstacles to full citizenship, but more recent discussion has shown how other important and often interlocking inequalities were overlooked. Social citizenship rights were defined on the basis of needs (what was *needed* 'to live the civilised life according to the standards prevailing in society' in Marshall's words), which were based on professionals' expert assessments of people's needs rather than on ordinary people's own understanding of them (Lund 2006) (see chapter 6 for further discussion on needs). The language of rights carries more power and has greater potential for exposing structural inequalities than the language of needs (Dickens 2010). The social movements in the 1960s and 1970s which fought for equal treatment for women and Black, disabled and gay people were rights-based and drew attention to the failure of needs-based citizenship entitlements to treat all citizens fairly. In the 1980s and 1990s both social policy and social work therefore became more sensitive to a range of social divisions and inequalities in addition to social class.

4.3 Social divisions, difference and inequality

Changing social attitudes and the social movements of the 1960s and 1970s led to legislation to outlaw sex and race discrimination in employment and other areas. The feminist, anti-racist and disability movements raised awareness of the ways in which social welfare was affected by discriminatory ideas and problematic social constructions (Williams 1989, 1992: 6). As a result, social policy gradually became less concerned with the technical administration of welfare, adopting a more sociologically informed perspective which recognized diversity and the social constructi of social divisions (Walker 2013; see also chapter 3).

People differ from each other in many ways. Some people are intellectual, others artistic, sporty or practical. Some people have blue eyes, others brown or green eyes. The colour of people's skin and their age varies. Some are religious whilst others are agnostic or atheist. Differences are rendered important when one characteristic becomes the basis for attributing differential social or moral status and resources – for example, the *good* Christian versus the *dangerous* Muslim, or the *normal* heterosexual versus the *deviant* homosexual. Stereotyping is one way this is achieved, and stereotypes are social constructions often built onto a single characteristic that homogenizes a particular group (Blum 2004) and thereby can have a significant impact on that group's life opportunities and outcomes. For example, homophobic peer bullying in schools is rarely effectively tackled because homosexuality is socially constructed as unnatural, deviant and undesirable, despite it being a protected characteristic under the 2010 Equality Act. Gay men, for example, have been traditionally stereotyped as effeminate and ineffectual pseudo-men, and lesbians as butch and aggressive man haters. Gay teenagers therefore, unsurprisingly, often suffer poorer mental health than their heterosexual peers, construing themselves in relation to society's wider negative attitudes and their treatment by others. Social equality, which requires changes in prevailing social attitudes, may therefore lag significantly behind the formal legal equality provided by anti-discrimination legislation (Seidman 2005; Fish 2008).

A *social division* incorporates social constructions and stereotypes but also refers to the way in which certain groups of people are differentiated from others in a way that produces enduring inequalities of status and resources. You may have been teased as a child because you wore glasses, rebelled or had acne or red hair. That experience, however, differs fundamentally from being consistently oppressed or discriminated against in a variety of spheres because you are Black, gay, female, an older person, a looked-after child or disabled. Social divisions are relatively long-lasting and extend from everyday small-scale interactions to wider societal norms, values and politics, influencing the way that institutions and organizations operate (Payne 2015). Through this process, people or groups with certain characteristics become homogenized and labelled as good or bad, natural or unnatural, desirable or undesirable persons. For example, old age is often constructed negatively as a time of decrepitude and passivity, and old people correspondingly are often stereotyped as unproductive, worthless and 'past it', many being abused in institutions or by their home carers and families (EHRC 2011). The negative perception of old age may help to explain why elder abuse, when exposed in the media, fails to elicit the kind of social outrage and action that child abuse does.

Intersectionality and interconnecting oppressions

Social class, gender and 'race'/ethnicity are generally accepted as the three most significant social divisions, with religion, age/generation, sexual orientation, mental health/illness and disability also identified as important (Spicker 2014; Payne 2015). Although there are varying definitions and understandings of oppression, including dictionary definitions which refer to the experience of being held or weighed down, it tends to occur socially when individuals are 'systematically subjected to political, economic, cultural, or social degradation because they belong to a [particular] social group [and it] . . . results from structures of domination and subordination and, correspondingly, ideologies of superiority and inferiority' (Charlton 1998: 8). Oppression generally involves systemic, widespread and repeated injustice, although this is not necessarily extreme or legally sanctioned (as in restricting certain groups from voting or imposing apartheid or slavery) and does not necessarily involve direct violence (Deutsch 2006). Oppression, therefore, is an enduring but dynamic multi-level process which restricts, dehumanizes and degrades certain groups of people and operates through a complex mesh of unequal power relations. It is often so effective that individuals in some groups internalize that oppression and come to believe in their own unfitness or unworthiness, whilst others may be unaware that they are oppressing others and benefiting from that situation.

Some theorists identify social class as the most important social division; others have prioritized gender or 'race'/ethnicity (e.g. Anthias 2014). In social work, although multiple divisions and oppressions have been acknowledged (Carr 2014; Healy 2014), racism has often been represented, explicitly or implicitly, as the most important division or oppression (CCETSW paper 30, 1989; Williams 1989; Macey and Moxon 1996; Graham and Schiele 2010; Wagner and Yee 2011) despite low social class / poverty being the defining characteristic of most service users. The concept of *intersectionality* represents an attempt to move away from identifying a single hierarchy of oppression (is 'race' more important than gender, or social class more significant than either?) in favour of looking at the ways in which social divisions interact to position individuals differentially. Social divisions may operate in ways that are mutually reinforcing or contradictory (Walby et al. 2012). An individual's characteristics may render them subordinate in one or more categories, for example, being female and/or Black, but privileged through being middle class; alternatively, they may be subordinate in all categories.

These intersections have important implications for how people construct their identities. Moustafa, a sixteen-year-old youth of Moroccan parentage attending a youth centre in Germany, when seeing he was listed in a register as male and foreign, pulled out his national identity card and stated: 'Wrongly registered. I am proud to be German' (Ploesser and Mecheril 2011: 796). He identified with the 'privileged' aspect of his identity (German), rather than his ethnic parentage (Moroccan). Under other circumstances – for example, an occasion bringing together wider family and friends to celebrate a significant family event – the same young man might have strongly identified with his ethnic parentage and dissociated himself from his nationality. Identity is inherently flexible and context-specific. However, groups competing for recognition and resources often put forward a static view of culture, in which flexible and multiple identity positions are denied (Van Zoonen 2013), and where the most powerful individuals within the community, generally men, effectively silence more marginalized members, often women or children (Harris 2001: 32). State practices also tend to manage identities through singularizing them – for example, some European countries advocate abolishing dual citizenship (Van Zoonen 2013); others make immigrants conform to mythical or exaggerated national rituals and values in order to gain citizenship or other valued statuses or resources (Byrne 2012).

Intersecting social divisions such as class, gender and 'race'/ethnicity may compound disadvantage, sometimes referred to as *double or triple jeopardy*, and involve not only individual factors but linked cultural and structural ones. These might include 'greater exposure to toxins, carcinogens and violence; fewer resources (parks, libraries, supermarkets); lack of access to healthcare; health-damaging behaviours such as use of cigarettes, excessive alcohol use, and lack of exercise and psychological states such as anger and a low sense of control, autonomy and trust' (Adler 2013: 680). The recognition of intersectionality produces complex real-world dilemmas about how to campaign most effectively for policies to address problems where there may be different and competing interests and claims for resources (Walby et al. 2012). This is particularly apparent in relation to disputes around sexuality, religion and women's and children's rights. For example, forced marriage, sex trafficking, female genital mutilation (FGM) and honour-based killing all constitute gender-based violence but also intersect with religion, ethnicity, gender inequality, nation and childhood. It is unclear whether it is possible to draw up policies that can effectively address the complexities of intersectionality or whether they have to be dealt with singly – for example, through policies to prevent gendered violence, violence against children or violence based on claims about religious beliefs.

4.4 Equality

The preceding section showed how social constructions rely on stereotypes and are the basis for social divisions, which reproduce inequality and disadvantage. We turn now to examine different ideas about equality and their implications for countering discrimination and achieving social justice.

There are different forms of equality (social, political, moral, etc.) and also different ideas about what constitutes equality and how to achieve it. Four possible alternatives are: (i) giving everyone equal (but not necessarily identical) opportunities to compete for a given reward or position; (ii) treating everyone uniformly (regardless of need or outcome); (iii) conceiving equality as the differential meeting of need; or (iv) ensuring that, even if starting positions are different, outcomes are made equal (Spicker 2014). Those on both the right and left of the political spectrum often claim a commitment to individual equality of opportunity, the most commonly accepted orientation towards equality in the UK, but they have different ideas about what this means. Frequently, understandings of equality are reduced to economic equality (often expressed as sufficient income, shelter and food), but White (2007) identifies different but integrally linked forms of equality. These are mostly associated with the different kinds of citizenship rights (civil, political and social) identified by Marshall and discussed earlier. White's final category, moral equality, however, seems to occupy a slightly different position and have more resonance with ideas about recognition and respect (identity) that will be examined later. White's different equalities are briefly examined and illustrated below:

> *Legal equality* means equal treatment for those who transgress laws and equal protection by the law. Rich people often have access to virtually unlimited expert legal advice and representation, whilst poor people's access to free or subsidized legal advice in the UK is increasingly constrained because of substantial cuts to both criminal and civil legal aid (Mayo 2013). Legal equality is a pre-requisite for citizens' exercise of their civil rights.
>
> *Political equality* encompasses the right to vote and to stand for public office; free association; and freedom of expression to enable grievances to be aired and to allow political debate. Formal political equality may be undermined by those with greater means being able to buy access to the media to promote a particular candidate or party campaign, or by charisma and oratory being used to persuade large groups to commit to something that they do not have the time, education or motivation to understand fully.
>
> *Social equality* refers not only to status equality, deemed important by Marshall, but to the absence of oppression within a society where everyone respects each other as equals. Women's lack of social equality in the last century is illustrated by the fact that in the 1950s women were prohibited from working in certain jobs, such as teaching, when they married. As late as the 1970s, wives were seen as the private property of husbands and rape in marriage only became criminalized in 1982 in Scotland and 1991 in England.
>
> *Economic equality* is more contested than other forms and has variable versions. From a meritocratic perspective (discussed further below), achieving economic equality involves a person's income and occupational position reflecting their

talent and diligence, rather than the type of family they are born into. By contrast, some socialists argue that workers should be rewarded according to how valuable their work is to society, while Marxists believe that need should be the primary determinant of resource allocation. Social citizenship rights are concerned with reducing social and economic inequalities to enable citizens' enjoyment of 'the civilised life according to the standards prevailing in society'.

Moral equality is the underlying principle motivating all other forms of equality (White 2007) and involves treating all people as of equal worth and with equal concern and respect (Dworkin 2000). White (2007) argues that moral equality is an attainable ideal but one that is difficult to realize if the poor are demeaned or coerced into doing things unwillingly because they depend on the rich for their basic livelihood. These ethical dilemmas raise the question of whether greater economic equality is a prerequisite for social and political equality or whether moral equality must precede all other forms of equality.

Equality as equal opportunity or same treatment

Equality legislation introduced in the UK from the 1960s onwards is concerned primarily with social and economic equality. The 2010 UK Equality Act harmonized and streamlined earlier anti-discrimination legislation and added some new 'protected' characteristics. The legislation now prohibits discrimination in relation to: age; disability; gender reassignment; marriage and civil partnership; pregnancy and maternity; race; religion and belief; sex and sexual orientation.

The Act places a legal duty upon public and private employers, including social services, to refrain from discrimination, harassment and victimization. It also requires employers to make reasonable adjustments for disabled people. Discrimination is defined as treating an individual or group less favourably on the basis of actual or perceived protected characteristics. Employers in the public sector are required to foster equality of opportunity, promote good relations, set equality objectives, have 'due regard' (proactively plan) for the need to eliminate discrimination, and publish information on their performance. Inequality resulting from social class is, however, *not* recognized under this Act or wider EU legislation (Walby et al. 2012), yet class, or more broadly socio-economic status (SES), is an important form of inequality which intersects with other inequalities (Hills et al. 2010) and is a key issue in social work and social justice debates.

Despite some of the legislation having been in place for almost fifty years, it is apparent that certain groups continue to suffer significant inequality, although selecting one characteristic or group or assuming everyone in one specific group will have the same experiences, without considering interconnecting or contradictory characteristics, clearly simplifies the issues.

- Even though sex discrimination legislation has been in force since the 1970s women still earn on average 22.6% less than men per hour.
- Less academically able but better off children outperform more able but poorer children by the age of six.
- A person from an ethnic minority is 13% less likely to find work than a White person.

- One in five older people fail to get quotations for motor, travel and car hire insurance.
- Six out of ten lesbian and gay children and young people experience homophobic bullying, many contemplating suicide as a result.
- Disabled people are twice as likely to be unemployed as non-disabled people.
  (Government Equalities Office 2009, cited in Gaine and Gaylard 2010: 14)

Evidence that at least some of these persistent inequalities are the result of direct discrimination is provided by a government study (Wood et al., 2009) in which three almost identical written applications were sent to public and private employers for just under 1,000 posts at different levels. The only difference between the three applications in each case was that the applicants' names were associated with different ethnic groups – White, and a variety of different ethnic minorities. One in nine applications from White candidates received a positive response, compared with only one in sixteen for those with names associated with ethnic minorities, which is evidence of continuing racial discrimination. Continuing discrimination and inequality, despite equality legislation, are not unique to the UK. Taylor-Gooby (2011) found that, despite formal equal opportunities policies in many European countries, informal mechanisms and social networks privileged those in the higher social classes, particularly men. Education was the most important factor in class advantage, even in more social democratic societies, with gender inequality particularly high in the UK, Germany and Poland.

One common understanding of equality, touched upon at the beginning of the chapter, is treating everyone in the same manner, sometimes known as 'formal or procedural equality'. However, the effect of treating everyone the same may be unfair if this produces divergent outcomes for different groups in the population. For example, a minimum height requirement of 5 ft 10 ins for joining the fire service excludes a much larger number of women than men. While historically the height requirement was justified, developments in technology (e.g. hydraulic ladders) have made this unnecessary, and it has been abolished. However, good eyesight remains a precondition for firefighters because it is necessary to perform the job competently. In terms of social work education, it might be considered fair only to accept applicants who have the same or equivalent qualifications. However, if it is accepted that those from privileged backgrounds are likely to have greater opportunities to gain such qualifications, then such a position may seem less fair. Therefore, as a way of widening participation to include those from traditionally under-represented groups, such as those who come from a deprived postcode area or an underperforming school, one could consider whether they might be offered a place with lower than expected or required entry qualifications in order to compensate partially for past disadvantage. This is known as positive discrimination or affirmative action and is an attempt to counter the historic discrimination and subsequent under-representation of certain groups in particular spheres. It was introduced in the USA in the 1960s to combat racial and then sexual discrimination in employment and later extended to education, but has been controversial. There have been numerous US court cases that challenge its constitutional legitimacy, alongside other claims that it is not effective because – amongst other reasons – it favours the most fortunate (but not necessarily the most able) in certain groups (such as upper- or middle-class, as opposed to working-class, Blacks) (Sowell 2005). These examples show that equality interpreted as uniformity is not always the most appropriate principle for achieving a fair outcome, but also that approaches such as positive discrimination have problems associated with them and do not always meet their aims.

All forms of feminism see women as oppressed in some way, but suggest different causes and solutions. The three principal perspectives are liberal, radical and socialist feminism. Liberal feminists seek to achieve gender equality by the reform of laws and policies that discriminate against women (or men) but do not fundamentally challenge the structure of society. However, the liberal approach, which focuses on equal treatment, risks simply trying to fit women into a male norm. For example, it is not enough to treat women and men equally in relation to employment, when employment and promotion opportunities are based on male patterns of work, and do not take into account women's and men's different socialization and education or the constraints on women because of their childcare and domestic responsibilities (Blackburn 1999). Radical feminists see the root cause of women's oppression as patriarchy, which involves men ruling society for the benefit of men, using violence to control and subordinate women. This does not mean all men are violent or misogynists or that they all equally benefit from or welcome such a system, but they may nonetheless collude with patriarchy by failing to challenge others' oppression or violence. Radical feminists advocate fundamental changes in society including breaking down gender roles and establishing new and completely different relationships between men, between women, and between men and women. Socialist feminists see women's oppression as being caused by the interaction of capitalism with patriarchy. Patriarchy results in women's subordination to men, servicing them through their domestic labour, which is often not recognized as a form of work at all. Women's subordinate domestic position in turn makes women a particularly useful source of labour for capital, as they can be drawn into the labour market and used to undercut working-class men's wages, or act as a 'reserve' to be drawn upon when there is a labour shortage. Even when in paid employment, women are often trapped in part-time caring or service jobs which are poorly paid and low status. Their poor pay and conditions are justified by reference to gender stereotypes which present women's capabilities as an expression of their 'natural' capacities rather than as learned skills. For socialist feminists the solution lies in the overthrow of both capitalism and patriarchy.

4.5 Key social justice theories

Equality is clearly an important condition for social justice, although, as the previous section indicates, there are different and sometimes conflicting interpretations of what equality means. This section examines five different theoretical approaches to social justice in the context of their different interpretations of equality. *Meritocratic* approaches adopt a narrow interpretation of justice as concerned only with *equality of opportunity. Rawls' theory of justice* is more concerned with *equal treatment and/ or outcomes*, particularly in relation to resource allocation. *The politics of recognition* sees social justice as being achieved principally through respectful accommodation of diversity and difference The fourth perspective equates social justice with '*parity of participation*' and addresses the distribution of cultural, political and economic resources so that all groups are equally able to participate in society. Finally, *the capabilities approach* is principally concerned with giving people the opportunities to live a life they value.

Meritocracy and equality of opportunity

Meritocrats believe that in a just society the most talented and hardest-working will receive the greatest rewards in terms of their income and social status. This is viewed as being both fair and to the benefit of society as a whole, with rewards and status linked to the social value of the work performed. There is an acceptance that within a meritocratic system there will be inequality in outcomes – less talented or less diligent people will work in lower-status jobs and receive lower pay, but in a fully meritocratic society equality of opportunity will ensure social mobility – the ability to move up or down social hierarchies and change your social and economic status. The central issue for meritocrats is how to ensure real equality of opportunity for those from very different backgrounds, since there is clear evidence, for example, of the very early effects of poverty in childhood on health, development and educational achievement (Dannefer 2003; Johnson and Kossykh 2008). It may also be difficult to achieve consensus about the societal value of different occupations. Consider the difficulties involved in comparing the social value of the work of care workers, town planners, bankers and neurosurgeons.

Many Western liberal democracies adopt meritocratic principles because these seem to be both a fair and an efficient way of organizing society. Welfare states demonstrate different degrees of commitment to meritocracy. States with a weak commitment, such as the UK, typically have anti-discrimination legislation but, as shown earlier, without other measures to address social and economic inequalities, this has had limited effectiveness. The UK's Commission on Social Mobility and the Child Poverty Commission examined the backgrounds of 4,000 leaders in business, law, politics, the media and other aspects of public life. They found that those from public/independent school and/or Oxbridge educational backgrounds were heavily over-represented and that diversity and talent were effectively being 'locked out' of the most socially and politically influential posts (Social Mobility and Child Poverty Commission 2014). A stronger commitment to meritocracy involves the recognition that, even without deliberate discrimination, wealthy and/or talented parents can negotiate or purchase better education for their children, cultivate their talents and access elite networks. More strongly meritocratic states therefore implement anti-discrimination legislation but also address the disadvantages that result from differential access to financial, social and cultural resources.

All forms of meritocracy are subject to the criticism that they are intrinsically unfair to the less talented. If, for example, a highly talented person can earn £500,000 per year working full-time but chooses to work one day a week and earns £100,000 a year, while another less able person receives £12,000 working full-time and often works overtime to pay essential bills – is this fair? Rawls (1999) and Dworkin (1985) therefore both argue meritocracy and equal opportunity are not a means to achieve social justice because people's opportunities are either enhanced or constrained by 'natural endowments' that they have no control over.

Rawls, social justice and luck egalitarianism

The political philosopher John Rawls in *A Theory of Justice* (1971) proposed a set of principles for achieving a socially just society. His method for arriving at these principles is an interesting one, involving a 'thought experiment'. The experiment was to think about what principles people would generally accept as the basis for distributing resources fairly if they had no knowledge of what their own position was in that society, e.g. whether they were male or female, able-bodied or disabled, young or old, Black or White – characteristics that are the result of what Rawls called *brute luck*. This method led him to three principles, which he believed balanced liberty with a fair distribution of resources:

*   each person should have maximum liberty, limited only by the need to ensure that this doesn't interfere with the liberties of others;
*   all positions in society should be open to everyone, and everyone should have the opportunity to acquire the skills necessary for any position;
*   any inequalities in society should be to the benefit of the least advantaged.

These principles, Rawls believed, would ensure a distribution of rights and liberties, income and wealth, status and opportunities that was just, and so would produce a just society.

Luck egalitarianism (Cohen 2000; Dworkin 2000) originates from Rawls' belief that people should not be disadvantaged by unpredictable factors – *brute luck*. It argues the state should prevent or compensate for factors that people have no control over, but luck egalitarianism does not endorse making allowances for, or penalizing, the outcomes emanating from poor or good choices – *option luck*. One problem with trying to balance liberty (the freedom to act as one chooses) with equality is how to deal with the outcomes of the different ways in which individuals use their liberty – in particular, where inequalities result from 'bad' or 'good' choices, such as a lucky win on the Grand National or a life-changing disability as a result of a drink-driving car accident. However, the distinction between brute luck (the effects of chance) and option luck (the effects of choices made) is not clear-cut. Someone of limited intelligence may make poor choices which lead to bad outcomes that might have been foreseen and avoided by others. Children may suffer from bad choices made by their parents about their upbringing and education. But those choices may be shaped by the parents' own circumstances. Is this brute luck or option luck? Luck egalitarianism has therefore been criticized for these reasons, and leaves those destitute or desperate through poor choices unsupported and vulnerable (Anderson 1999).

Social justice, recognition and participation

The anti-racist, feminist, disability and gay social movements of the 1960s and 1970s demanded equal treatment and played a key role in initiating anti-discrimination legislation in the UK and the USA (Martin 2000). However, as we have seen, these measures have had limited effect. Some people have argued that disrespect and lack of recognition for disadvantaged groups such as women, gay couples, Travellers (established itinerant ethnic groups), asylum seekers or religious minorities are more damaging than unequal distribution of resources, and that the key to social justice is therefore about identity formation and validation: *recognition* (Young 1990).

Fraser (2008) conversely argued that the focus on identity, which equates social justice with recognition, jeopardized equality claims (see also Fraser and Honneth 2003). She argued that social justice involves integrally linked political, cultural and economic dimensions, none of which is reducible to or takes precedence over another. Fraser sees *parity of participation* as the ultimate goal of social justice, requiring 'social arrangements that permit all to participate as peers in social life'. The obstacles to achieving this are: (i) *distributive injustice* or *maldistribution*, which involves people being denied material resources required to interact with others; (ii) *status inequality* or *misrecognition* – that is, cultural hierarchies which devalue and disrespect some groups and elevate others. Examples include the stereotyping of Muslims as religious fundamentalists and terrorists, women's subordinate position in numerous cultures, and the criminalization and stigmatization of gay people in many countries (Green and Grant 2008). Fraser's third dimension, *misrepresentation*, relates to decisions that exclude some people from participating as equals in political and other spheres. Misrepresentation is essentially the denial of an equal or valued voice in democratic decision making and public discussions. In this way, people may be nominally included – for example, having the formal right to vote or air their opinion in public debates – but may not feel sufficiently worthy or informed to contribute. Alternatively, they may be disregarded, manipulated or have their opinions discredited. This dimension of representation is similar to White's conception of political equality. Fraser argues that to subdivide social injustice into separate spheres, and argue that one, such as identity misrecognition, is separate from or more important than another, is misguided.

The capabilities approach

The capabilities approach, developed by two political philosophers, Nussbaum (2011) and Sen (2009), is concerned with the multiple conditions that enable individuals to make informed choices about how to lead a worthwhile life and gain self-respect and the respect of others. 'Capabilities' refer to the material, social or psychological resources that enable each individual to 'do' or 'be' something they see as valuable. This will vary between cultures and individuals and the theory is therefore not predominantly concerned with equal resources or equivalent or identical outcomes but with the conditions that allow an individual to flourish. Good mental health might involve the freedom to go where one wants in public, or to associate freely with whomever one chooses. Achieving this requires social and moral equality which does not necessarily depend on material resources. The capabilities approach – like luck egalitarianism, but unlike Rawls' theory of justice – incorporates a particular theory of responsibility. A person who has the capability to perform specific functions, but fails to do so, is deemed responsible for the consequences. This approach is concerned principally with human *agency* and processes, as opposed to *outcomes*. Both the capabilities approach and Fraser's view of social justice as parity of participation adopt a multidimensional approach to achieving a just society.

The preceding discussion reveals equality and social justice as contested, multifaceted and interlinked concepts that have developed from understandings of citizenship, human rights and social divisions. Some theories are predominantly focused on equal treatment, equal opportunities or equal outcomes; others stress the pre-eminent importance of respecting and accommodating difference, or making people responsible for freely chosen actions but not for unpredictable events. Some concentrate on one particular aspect, such as economic equality, whereas others are multi-dimensional. Social workers need to think through what their views and commitments are in relation to social justice, rights, equality and difference, both generally and in response to specific situations that they may encounter.

The next section examines social work's understanding of social justice and equality, concepts which it has tended to interpret and then deploy in fairly narrow ways that focus on anti-discriminatory practice at the level of the individual. This obscures the wider structural causes of inequality and shifts attention away from a broader conception of social justice to the accommodation of individual diversity. However, even this narrow focus has proved problematic. An uncritical and simplistic acceptance of multiculturalism has sometimes resulted in social workers who are fearful of being labelled as discriminatory towards others' cultures or religions, condoning oppressive behaviours. They have consequently failed to assess and intervene appropriately in complex safeguarding situations where vulnerable children, or perhaps adults too, are at significant risk. We therefore examine some complex practice scenarios and issues and outline some of the factors social workers may need to take into account when analysing and assessing such situations.

4.6 Social work, justice, equality and difference

> The social work profession promotes social change, problem solving in human relationships and the empowerment and liberation of people to enhance well-being. Utilising theories of human behaviour and social systems, social work intervenes at the points where people interact with their environments. Principles of human rights and social justice are fundamental. (BASW 2012a: 5)

This internationally accepted definition presents the social work profession as informed by social science and committed to social justice and human rights. Social work's clientele is drawn from the most marginalized and multiply disadvantaged groups in society across the life course (from the neglected child, the juvenile offender, the mentally ill adult, to the older person requiring residential care) (Marmot 2010). Social workers need to be able to address intersecting injustices and inequalities competently at individual and structural levels and intergenerationally, and this involves ensuring that their practice is based on a thorough understanding of ADP/AOP principles. Some commentators view ADP as narrowly concerned with the legal context and individual discrimination whereas others link AOP with a wider commitment to combatting oppression, with a third group perceiving little difference (Healy 2014). Most writers on ADP/AOP would, however, underline the importance of social justice, encourage multidimensional analysis and support both a micro- and a macro-level approach (e.g. Dominelli 2002; Thompson 2003; Dalrymple and Burke 2006; Okitikpi and Aymer 2010). In the remainder of this chapter, we use the term 'AOP' rather than 'ADP' because it shifts the semantic focus away from a narrow concern with individual discrimination to a wider understanding of oppression as operating, and requiring responses, at different levels.

The history of ADP/AOP in the UK

Social work's commitment to AOP appeared in the late 1980s, although in the 1970s and 1980s there was a radical social work tradition influenced by Marxism which focused on state oppression and social class inequalities. In 1989, the Central Council for Education and Training in Social Work (CCETSW), the body with responsibility for social work training, published *The Rules and Requirements for the Diploma in Social Work* (referred to as 'Paper 30'). This set out, for the first time, the need for social work training providers to show that their programmes included anti-discriminatory and anti-racist policies and that they had policies and procedures for implementing and monitoring these. A modified edition concerned predominantly with 'race' appeared in 1991. CCETSW's requirements also need to be understood within the context of changing responses to ethnic diversity in the UK (discussed further in the section on 'race' and ethnicity), as well as different perspectives within feminism, briefly outlined earlier. It is therefore unsurprising that CCETSW Paper 30 did not specify that social workers should take action against social injustice, or itself clearly explain what it understood social justice to mean. It specified social work students should merely possess *awareness* of the inter-related processes of race, class and gender oppression, which, as this chapter has shown, is highly challenging, involving differing interpretations of what constitutes oppression and how it might successfully be addressed. Subsequent revisions to Paper 30 removed the explicit references to structural oppression and anti-racism (McLaughlin 2005: 295) but still required students to challenge their own prejudices, value diversity and counteract disadvantage, discrimination, injustice and inequality (CCETSW 1995: 18).

Social workers, whether employed by the state or by voluntary or for-profit organizations, have to comply with the provisions of the 2010 Equality Act. Professional codes and guidance from the late 1980s onwards also deal with social justice, diversity and equality, although the emphasis on inequality and social justice has lessened in recent years, with attention focused on diversity. The professional capabilities framework (PCF) guides pre- and post-qualifying social work education. The PCF was initially developed by the Social Work Reform Board and later adopted by the College of Social Work (TCSW). After the dissolution of TCSW in 2015 (see chapter 5), responsibility for the PCF was transferred to BASW (BASW 2015a). The PCF was still operational at the time of writing, but it is possible other professional codes and guidance may be developed later and it may be superseded. It specifies that social workers should understand and respect difference in self and others and challenge discrimination, oppression and cultural assumptions, although this in itself is confusing (as later examples evidence) because it may require understanding different cultural assumptions and showing respect for service users' difference, while at the same time challenging their values or practices. Rights, justice and economic well-being are also key aspects of the PCF.

AOP in the UK was positively influenced by Marxism, anti-racism and feminism, hence the early focus on class, 'race' and gender. There were originally high hopes among some social work academics for the potential achievements of AOP. Dominelli (2002) saw it as offering social work the possibility of going beyond its control, maintenance or casework focus and influencing public policy by winning ideological debates. Beresford and Croft (2004) envisaged collaboration with service users leading to public policy advocacy and change, but neither occurred (Rush and Keenan 2014). AOP became more individualistic and apolitical from the late 1980s onwards as neoliberal ideology became dominant. Supporting a more individualistic expression of difference was more consistent with neoliberal ideology and it fractured equality claims and collective action by different groups, who increasingly saw themselves as competing for scarce resources and requiring different responses. McLaughlin (2005, 2008) is deeply pessimistic about the direction AOP has moved in and its current state. He argues that AOP has now degenerated into a micro-level impression management enterprise, with social work students being aware of how not to discriminate against individuals at a personal level but simultaneously complying with oppressive state- and organizational-level policies.

Misunderstanding ADP/AOP and its complexity

Some commentators question whether social workers can ever be genuinely anti-oppressive, given their power (Sakamoto and Pitner 2005), particularly in relation to safeguarding and resource allocation, and in the context of the popularity of individualistic, psychologically oriented methods (Reisch 2013; see also chapter 6) which ignore the structural causes of exclusion, discrimination and disadvantage. Reisch and Jani (2012: 1141) therefore recommend that social work education focuses on developing 'critical consciousness' about the pervasive effects of power differentials on institutional policies, practices and social relations.

The success of AOP education in terms of producing self-aware, critically conscious practitioners is, however, difficult to evaluate, as academics must successfully 'challenge years of socialization and internalized ideologies of superiority that make hierarchies of privilege appear to be the natural order, with classic victim-blaming . . . aided by the ideology of equal opportunity' (Lichtenwalter and Baker 2010: 305–6). This difficulty is compounded by the 'personal–professional dialectic' which produces ethical tensions when professional values conflict with students' often long- and deeply held personal values. This may cause discomfort, anger, disorientation, guilt, defensiveness or students feeling they are being personally attacked (Bernard and Campbell 2014), all of which need to be worked through. An analysis of thirty second-year postgraduate students' practice portfolios in Scotland showed that, although they had a basic understanding of power, empowerment and partnership working and some social divisions, their engagement with class, religion and sexuality was minimal and they tended to accept agency policies and wider structural oppression unquestioningly (Collins and Wilkie 2010).

A number of other studies across Western countries reinforce these findings, showing students' understandings of various forms of oppression, particularly early on in their education, are uneven and often superficial. Some students negatively stereotyped certain groups, such as disabled, older and unemployed people and substance misusers (Weiss et al. 2002; Heenan 2005; Smith 2013; Theriot and Lodato 2012), and they rarely saw social work practice as extending further than the micro context. Studies of students at later points in their education tend to be contradictory and inconclusive. One small-scale-snapshot British study suggested social work education can lead to students competently practising in an anti-oppressive manner (Hughes 2011). However, a longitudinal Australian study found the reverse, with students, even towards the end of their training, resorting to stereotypes and victim-blaming in assessments and interventions (Ryan et al. 1995). Because these studies have been conducted with diverse methodologies, at different times, across countries with dissimilar cultures and political systems, and have often focused on different aspects of diversity, oppression, moral reasoning or ethical reflexivity, they are understandably difficult to compare. Nevertheless, even the most optimistic studies show that shifts in attitudes towards minority groups during social work education and training are not huge, and although a wide range of different educational techniques may support anti-oppressive education, students must be continually prepared to work on and challenge themselves as well.

Forcing social work students to adopt a 'correct' discourse, or them deciding to camouflage their true beliefs under politically correct terminology and language, is unlikely to lend itself to meaningful learning, critical reflection or attitude change (Macey and Moxon 1996: 310; Green and Featherstone 2014). Psychological research shows that individuals may hold inconsistent attitudes or be unaware of the attitudes they hold, and that their behaviour does not always reflect their attitudes (Pugh 1998; Sullivan 1998). Denying or suppressing internalized negative stereotypes in order to conform to professional requirements may result in these stereotypes resurfacing, particularly when under stress, resulting in victim-blaming or acting against the interests of certain groups (Macrae et al. 1994; Pugh 1998). These findings point to the need for critical reflection to help students resolve tensions between professional and personal values relating to AOP and to recognize how people are 'othered' and marginalized through subtle acts of normative violence (Green and Featherstone 2014). 'Normative violence' is a term taken from Judith Butler (see Boesten 2010). It refers to the often inadvertent misrecognition of people who diverge from cultural norms and become labelled as dangerous or perceived of as unintelligible because of this. Normative violence does not include direct physical violence but may precede it. For example, intersex people, such as hermaphrodites, are born with chromosomal configurations, reproductive organs and/or sexual anatomy that do not allow them to be easily categorized as either male or female. Others may therefore struggle to know how to define, treat and understand intersex people in the context of what they see as an abnormal, liminal, seemingly indeterminate state. Intersexuals have therefore traditionally been subjected to painful, unrequested and repeated genital and other surgery as children (if their situation is known then) so they can conform visually more easily to being male or female. This is seen to be for their benefit so they fit better into society, whilst at the same time no longer destabilizing our and society's dependence on binary categories of biological sex.

Green and Featherstone (2014) exhort social workers to embrace the 'stranger' or 'other', recognizing our shared humanity, and to step away from binary hierarchies of victim or villain, 'normal' or 'abnormal', deserving or undeserving. A focus on internalized attitudes is consequently important for anti-oppressive understanding and practice, both micro and macro. Challenging the dominance of normative or privileged categories such as able-bodiedness, whiteness or heterosexuality, and understanding their impact on those who diverge from them, requires critical analysis. This should lead to greater awareness of the extent to which privilege is unconscious and unacknowledged. This is not always easy and the following paragraphs therefore deal more fully with the potential impact of simplification, stereotyping and ignoring intersectionality.

Stereotypes and simplification

'Race' and ethnicity

In the nineteenth and early twentieth centuries, a colonialist belief (since disproven) prevailed: that biologically and intellectually different races existed, with the White European race being more evolved. This view has been discredited but the concept of 'race', as a socially constructed category (see chapter 3), has been retained to refer to a set of ideas that shape social institutions and practices. The concept of ethnicity, like 'race', is a social construction that is often used in preference to, or (inaccurately) interchangeably with, 'race'. It refers to a group of people with shared ancestry, culture or nationality, and in this way is more narrowly defined than 'race'. For example, 'White' as a racial category includes many different ethnic groups, who may be defined in terms of nationality, or religion or some combination thereof – Poles, Irish Catholics, Gypsies, English. The concepts of 'race' and ethnicity are both problematic and carry the danger of essentialism – the idea that there are certain fixed characteristics which are inherent to a particular ethnicity or 'race' (see Bloch et al. 2013: ch. 1).

As immigration to the UK from former colonies increased from the 1950s onwards, those from other mostly 'Black' cultures and countries were often marginalized for preserving some of their 'inferior' indigenous practices. Policies initially concentrated on integrating these immigrants into the culturally 'superior' host nation by *assimilation*. As Black activism in the USA and UK gained momentum in the 1960s and 1970s and encouraged ethnic minorities to be proud of their distinctiveness, assimilation was gradually replaced by a greater acceptance of the co-existence of different cultures: *multiculturalism*. From a social work perspective, this might mean that different dietary requirements, religious practices, clothing and belief systems should be catered for and celebrated. However, multiculturalism was criticized because it did not challenge racist beliefs that were deeply ingrained in the White population. This limitation was addressed in the 1980s by *anti-racism* which was concerned with challenging covert or overt racism, addressing racial discrimination and promoting race equality within society and its institutions. Anti-racism also had limited success and it has been argued it oversimplifies 'race' and racism, dividing Black and White people into oppressed and oppressors, elevating 'race' above all other social divisions, and ignoring the importance of intersectionality. A further shift in policy on race took place after 2001, precipitated by a series of violent outbreaks between South Asian young men, White racists (both groups from relatively impoverished and disadvantaged areas) and the police in several towns in northern England. A number of inquiries into these events drew attention to the segregation of different communities within these towns. They called for policies to promote *community cohesion*, which would combine respect for diversity with promoting inter-community relations, a common set of 'British' values and shared identity. The London bombings in July 2005 by young British-born Muslim men gave added impetus to policies to promote a common set of 'British' values in order to counter 'extremism' in some minority communities (for a fuller discussion of these issues, see Bloch et al. 2013: ch. 2).

Multicultural social work practice traditionally incorporated two components: (i) acquiring cultural information about the 'other' – their history, worldviews, communication styles and social and family norms, as well as understandings of health and illness and help-seeking behaviours; and (ii) a sensitivity to cultural differences which tries to guard against professionals inevitably evaluating service users' cultural values negatively because they see them as inferior to their own. One example of this might involve investigating and perhaps challenging the assumption that arranged marriages are less desirable and successful than those associated more with romantic love and individual choice. More recently, the aim has been to develop social workers' *cultural competence*, encompassing the first two elements but additionally aiming to equip practitioners with skills to work at three levels: direct practice (micro), agency/ service (meso) and policy (macro). Advocates argue cultural sensitivity and knowledge of the 'other' are insufficient in themselves and that a critical awareness of one's own cultural attitudes, prejudices and understandings of cross-cultural encounters needs to be developed. Since the mid-1990s, cultural competence has become an important approach in social work but has sometimes been misinterpreted to mean uncritically embracing all cultural diversity and difference (Laird 2008), thereby contributing to some tragic errors in child protection practice. However, both traditional multicultural social work practice and its successor, cultural competence, have been criticized for reflecting conservative and liberal viewpoints which either covertly reintroduce an assimilationist view or ignore cultural dynamism, wider interconnected global justice issues and intersectionality (Nadan and Ben-Ari 2013).

Nadan and Ben-Ari (2013: 1091) therefore advocate an anti-oppressive critical multiculturalist perspective, emphasizing the conditions that disadvantage groups and the political and institutional forces that oppress, restrict and exclude them from social justice. In Australia, for example, although various forms of cultural competence have featured in healthcare for many years, there have been few robust studies of their effectiveness at a micro interpersonal level and no evidence that they have improved vast structural health disparities between indigenous Australians and the wider Australian population (Thackrah and Thompson 2013). Hollinsworth (2013), in comparison, advocates a less activist, more reflexive approach, challenging students to become self-critical about unacknowledged dominance and unearned privilege, and to build trust with and learn from service users rather than adopting a rigid view of how they think a particular culture operates. Both Nadan and Ben-Ari and Hollinsworth make important points, one suggesting understanding the operation and effects of wider structural oppression on minority groups is imperative and the other stressing the importance of not relying on static perceptions of how different cultures operate and urging social workers not to make assumptions but rigorously to investigate every situation anew.

Batson et al. (1997) argue that attitudes towards stigmatized groups can be improved by presenting information incompatible with negative stereotypes and compatible with multiculturalism, and improving knowledge of, contact with and empathy with these groups. However, much depends on the type and nature of the contact and the understandings drawn from it, as frequent contact in itself may not engender empathy or a lead to a deep understanding of the systemic and institutional injustices certain groups might experience. Cultural competence has also concentrated more on 'race' than other aspects of culture which may also be important

(Thackrah and Thompson 2013). Group identity, furthermore, is not fixed, and early anti-racism strategies, whilst dismissing multiculturalist approaches, themselves depended on a fixed, essentialist notion of what it was to be Black (Rattansi 1992). Social work has traditionally concentrated on the 'White on Black' paradigm of structural racial oppression (Laird 2014). Little attention has been paid to 'White on White' racism, such as discrimination against Eastern European or Irish people (e.g. Garrett 1998; Mac an Ghaill 2002) or to 'Black/Brown on Black' racism (Washington 1990; Sautman 1996; Yancey 2005; Waters and Kasinitz 2010). This involves lighter-skinned individuals such as Asians, who sometimes experience less discrimination from the White population, discriminating against darker-skinned groups, such as Africans (Deliovsky and Kitossa 2013). One cannot, however, always assume that depth of skin colour determines the levels and extents of racism, and other factors such as culture, class and community are very important. Les Back's ethnographic study (1996) of an urban mixed ethnic community in England found, for example, that although many White and African Caribbean youths socialized amicably together, both these groups harassed and excluded Vietnamese young people.

Mixed-heritage/parentage children may also confound or throw into confusion assumptions around racial identity or cultural belonging. Some of these children primarily identify as either Black or White, mixed heritage or mixed race, or by their country of origin. Alternatively, they may completely reject identity linked to nationality, skin colour or ethnicity, or may self-identify differently depending on the context, thereby manifesting a fluid and shifting sense of self (Tizard and Phoenix 1993; Alibhai-Brown 2001; Brunsma and Rockquemore 2002). The example given by Ploesser and Mecheril in the earlier section on intersectionality offers a good example of this potential fluidity. Debates about the fostering and adoption of mixed-heritage children appear almost to have gone full circle. Many mixed-heritage children in the 1960s–1980s were placed, in an unthinking way, with White families. Between the late 1980s and the 2000s, policy and academic views changed, stipulating that these were unequivocally Black children who were only to be placed with Black families (e.g. Small 1991; Robinson 2005). Little attention was accorded to other considerations such as nationality, social class, culture and religion, the children's mixed parentage or their own choice or self-identity. In 2003, statistics showed mixed-heritage children were more likely to be in care or 'looked after' than any other ethnic group (Thoburn et al. 2005). Colour-blind exhortations to ignore 'race' and culture re-emerged in 2012–13 when it was found that mixed-heritage children were languishing in care for long periods of time because no suitable 'racial' matches could be found.

This brief examination of 'race'/ethnicity initially outlined changing demographics, definitions, understandings and responses to different 'races' and ethnic minorities in the UK, whilst showing some common responses still involve resorting to stereotypes and simplification. Some early responses to immigrants in the 1950s/1960s were colonialist and superior; others uncritically celebrated all cultural diversity. Later responses focused on tackling racism throughout society, assuming a simple White/Black hierarchy of the oppressors and oppressed. The most recent approach attempts to counter 'racial' segregation and hostility by encouraging intercommunity interaction and shared values, but without an acknowledgement that other factors, some associated with poverty and deprivation, might also be important. Not all racism is linked to the Black/White binary or continuum, and 'race' may intersect in complex ways with other social divisions. Societal and historical contexts are very important, as are the self-identification of the service user and the social worker's understanding of the service user's perspective. Given the complexity of such issues, it is not surprising social workers have struggled to respond to them in a nuanced and sensitive way, often resorting to binaries or stereotypes. Heated debates therefore surround what constitutes good social work with 'racial' or ethnic minorities (for example, between multicultural, culturally competent and anti-oppressive critical multicultural approaches with some commentators advocating ignoring racial or cultural considerations completely). The most productive ways of working, however, seem to combine close interaction with an understanding of individual service users and their wider communities, with a more holistic understanding of oppression and an ability to take into consideration intersectionality and multiple oppressions and social divisions.

Sex, gender and sexual orientation
The term 'gender' refers to the social construction of femininity and masculinity in a particular society at a particular time. The biological difference between the sexes is the starting point for the development of a set of culturally specific norms about what it means to be a man or a woman (gender identity) and how this is expressed in behaviour (gender expression). Individuals are expected to conform on the basis of their *biological sex*, including expectations in contemporary Western societies that 'normal' men and women are physically and romantically attracted to the opposite sex – in other words, that their *sexual orientation* is heterosexual. The reality is somewhat different. Although it is often assumed that a clear and fixed binary exists for sex, gender and sexual orientation – you're either biologically male or female, you're either a man or a woman, you're either 'gay' or 'straight' – there is great diversity and dynamism in people's sexual preferences, behaviour and gender identity. Some people may always identify as heterosexual, gay, lesbian or bisexual; others change their sexual orientation during their life course or reject any definitive label. Some people may identify as heterosexual, and perhaps express homophobic attitudes, but will simultaneously engage in sporadic, casual same-sex sexual encounters. Table 4.1 provides a summary of the relationship between the concepts of biological sex, gender norm, gender expression, gender identity and sexual orientation. There are, however, strong social pressures against acknowledging the fluidity of gender identity and expression, and widespread discrimination against and oppression of individuals who do not conform to gender norms. Given the centrality of gender identity and sexual orientation to people's identity, it is not surprising that these issues provoke very strong feelings and that, in relation to social work, there are examples of misunderstandings about anti-discriminatory practice in relation to gender and sexual orientation.

The Wakefield Inquiry into the sexual abuse of 'looked-after' boys by two male homosexual foster carers found that the social workers' fear of being seen as homophobic clouded their professional judgement about the risks to these children (Parrott et al. 2007). In this case, the social workers were not acting in an anti-oppressive manner but seemed to assume they would be accused of being oppressive if they challenged the foster carers because they were members of an oppressed group. Assuming that all gay men are *never* or are *always* automatically a risk to children are equally

Table 4.1 Sex and gender: five dimensions of variation

Biological sex	*Physical* characteristics: genitalia, hormones, body shape, voice pitch
Gender norm	*Culturally and historically specific* norms which specify the socially approved characteristics of men and women (masculinity/femininity) in a particular society (e.g. behaviour, demeanour, dress)
Gender expression	*Presentation by an individual* of gender based on gender norms (femininity/masculinity); degree of conformity, e.g. in relation to behaviour, demeanour, dress
Gender identity	Degree of *identification* with gender norms
Sexual orientation	Degree of *sexual attraction* to people of same and opposite sex

Source: based on *The Genderbread Person v.3* (http://itspronouncedmetrosexual.com).

problematic stances. Members of oppressed and privileged groups both have the potential either to oppress others in their own group or members of other groups or, alternatively, to act sensitively or fairly towards them. The social workers responsible for the 'looked-after' boys therefore should have subjected the gay couple to the same sort of professional assessment they would have subjected any heterosexual couple or single foster carer to and should have followed up on, rather than ignored, any potential concerns. Such action would not be discriminatory but would be a professional response to concerns about another minority and often-oppressed group, children. In another example some social workers who said they did not want to discriminate against lesbian and gay prospective adoptive or foster couples revealed their stereotyped views about gender roles in the heterosexual nuclear family through the questions they asked (Hicks 2011, 2014). They were bemused by the different and non-gender-stereotypical relational practices of some same-sex couples, asking male couples if they knew many women and how they would ensure any child placed with them was exposed to female role models: 'The social worker did ask us a lot about role models, and female role models . . . It must have been difficult for her. I think she struggled with it . . . But we don't define who does what . . . It was almost as if she wanted us to be these stereotypical roles' (Hicks 2011: 120–4).

Here may be another example of Butler's concept of normative violence, whereby people who diverge from social norms are found unintelligible because they are difficult to fit into accepted categories (regarding gender and sexual orientation). Consequently they may be judged negatively, marginalized and potentially discriminated against. Hicks' analysis shows not only the importance of an understanding of intersectionality in social work (in this case between gender expression and sexual orientation) but also how an understanding of all social divisions and the stereotypes that inform them is important, even when apparently considering just one. Learning about and developing empathy for stigmatized and often unfamiliar groups who may have fluid lifestyles and norms is complex. Students must be prepared to live with uncertainty and constantly revise their knowledge and challenge previously held assumptions and values. They must guard against the fear of being seen as discriminatory when safeguarding issues are the main concern, whilst simultaneously ensuring they do not inadvertently oppress certain groups through simplistic acceptance of problematic stereotypes.

Social class, 'race'/ethnicity and childhood

The case of eight-year-old Victoria Climbié who was murdered in 1999 by her great-aunt and her aunt's partner also raises questions about the role of stereotypes, but around 'race', ethnicity and working-class children, and demonstrates the complex issues and dilemmas both social work and healthcare professionals confront in some child protection scenarios. They were faced with a dirty withdrawn child who apparently had scabies, spoke a foreign language and came from a different culture, and they were unnerved by her hostile adult carers. Fears of aggression, of contamination and communication barriers, alongside concerns they would be seen as racially discriminatory if they challenged different cultural norms (they equated Victoria's quietness with African cultural norms of deference to elders), effectively paralysed their judgement of the situation. The subsequent inquiry criticized social workers for being too trusting of the family and making uncritical assumptions about culture and extended family networks (Cocker and Hafford-Letchfield 2014). Seeing cultural norms as static and homogeneous, and adopting a position of cultural relativism also meant social workers made assumptions, rather than sensitively and rigorously investigating and assessing that specific situation and being prepared to make judgements. Arguably, the emphasis on 'race' and ethnicity in social work over the years has led social workers (and the subsequent inquiries) to over-privilege racial/cultural considerations and disregard other social divisions associated with intergenerational, social class and gender inequalities (Collins and Wilkie 2010). Attending to these other sources of inequality and to their intersection might have resulted in a more balanced analysis and possibly averted a tragedy of this kind. Ferguson (2007), for example, found the early philanthropists saw working-class children as 'moral dirt'. Over 100 years later, Steckley (2012) argues, children in residential care are the 'new untouchables'. A multi-professional failure to intervene with children, such as Victoria, who are later killed by their carers may therefore be partially attributable to professionals subconsciously viewing them as objects of contamination (Ferguson 2011), so clearly ethnicity or culture should not be the only considerations. In the case of Victoria Climbié, the intersection of childhood and social class, both social divisions and sources of oppression and subordination, needed to be considered alongside sensitive and nuanced understandings of 'race' and culture. These intersections seem to have produced not only misunderstandings about cultural issues, but also possibly subconscious perceptions about children as naturally subordinate because of their childhood status, and of working-class children as inevitably dirty and a potential pollutant and object of disgust.

Social workers frequently face complex and ambiguous situations in relation to justice, recognition, diversity, equality and safeguarding duties. Many are confused about how to respect difference and challenge oppression and discrimination, yet simultaneously question and perhaps ultimately judge the cultural norms of marginalized groups in the context of safeguarding – for example, in order to assess whether or not a child or adult is at risk. They often work with damaged and profoundly disadvantaged service users who have suffered substantial injustice. However, in a process of *double suffering*, some service users perpetuate that injustice by inflicting harm on themselves and others (Frost and Hoggett 2008), perhaps because oppression is their only role model (Freire 2000). Social workers are responsible for child and adult protection/safeguarding but must at the same time try to build trusting relationships with people from low-status marginalized groups. They often express stigmatizing attitudes towards such damaged clients and treat them in disrespectful ways (Pithouse 1987; Featherstone, White and Morris 2014), thus reinforcing a long history of professionals pathologizing poor working-class families (Fink and Lomax 2012: 5). Completing an assessment, which concludes a child is at significant risk of harm and needs to be removed from their carers, does not constitute discrimination simply because the family is Black and/or poor or the carers self-identify as gay, but treating them with a lack of respect in the process is unacceptable. However, any assessment should take into account whether poverty, oppression or injustice has further jeopardized a child's or adult's safety because this evidence could support broader social justice arguments.

The next section examines some examples of contentious or difficult issues social workers may engage with, and the complex debates they provoke. The discussion aims to demonstrate the importance of avoiding unthinking politically correct dogma and fixed binary categories. It encourages social workers to think through issues of diversity, equality and social justice carefully when they encounter them, and to challenge their own as well as others' conceptions and values. The first example deals with the potential social work role in dealing with FGM. The second questions the extent to which social workers should respect cultural and religious difference. The third example engages with debates about the role of the service user in relation to services: the 'expert through experience' and the 'informed consumer'.

4.7 Engaging with difference

FGM

What should social workers do when working with families with young daughters, originating from the twenty-eight countries where female genital mutilation (FGM) is known to be practised? FGM is defined by the World Health Organization (WHO) as 'all procedures involving partial or total removal of the external female genitalia or other injury to the female genital organs for non-medical reasons'. FGM is often seen as a ritual which is imperative for the girl's future marriage prospects and secures her sexual subordination. A study in 2007 estimated that there were 21,000 girls under fifteen in the UK at high risk of having FGM performed on them, either illegally in the UK or in their country of origin – 'vacation cutting' – with a further 11,000 likely to have already been subjected to it (Dorkenoo et al. 2007). Few social workers would condone such actions. Wade (2011a), however, analyses the debates surrounding a real-life case in which it was proposed that the cultural needs of immigrants from ethnic regions where FGM is the norm should be partially met by allowing doctors to make a superficial incision of 1 cm in the young girls' clitoral foreskin. This was intended to prevent more damaging FGM being performed illicitly and improve community relations, whilst providing culturally sensitive healthcare. Physicians working with Somali families in the USA interviewed thirty-six mothers who were amenable to modified genital cutting. The mothers had all undergone FGM themselves and did not want to subject their daughters to the same suffering, but neither did they want to abandon this practice entirely, for cultural reasons. The doctors saw their proposed action as a purely medical issue and failed to consult other professionals or interest groups, likening it to the Jewish/Muslim ritual of circumcising boys (although some might argue this too constitutes genital mutilation and child abuse). However, when other interested parties found out, there was huge opposition and the proposal was eventually withdrawn.

Wade argues that the doctors had a dynamic view of cultural change, whereas the opponents adopted a static view of Somali culture, and perceived 'the ritual nick' as a barbaric patriarchal procedure. Wade seems sympathetic to the physicians' empathic position but acknowledges important questions needed to be asked about whether social pressure and gender or generational inequalities might make their mothers', or the adolescent girls' (if they were asked), agreement with the practice relatively meaningless. A social worker involved with a family from a culture where FGM was practised would need to reflect on a number of interconnecting social divisions/oppressions and visions of justice and apply a nuanced understanding of 'race' and ethnicity, immigration, religion, culture, gender and age. This would involve taking into account the status of children and women, not only in relation to where they came from, but in their new context, and require social workers to be attuned to both safeguarding and support issues. For example, persecution and racism might make an immigrant family isolated and inclined to adhere to older cultural practices. Alternatively, positive experiences of a new country and culture with different laws and norms might make them willing to re-think, and discard or modify old customs and practices. Assumptions that such a family will automatically want FGM performed on female children may be misconceived. However, the ability to empathize with such a family and understand that cultural practices are dynamic might help the social worker to assess the situation. Even if a social worker assesses there to be a significant safeguarding risk, this does not mean they should label the parents as 'evil' or 'backward religious fanatics' or treat them with disdain. It may, however, mean that, with some families, statutory intervention to safeguard a child is necessary.

Religious expression

Religion and belief are protected characteristics in relation to discrimination, but so are other characteristics such as age, sex and sexual orientation. A number of recent European legal cases illustrate how respect for religious beliefs may conflict with upholding other people's rights not to be discriminated against. The cases all centred on the refusal of services to gay couples because of a religious belief that homosexuality is wrong. The situations were diverse: a marriage registrar who refused to conduct a civil partnership ceremony for a gay couple; two heterosexual married hoteliers who refused a gay couple bed-and-breakfast accommodation; and a RELATE relationship counsellor who would not work with a gay couple. In all cases, the right to express religious belief in this way was rejected by the court because it discriminated against gay people. By contrast, the right of a BA check-in employee to wear a cross at work was upheld by the European Court of Human Rights on the basis it expressed her religious beliefs in the same way as a Sikh wearing a turban, and did not adversely affect other people's rights: 'The dividing line, it seems, is between indicating one's faith and spelling out what it means in practice: devout Jews or Muslims, say, may wear kippahs or hijabs at work, but any manifestation of traditionalist religious views on morality would still be unacceptable – such as shunning colleagues of the opposite sex, or expressing disapproval of homosexuality' (*The Economist* 2014).

These examples are interesting and provide social workers with food for thought, but many situations that they encounter may be more difficult to negotiate. What should a social worker do, for example, if assigned to work with a man who refuses to shake hands with a female (social worker) because his religion precludes it and positions women as having lower status? What would be an appropriate response to a mother or father who refuses to let a male social worker engage with their teenage daughter on the grounds the family's religion precludes young females from being alone with unknown men from outside the family? Should service users' religious beliefs allow them to dictate the sex of the social worker they or their daughter will work with, and how should the social worker and the local or health authority respond? Alternatively, should considerations about children's rights and gender equality override religious demands? Serving culturally appropriate meals and accommodating worship in certain places or at certain times for people living in residential care are reasonable provisions that respect religious difference. Other adjustments that devalue, harm or deprive, for example, women, children or disabled or gay people are problematic in a society where certain characteristics or groups are protected under both UK and European legislation. Balancing rights and achieving justice is not easy. Social workers have to try to build relationships with the service user and fully understand their perspective, as well as challenge behaviour that is prejudiced, oppressive and contravenes others' rights. In doing so, they need simultaneously to be aware of intersecting oppressions and to consider the rights of not only the service user, but also other family members and the wider community. They need to perform a delicate balancing act guided, but often not entirely decided, by legislation and wider social work values and be prepared to explain to service users why sometimes the rights of some people over-ride those of others, particularly where the behaviour of some groups devalues or dehumanizes others.

'Experts through experience': who speaks for whom?

This section examines debates around service user involvement, autonomy and rights associated with the shift from seeing users as passive objects of expert intervention to perceiving them as people who are equal to professionals and are sometimes presented as even more knowledgeable because they are 'experts through experience'. This transition was initially influenced mainly by the disability and mental health survivor movements which claimed services had misunderstood them and not met their needs. Their members also felt services had stigmatized, stereotyped and dehumanized them in the process, with some of their basic human rights, such as respect and dignity, being contravened (e.g. Charlton 1998). The requirement to listen more carefully to users was further strengthened, although in a more individualistic and apolitical sense, by the marketization agenda championed from the 1980s onwards (Carey 2010), which depicts users of health and welfare services as active, informed consumers who should have a voice and choice of services (for more detail, see chapter 6). In social work education, it has been suggested, and sometimes stipulated, that service users, as 'experts through experience', should be involved at all stages of planning and delivering social work services and education (DH 2002;

HCPC 2013). However, there are a number of problems with the way in which the concept of experts through experience has been applied.

- Those service users who are the most involved in advising on services and in delivering social work education may often be disproportionately drawn from specific groups, such as articulate physically disabled people or those with mental health issues, and are therefore not representative. Children with severe learning disabilities, for example, may struggle to be involved and often be overlooked or misunderstood (Mitchell et al. 2009), or the resources required may mean that it is not feasible to involve them. Equally important are questions surrounding whether it is ethical to ask those who are extremely distressed, such as people whose children have been removed and adopted, to be involved in social work education (Carey 2013).
- Consideration needs to be given to what sort of support and training service users need if they do want to be involved, to ensure they are competent and well prepared, and neither are exploited nor use their position as a platform to vent their discontent unreflectively.
- There is a lack of clarity about whether expertise lies in the fact of being a service user or in being a member of one or more marginalized groups, or both, and whether one individual's experience can be extrapolated appropriately to others in similar situations. For example, those with mental health problems who identify as psychiatric system survivors, reject the medical model of mental illness and see psychiatry as oppressive have very different messages to convey to services and social work students from those who embrace the medical model and experience having a diagnosis and the treatment and support that come with it as supportive and helpful (Hopton 2013).
- The service user expert paradigm often ignores intersectionality (Carr 2014). An individual is not wholly defined by a single characteristic in terms of identity and experience – such as being a service user or being Black, working class, female or gay. The concept of expert by experience, by focusing exclusively on the experiences of individual service users as representatives of a particular group, hides a multiplicity of structural oppressions. It thereby obscures how such oppressions are seen, what responses are needed and who is responsible. The wider canvas of social injustice in terms of poverty and other social divisions then becomes less visible.
- It is unclear what criteria should be used to identify someone as an expert through experience. Some service users may have some insight into their experiences and important messages to communicate to professionals and students about respect, humility, communication and empathy as well as oppressive practice, and they may influence attitudinal change in respect of marginalized groups (Scheyett and Kim 2004). Service user knowledge has traditionally been undervalued and it is important to engage with it, despite few robust studies evidencing its effects (Robinson and Webber 2013). Their experience therefore may complement a theoretically informed analysis, but it cannot replace it (Evans and Hardy 2010).

While service users' views clearly have an important contribution to make, despite these difficulties, they need to be put into a broader context and balanced with other appropriate expertise. The Social Care Institute for Excellence argues, for instance, in their guidance on creating a Knowledge Review, that there are five kinds of knowledge that need to be considered in social care, and these bring different 'expertise' to a subject – research, policy, organizational, service user and practitioner. But when conflicts occur, whose knowledge should take precedence? Some patients may be able to teach student doctors a lot about communication, respect and listening to people, but pharmacology, anatomy and physiology need to be taught by specialist practitioners and academics. In a similar vein, how many service users have the necessary skills to teach the kind of complex subject matter covered in this chapter? Similar questions could be asked about whether social workers from particular cultural or oppressed groups should be assigned to service users from those groups (as they sometimes are), or be able to claim that they are experts about all service users in that group and as such are immune from making problematic cultural assumptions about their own or others' cultures (Singh and Cowden 2013; Laird 2014).

4.8 Conclusion

This chapter has provided an introduction to some of the literature on social justice, citizenship, human rights, equality and diversity. It has used these concepts to examine critically social work's claims to be committed to social justice and anti-oppressive or anti-discriminatory practice. Deconstruction, self-awareness and reflexivity, which can acknowledge both individual experience and wider structural contexts, are important components of AOP/ADP. Social workers can use their understanding of citizenship and awareness of national, European and global human rights to challenge unjust and oppressive policies and practices. The human capabilities approach offers a useful way to understand the debates between social work, social justice and human rights (Spatscheck 2012), as do the other social justice theories examined. Having a critical understanding of the concepts of diversity, inequality, oppression and injustice should enable social work students to understand and challenge their own and others' preconceptions and prejudices. A piecemeal understanding of ADP and AOP and a lack of awareness of the broader political canvas can lead to dangerous practice and an approach that focuses on processes at the individual level, excluding the importance of social divisions and their complex intersections. This chapter warns social workers against adopting a simplistic and apolitical attitude to social justice and AOP, by giving them an initial introduction to literature which will help them think through these difficult issues.

Social workers need to choose carefully how far their commitment to equality or diversity extends beyond the micro context, or whether it is even possible to promote social justice from within such a context. Challenging the powerful is not easy, and working with oppressed and relatively powerless people does not prepare social workers to make such challenges (Philp 1979). Although, clearly, categories of oppressor and oppressed are not mutually exclusive, people in positions of power have much greater knowledge and resources for preserving and perpetuating their privilege. By remaining silent or uninformed about issues such as the inadequacy of resources or the plight of specific minorities who are being oppressed or persecuted, social workers are never neutral. They are acquiescent and complicit by their very silence. Reisch (2013: 728) suggests:

A vision for social work might . . . include a reassertion of its historic commitment to social justice purposes and recognition that it is a value-based profession, not merely an agglomeration of sophisticated research and practice techniques . . . If our profession's commitments to diversity, social justice and multiculturalism are to have more than rhetorical significance, we have to find ways of defining these terms clearly and carrying out our scholarly and practice activities in the context of this philosophical orientation.

Discussion questions

•   Could a social worker who personally holds prejudiced views about certain groups, such as Travellers or gay or disabled people, or who strongly disagrees with certain behaviours (e.g. having a pregnancy termination or taking illicit drugs), genuinely practise professionally in an anti-oppressive manner?

•   Can social workers ever work in a genuinely anti-oppressive manner with any group in view of their professional, organizational and statutory powers? If so, how?

•   Why is it important in social work to have a nuanced understanding of both intersectionality and cultural dynamism and change? Illustrate with reference to specific examples.

•   Choose a real-life or imagined case scenario and explain how you might interpret and apply some of the key concepts examined in this chapter, such as equality, justice and difference.

Further reading

Dominelli, L. (2012) 'Anti-Oppressive Practice' in M. Gray., J. Midgley and S. A. Webb (eds.) *The Sage Handbook of Social Work*, London: Sage.

Healy, K. (2014) *Social Work Theories in Context: Creating Frameworks in Practice*, 2nd edition, Basingstoke: Palgrave, ch. 9.

Lister, R. (2010) *Understanding Theories and Concepts in Social Policy*, Bristol: Policy Press, chs. 7 and 8.

McLaughlin, K. (2005) 'From Ridicule to Institutionalization: Anti-Oppression, the State and Social Work', *Critical Social Policy*, 25 (3), 283–305.

Payne, G. (ed.) (2015) *Social Divisions*, 3rd edn, Basingstoke, Palgrave.

5 How Social Work is Organized: Institutional Arrangements and Governance

5.1 Introduction

Chapter 1 traced the development of social work in the post-war period in the wider context of the changing welfare state, from the fragmented post-war local authorities through to Seebohm's 1970 unified local authority social services departments, staffed by professionally qualified generic social workers. From the 1980s onwards there was a return to more specialist social work, albeit in a very different policy context. There have been major changes to where social workers are located institutionally, the role of the market in service delivery, the relationship between central and local government in determining social work services, and to social work's professional identity and relationship to other professions. These developments have important implications for what social work is and how social workers are trained. This chapter examines current structures for delivering social work services and for co-ordinating them with other relevant services, alongside the systems developed for ensuring quality and accountability, including both professional governance and social work training.

5.2 Institutional arrangements: Seebohm and after

A major benefit of the establishment of a single local authority social services department following the Seebohm Report was that these departments had the capacity to work holistically with families. However, the removal of one set of divisions, for example between adults' and children's personal social services, was inevitably replaced by new divisions between social services, health and education, which produced new problems of communication and co-ordination. There were significant difficulties in bringing together the different occupational groups involved in delivering personal social services, with their different areas and levels of expertise, to form a single department offering a generic service, and there was confusion and debate about whether 'generic' meant generic departments, generic teams or generic social workers (Stevenson 1999: 86). Considerable time and effort was devoted to trying to work out the best way of organizing the delivery of the new personal social services: 'The creation of Social Service Departments did not resolve the problems of communication and cooperation as had sometimes (unrealistically) been suggested. Inside and outside the local authority were agencies or other professionals critical to the well-being of children and families and others needing service' (Stevenson 1999: 88).

As this chapter will show, the attempt to find structural solutions to the problem of how best to co-ordinate the work of different professions and agencies in order to provide adequate support and protection for children, adults and families has preoccupied successive governments. These issues became an increasing concern as local authority power was gradually eroded from the 1980s onward, in favour of greater control of policy and resources by central government. The work of social services departments was overseen by the Department of Health and Social Security, and from 1988, when this department was re-organized, the Department of Health.

A return to specialization

Whilst the formal institutional arrangements for personal social services remained unchanged during the 1980s, social work fragmented again into more specialized work under a single social services organizational umbrella. There were several reasons for this. First, a series of high-profile inquiries into child protection scandals in the 1970s and 1980s consistently uncovered failures of communication between social workers and other agencies involved with the families, and also identified inadequately trained and supervised front-line workers as a contributory factor. The complexity of child protection work and the need for good communication with other agencies led to greater specialization by social workers, with child and family social work increasingly narrowly focused on child protection.

Second, two major pieces of legislation, the 1989 Children Act and the 1990 NHS and Community Care Act (discussed further later in this chapter and in chapter 6), signalled a new role for social workers as enablers and managers of services working in partnership with other agencies. Both pieces of legislation involved a move away from state social work's centrality in *providing* services, to a much expanded role for the private and voluntary sectors as service providers (albeit with state funding), with social workers assessing situations and facilitating appropriate service delivery. The main exception was in child protection where local authority social workers retained central responsibility for assessing whether children were at risk of significant harm, and making arrangements for their protection (Langan 1993; Langan and Clarke 1994: 76). The legislation reinforced divisions which had already emerged for pragmatic reasons between social workers working with older and disabled adults, those focusing on children and families, and mental health social workers.

This return to more specialist roles for social workers led in the 2000s to institutional changes which continued the reversal of the Seebohm reforms and created new local institutional structures for social work with different client groups. These changes were driven by longstanding concerns about the rising cost of adult social care and New Labour's focus on 'joined-up government' to achieve better co-ordination between different services and agencies as a means to deliver more effective and efficient services through the synergy they hoped this joint working would produce. Some changes also involved 'de-professionalizing' social work to some extent, as many new roles were no longer restricted to qualified social workers. So, for example, care managers, working with elderly people or adults with disabilities, may have qualified as occupational therapists, and those working with adults with mental health problems may be health professionals (Harlow et al. 2013: 240).

From the 1990s, social work also began to be referred to under the broader canvas of *social care* and from 2000 the organizations regulating social work adopted the term 'social care' to include both social work and the wider social care workforce (the General Social Care Council and the Health and Care Professions Council), as opposed to the original Central Council for Education and Training in Social Work. These changes also risked undermining social work's professional status because 'social care' was traditionally a Cinderella service, subordinate to medicine and healthcare, associated with the more 'tending' and 'hands-on' practical aspects of looking after vulnerable people, and carried out by people with few or no qualifications. Furthermore, some authors have argued that the incorporation of social work into the broader social care agenda has distracted attention from the more controlling and political aspects of the social work role, led to lay confusion about the difference between social work and social care, and has often resulted in social work, configured as part of social care, being viewed as inferior to healthcare or as an adjunct to it (Barnes et al. 2007). Higham (2006: 8), however, claimed that 'the emergence of social care in its own right has set social work free to become a profession which can now focus on higher level practice, skills and values'.

New institutional structures

The institutional structures for social work with children and families were radically re-organized after the Laming Inquiry (2003) identified poor communication between health, education, social services and the police as the underlying cause of the failure to protect Victoria Climbié from the abuse she suffered, which eventually led to her death. The government's response, *Every Child Matters* (Chief Secretary to the Treasury 2003), led to the Children Act 2004 which introduced a duty on many organizations to work collaboratively to safeguard children and promote their well-being. Section 10(2) of the Act defined well-being as involving five aspects: physical and mental health and emotional well-being; protection from harm and neglect; education, training and recreation; the contribution made by children to society; social and economic well-being. These were abbreviated in subsequent policy documents to five outcomes: being healthy; staying safe; enjoying and achieving; making a positive contribution; and achieving economic well-being (see, for example, DfES 2004: 4). The Act required local authorities to appoint a Director of Children's Services, with responsibility for both education and children's social services. This led to the creation of children's services departments, answerable to a councillor holding lead responsibility for children's services within the local authority.

Changes at local government level were matched by changes in central government. From 2004, responsibility for social work was divided between different central government departments. The Department of Health retained responsibility for adult social services and mental health social work. Children's education and social care were brought together under a new Minister for Children, based in the Department for Education and Skills (DfES, subsequently the Department for Children, School and Families, DCSF). In 2010, under the Coalition government, the department name reverted to Department for Education, with responsibility for children and families resting with an Under Secretary rather than a Minister. This had the effect of significantly reducing the profile of social work with children.

Directors of Children's Services did not have to have a specific professional background and the majority of the initial appointments to these posts came from education, with only about 25 per cent coming from a social work or social care background (O'Brien et al. 2006). Furthermore, only a small proportion of the total budget was allocated to social workers, who were limited to working with the most vulnerable children – 'children in need' – including children in need of protection, disabled children and looked-after children (Parton 2009). Broader community-based family support roles were given to the education sector in the form of extended schools, and to the recently established Children's Centres staffed by workers from a range of professional backgrounds.

The 2004 Act therefore removed social work from its more generic aspirations by replacing Directors of Social Services with Directors of Children's Services and separate Directors of Adult Social Services (Jones 2014). Seebohm's vision of social work providing a universal preventative family service was also replaced by a focus on high-risk families and child protection, while more universal family support services became the responsibility of other professionals. Children's social work was effectively subsumed within education from 2004 onwards, whilst adult social work became further colonized by health under New Labour and the Coalition and submerged under the banner of 'health and social care'. New Labour also created new multi-agency bodies such as Youth Offending Teams, where social work's influence and distinctiveness waned (Rogowski 2010). This fragmentation of services meant that social work lost its rather fragile identity as a generic but distinctive profession.

5.3 New public management and marketization

As chapter 1 showed, since the late 1980s the organization and delivery of welfare services has been shaped by neoliberal ideology, with a central role given to the operation of the market and to methods of management drawn from the private sector. This organizational change in the public sector is referred to as 'new public management' (NPM). It is characterized by:

- *Disaggregation*: Splitting up large public sector hierarchies into smaller units; wider, flatter hierarchies internally; introducing new information and managerial systems to support this.
- *Competition*: Introduction of a purchaser–provider split to create (more) competition among potential providers; use of competition as the basis for allocating resources; diversification of suppliers.
- *Incentivization*: A move away from rewarding performance in terms of a diffuse public service or professional ethos to its replacement by performance-related pay. (Dunleavy et al. 2006: 470)

Although NPM was developed in slightly different ways by the New Labour governments (1997–2010) and the 2010–15 Coalition government, the underpinning philosophy has remained fundamentally unchanged. While the post-war welfare state has always involved a *mixed economy* of welfare, with services provided by the state, the market, the voluntary sector and the family, the balance shifted under the influence of neoliberalism to give a much greater role to the market (and to some extent the family). The state continued to be responsible for *funding* the majority of welfare services, but service *delivery* shifted away from the state to the private and voluntary sectors. This introduced a whole new layer of bureaucracy into public services, associated with the process of tendering and contracting for services. In some areas of welfare provision, such as the NHS, where it was not politically feasible to introduce private contractors, a system of *quasi-markets* was introduced where one section of the service contracted with another for particular services. Most notably, GPs were given funds to purchase hospital services for their patients, with hospitals competing with each other to be awarded a contract. Such competition was supposed to ensure that hospital services were delivered as cheaply as possible.

In social work, marketization involved the state paying for services co-ordinated by social workers but purchased from outside the local authority. Until the early 1990s, the majority of services social workers drew on were 'in house', i.e., local authority-run resources, such as day centres, residential homes, and community provision, such as home help services, with a few highly specialist services being bought in. Clients were rarely charged for services or means-tested to determine their eligibility for them. Residential care was free for many older adults and paid for from central government's social security budget.

In an attempt to contain costs, the 1990 NHS and Community Care Act shifted responsibility for meeting the cost of residential care to local authorities, as well as placing the onus on families and neighbours to provide as much unpaid 'community care' as possible. Local authorities only retained the money transferred to them from the social security budget for residential care if 90 per cent was spent on contracted-out services, and, again in an attempt to control costs, means-testing for these services was extended.

By 2005, 90 per cent of all residential care homes were in the private sector, many owned by large multinational conglomerates that effectively monopolized the market (Jordan and Drakeford 2012). Social workers, with the exception of those working in child protection, were correspondingly recast from a traditional social administration role into an NPM incarnation (Farrell 2010): social worker as care manager rather than caseworker. Furthermore, because one of the key reasons for the introduction of community care policies was to restrict expenditure (Lewis and Glennerster 1996), the social work role was transformed into one of gate-keeping and rationing (Lymbery and Postle 2010), which, many argued, de-professionalized social workers. It is important to note, however, that other motives for the changes introduced into adult social care – at least rhetorically – included de-institutionalization of older people and those who were mentally ill or disabled, in order to give them a better quality of life.

A similar process of marketization has occurred in children's services in relation to the provision of foster care and residential care for children (Sellick 2011). This was further extended in 2009 when the New Labour government piloted independent Social Work Practices (SWP), analogous to GP practices, as a model for delivering services for looked-after children. The pilot SWPs took a variety of forms: voluntary or community organizations, social enterprises and private businesses. The aim was for social workers to be freed from the restrictions of local authority procedures and high caseloads to enable them to focus their efforts and energies on looked-after children (Stanley et al. 2012). Controversially, the pilot involved outsourcing some aspects of children's social workers' *statutory* roles and tasks, although the local authority remained the 'corporate parent' with ultimate responsibility for the child. The findings from the pilot were mixed and it was difficult to determine how far positive outcomes for children, parents and carers were attributable to the model or to other factors (Stanley et al. 2012). A proposal in 2014 to extend the contracting out of statutory responsibilities further by allowing local authorities to contract out child protection services was modified to exclude for-profit organizations bidding for the work after widespread objections from social workers, academics and the wider public (Munn 2014).

Wrennall (2013: 172) documents three potentially corrupting processes linked with NPM that may eclipse service user needs: (i) *economic conflicts of interest*; (ii) *perverse financial incentives*; and (iii) *NOMBism* (NOMB being an acronym for 'not on my budget'). *Economic conflicts of interest* occur when the boundaries between public and private services become blurred (Penna 2003). This might involve public officials, such as social workers or doctors, also acting as directors of private companies (for example, residential care homes), leading to a lack of clarity as to whether local authorities are purchasers, providers or both, with the two being governed by different rules. Take-overs and mergers of different private companies can also result in a monopoly or cartel in particular areas of service provision, such as adult or children's residential care.

Perverse financial incentives occur when local authorities are financially penalized for investing in 'worthy' outcomes or rewarded for less worthy ones. For example, in 2006 looked-after children who entered higher education became the financial responsibility of their local authority, meaning that there was a financial disincentive for local authorities to encourage these young people to go to university. By contrast, the cost of maintaining looked-after children in young offender institutions was met from the Home Office budget, 'rewarding' authorities when young people in care were sent to these institutions (Wrennall 2013).

NOMBism can mean that cost-cutting on one budget increases demands on others. A reduced budget for social care may result in additional costs to other welfare services such as the NHS. This was illustrated by the crisis in the NHS early in 2015 when a number of hospitals declared a 'major incident' and were forced to cancel all non-emergency operations and direct patients elsewhere because of intense pressure on A & E departments for a combination of reasons, including 'bed-blocking' by elderly patients who could not be discharged because there was no appropriate community care package in place (*Guardian*, 6 January 2015). Wrennall's analysis illustrates how the apparent efficiencies of the market may be compromised by other countervailing interests.

5.4 Ways of working: joined-up government, partnership and inter-professional working

Marketization of welfare services resulted in a new kind of fragmentation of provision, with different agencies responsible for different services. The pressures to meet performance targets, created by NPM, also undermined cooperation because of the different targets that different agencies had to meet. Responsibility for older people was frequently passed between health and social care, with mutual recriminations between health and social services over avoidable hospital admissions and delays to hospital discharges because of a lack of clarity about what constitutes 'healthcare' and what constitutes 'social care'.

New Labour aimed to 'modernize' public services by promoting greater cooperation and communication between agencies whose joint working was necessary to address a wide variety of 'wicked issues'. Wicked issues are multi-faceted problems with complex underlying causes and no clear solution, such as the poor educational outcomes of children in care, teenage pregnancy, neighbourhood deprivation and re-offending by ex-prisoners. Units and task forces were created, working across different government departments, to develop integrated policies to address these entrenched social problems. The Social Exclusion Unit (SEU), for example, established in 1997 and later transformed into a 'taskforce', had the remit of providing 'joined-up solutions to joined-up problems' (SEU 2004). Early SEU reports focused on rough sleeping, school exclusion and teenage pregnancy, making recommendations affecting central and local government departments responsible for health, education, housing and social security.

Joined-up government

The Labour governments from 1997 saw 'joined-up government' – bringing different government departments together to develop more coherent policies – as key to its project of modernization of the welfare state, demolishing the 'silo' mentality which separated policy making in health from social care, or separated policies to promote children's health from those aiming to reduce poverty and poor educational outcomes. Joined-up government aimed to: (i) increase effectiveness by removing contradictions and tensions between different policies; (ii) make better use of resources by avoiding duplication or contradiction; (iii) promote synergy between different agencies addressing a particular problem; and (iv) forge closer cooperation between services for service users' benefit (Pollitt 2003). At the level of local service delivery, this is exemplified in the creation of 'one-stop shops', such as children's centres, where parents can access child health services, play facilities and advice on welfare benefits, training or employment opportunities or childcare in one place, and where different service providers can hypothetically more easily exchange information and develop a more holistic understanding of their clients/users.

The problem of poor service co-ordination was addressed through the promotion of 'partnership working'. This sought to identify a 'Third Way' between the old bureaucratic hierarchical methods in which different government departments functioned relatively autonomously, each subjecting 'their' services to central government 'command and control', and the chaotic competition of the previous Conservative government's markets and quasi-markets where the principal instruments co-ordinating services were local authority-issued contracts. A number of measures were introduced to bring this about. The 1999 Health Act, for example, introduced a number of 'flexibilities' to remove legal and structural obstacles to joint working: (i) *pooled budgets*, allowing local health and social care budgets to be combined; (ii) *lead commissioning*, allowing the local authority or health body to commission services on behalf of both bodies; and (iii) *joint provision*, enabling staff, resources and management structures to be combined to integrate service provision from management to the front line (Birrell 2006). These measures were intended to promote greater collaboration between health and social care for older people's services and for learning-disabled and mentally ill adults. This legislation also provided for the creation of a new local organization, in the form of a Trust merging health and social care, to enable more effective organization of services. Trusts for mental health and learning-disabled services were successfully established in a number of areas; the proposal to establish Care Trusts for older and disabled adults in every local authority was eventually abandoned in favour of continuing with a variety of arrangements for joint funding of services. The model adopted has been one in which health has tended to be very much the dominant partner, with social workers generally brought into health settings, rather than the reverse (Penna and O'Brien 2006; Barnes et al. 2007).

Children's services departments, established under the 2004 Children Act, aimed to improve 'joined-up' working by bringing together education and children's social services; introducing an electronic database holding records on every child in England and accessible to all agencies; and establishing a statutory inter-agency body for child protection, a Local Children's Safeguarding Board (LCSB), in each local authority, made up of senior managers from different agencies in contact with children and families.

Inter-agency partnership

To promote local partnership working, government funding for various initiatives was conditional on many different 'stakeholders' from public, private and voluntary sectors all being involved in planning and delivering services. The term 'partnership' covers a variety of institutional arrangements from cooperation between two or more agencies which retain their own distinct financial and administrative arrangements, to highly integrated structures with a single budget and a unified management structure for different professionals working within it. At an abstract level, partnership between agencies concerned with different aspects of a social problem seems logical but there are various obstacles to implementing effective partnerships in practice:

- Power and resource imbalances may mean that some partners (such as voluntary or community organizations) may have less influence within the partnership than others. Social care tends to be the 'junior partner' in health and social care partnerships, with users or local communities having even less influence.
- Members of the partnership may not cover the same geographical areas, making joint planning difficult.
- Ensuring that all relevant agencies are represented on a partnership board may be challenging. France et al. (2010) in their study of LCSBs found that 21 to 26 members was optimal, although the legislation provides for boards with over 30 members. (Horwath and Morrison 2011)

Most research on partnership working has focused on identifying the factors contributing to good working relations between partners, with less clarity about whether partnership working actually produces better outcomes for users, and what particular aspects produce good outcomes for which groups of service users (Dowling et al. 2004). A study of health and social care partnerships for three different groups of service users – older adults, adults with mental health problems, and learning-disabled adults – identified three broad types of outcome significant to service users: (i) *quality of life* (including issues like feeling safe, having things to do and seeing people, living where and in the way you want and staying as well as possible); (ii) *process* (feeling listened to, having choices, being treated as an individual, reliable and responsive services); and (iii) *change* (greater confidence and skills, greater mobility, reduced symptoms) (Petch et al. 2013). Service users identified four features of partnership that contributed to these positive outcomes. Services based in the same building (*co-location*) enabled easier contact between different relevant staff, and improved inter-professional communication, enhancing services' reliability and responsiveness. Services that met health and social needs simultaneously (*multi-disciplinary teams*) contributed to change outcomes – helping users recover confidence and skills after a fall, or providing environmental modifications that made mobility easier – and at the same time contributed to quality of life by helping them to feel safe or live where and how they wanted. *Specialist partnerships*, mainly created to serve the needs of specific groups of users, led to users feeling they were understood in a non-discriminatory way, which contrasted with acute services. *Extended partnership*, including housing, benefits advice and the voluntary sector, provided more comprehensive user access to relevant services.

Partnership working has benefits for agencies and the professionals who work in them. Dowling et al. (2004) found a common outcome of partnership working was increased understanding of the roles of the other agencies and professionals in the partnership. This is likely to assist inter-professional working, which we examine next.

Inter-professional working

Policy emphasis on partnership working between different agencies has resulted in professions which historically had relatively distant relationships now working much more closely together. This may occur within the same organization or across different agencies and may involve co-working a case or trying to meet common strategic goals, but it does not guarantee better working relationships, even with co-location (White and Featherstone 2005). A variety of factors may contribute to difficulties in inter-professional relationships, ranging from different statuses, language and conceptual understandings of problems to different expectations about each profession's role and ways of working with service users. A study by Rose (2011) illustrates some of the issues that arise. She interviewed members of eight inter-professional teams in children's services (Child and Adolescent Mental Health Services (CAMHS), Special Educational Needs and Social Care) including clinical psychologists, speech and language therapists, primary mental health workers, social workers, nurses, teachers and police officers. They all concurred that shared goals and agendas were important, but felt agreeing and achieving them was problematic. Some respondents felt their specialist professional perspective and expertise were threatened both because of overlapping skills and because they were encouraged to work generically to meet common goals. It was sometimes difficult to define the appropriate activities and role boundaries for different professionals. These were partly determined by their employing agency and also by professionals' different levels of *power and status*, which affected parity in team decision making. Overcoming these difficulties required negotiation and compromise: 'professionals may have to adjust to a conceptualisation of themselves as non-specialists; or accept that achieving the team's goals may not always entail use of their specialist knowledge; or . . . [carry] out roles that would traditionally fall to someone else; or cope with someone else being given disproportionate decision making power due to the setting of the joint work' (Rose 2011: 161).

In most multi-disciplinary teams, particularly those involving health, social workers are in the minority and may not be accorded the same esteem as other professionals (All Party Parliamentary Group (APPG) 2013: 20). Research on multi-professional health and social care teams dealing with people with mental health difficulties, learning and physical disabilities and older people supports this (Jones et al. 2013). Mental health social workers in multi-disciplinary teams reported they felt that medical-model psychiatric diagnostic labels were all-pervasive and that their colleagues were perceived in their professional identity, such as nurse or psychologist, first, and care co-ordinator second, whereas social workers' own specialist contribution was unacknowledged. They therefore began to see themselves, and were viewed by other professionals, only or primarily as care co-ordinators (Bailey and Liyanage 2012). This suggests that partnership and multi-professional working are most effective when there is clarity about each agency's or service's contribution, and respect for each other's specific expertise, rather than an attempt to erase difference and blur professional boundaries (Statham et al. 2006; Boddy and Statham 2009: 4).

One aim of the 'joined-up working' agenda is greater information sharing between agencies and professionals. This may, however, be adversely affected by new organizational working patterns, often linked to budget reductions, such as home working, 'hot-desking' and agile working, where workers have no permanent fixed location (Jeyasingham 2014), all of which sap morale and reduce opportunities for sharing information and direct communication. Continuity and stability are also impeded by adult service users being passed through different teams which deal with different types of information and advice, assessments and reviews (Jones 2014: 497), with generic call centres further depersonalizing the service user experience. This suggests that the aspirations for inter-professional and inter-agency 'joined-up' working are not matched by reality and some current arrangements benefit neither workers nor service users.

Inquiries into child deaths have repeatedly identified the failure to share information as the cause of the breakdown in child protection. The report into the death of a two-year-old child, Keanu Williams, in 2013, echoed the conclusions of many previous enquiries when it stated: 'Professionals in the various agencies involved had collectively failed to prevent Keanu's death . . . They did not meet the standards of basic good practice when they should have *reported their concerns, shared and analysed information* and followed established procedures for . . . child protection investigations and a range of assessments including medical assessments and child protection conferences' (Birmingham Safeguarding Children Board 2013: 6, emphasis added).

Poor information sharing, different professional agendas, language and levels of power also contributed to the failure to prevent the death of Peter Connelly in August 2007. It is clear inter-professional and inter-agency communication in this case were poor, but it was social work which bore the brunt of the subsequent blame, with the public sacking of the Director of Children's Services by the then Minister for Children, Schools and Families, Ed Balls, despite the fact that other agencies, such as the health service and the police, had an equally significant role in failing to protect the child.

Technologies of inter-professional working

The New Labour government placed great faith in technical solutions to some of these problems, deploying information technology to address longstanding difficulties in achieving effective inter-agency and inter-professional communication and cooperation (Garrett 2005), a faith also shown by the Coalition government. The 2004 Children Act's 'electronic turn' led in 2007 to the rolling out of the Integrated Children's System (ICS), an electronic system intended to hold records of professional involvement with children from initial contact to case closure, with local authorities that failed to adopt the centrally devised electronic forms losing funding (White et al. 2010). Another proposed initiative was ContactPoint, a database containing details of all children in England, accessible to all relevant professionals, on which they could enter concerns about children, triggering further action once a certain threshold was reached. There was considerable opposition to the proposal on the grounds of the unacceptable degree of state surveillance of families and the threats to confidentiality of information given to professionals that the database would entail, and ContactPoint was eventually abandoned in 2010. The government also created a standard assessment tool for identifying and assessing children with additional needs – the Common Assessment Framework (CAF). This single electronic form, intended to be used by different professionals, aimed to promote a common language among them, encourage early intervention and reduce referral rates to local authority children's services (White et al. 2009). CAF's implementation showed considerable variation across local authorities, with some using it for referrals as well as assessments. It also produced a fragmented rather than a chronological and narrative account of the child and his/her family, and precluded specialist professional knowledge being entered because of its standardized questions and 'tick boxes' (White et al. 2009). Furthermore, social workers' anxiety about being held responsible for failing to note something which later turned out to be significant in the death of a child sometimes led to indiscriminate recording at the expense of deeper analysis (Horwath 2011). Social workers consequently became preoccupied with targets and procedures, deferring professional judgements and taking dangerous short cuts in order to meet timescales (Broadhurst et al. 2010a and b).

Peter Connelly's death in 2007, occurring so soon after the reforms precipitated by the Climbié case and in the same London borough, publicly challenged the government's faith in electronic systems. A further inquiry by Lord Laming (2009) indicated that social workers were spending too much time at their computers completing inordinately long and complex forms, with insufficient time to undertake specialist work with children and families. This finding was also reiterated in a number of other reports. The first report of the Social Work Task Force, established to advise the government about comprehensive reform to child and adult social work, found social workers stressed and hindered by unfit IT systems and electronic performance monitoring (Dickens 2011). A 2010 literature review on safeguarding found that social workers responsible for dealing with an increase in safeguarding referrals, in the absence of any limit on their caseload and in the context of limited resources, were additionally hindered by multiple performance indicators and rigid ICT systems (Martin et al. 2010). The Munro Report (2011), commissioned by the Coalition government to investigate child protection, also identified excessive centralized prescription, implemented in part through national IT systems for case record-ing, as hampering the effectiveness of social workers. In 2013 the BASW All Party Parliamentary Group *Inquiry into the State of Social Work* (APPG 2013) still cited poor IT systems, compounded by unrealistic timescales and rigid procedures, as signifi-cant problems.

5.5 Service quality and performance management

In the post-war welfare state (1945–79), social work operated as a *bureau-profession* (Parry and Parry 1979). Local authority bureaucracy provided rules and procedures for implementing government policy within a legal framework, but complex indi-vidual cases and trust in professionals' discretion meant variable responses were acceptable, with appropriate practice monitored by face-to-face supervision and local review. The managerialist approach to public services that emerged in the 1980s was founded on a lack of trust in professional standards and motives, and expanded central government systems for monitoring performance, imposing uni-formity across practitioners and geographical areas. Subsequent governments have shown equal enthusiasm for centralized performance management although with modifications in how this has been administered.

Centralized inspection of local authority social services departments was intro-duced in the 1980s. From the 1990s onwards, standardized, centrally determined quantitative *performance indicators* were introduced, which increased central government's power to specify and monitor service outcomes. New Labour used league tables, star ratings and 'naming and shaming' of poor performers to drive improvement in local services (Harris and Unwin 2009).

The return to specialization in social work has led to the establishment of separate inspectorates for adult and children's social work. The CQC is responsible for adult services including nursing and residential care homes, home care agencies and other community provisions, such as supported living accommodation. The Office for Standards in Education, Children's Services and Skills (Ofsted) inspects local authority children's services as well as independent fostering and adoption agencies, residential children's homes and special schools (increasingly provided by the pri-vate and voluntary sectors) and other specialist children's services outside the local authority.

Concerns have been expressed about the under-resourcing, statutory duties, auditing techniques, autonomy and expertise of these two audit bodies. For example, Roger Singleton was appointed in 2009 as independent chair of a cross-departmental National Safeguarding Delivery Unit. He resigned in 2010 after the Unit was closed and all safeguarding and 'looked-after' children inspections were transferred to Ofsted, arguing Ofsted had insufficient knowledge to undertake the task successfully. The CQC came under serious criticism in 2011 after its failure to respond to reports by a whistleblower of serious abuse at Winterbourne View, a private hospital for people with learning disabilities and challenging behaviour. Action to close the hospital was only taken after the BBC's *Panorama* showed film of patients being abused by staff. The hospital had been inspected by the CQC on several occasions in the previous two years and been assessed as 'compliant with essential standards of quality and safety', calling into question the adequacy of its inspection regime (*Guardian*, 27 June 2013).

In the CQC's inspection of adult social care, only one out of the eight outcomes for 'social care related quality of life' is about how people are treated. This is derived from a questionnaire completed by service users which, for valid reasons (such as capacity, fear or harassment), may not be completed candidly or even at all (Lewis and West 2014). The Coalition government abolished the minimum care home standards established by New Labour, and in June 2010 the CQC was instructed to adopt a risk-based approach (House of Commons 2011), with the government justifying this with the claim that most carers were well motivated, adequately trained and 'naturally' caring (Department of Health 2011). Even with this 'soft touch' minimalist approach, after inspecting 13,000 homes in 2011–12 the CQC still, *contra* the government's claims, expressed significant concern, particularly in relation to nursing homes, about inadequate staffing levels, poor nutrition, little dignity and providers' failure to monitor the quality of their care reliably (CQC 2012, 2013a and b). The CQC, however, paradoxically stressed it was the public's responsibility to tell the government about 'inadequate staffing' (House of Commons 2011), thereby placing responsibility for quality control with providers and then service users and their families. The 'Delivering Dignity' (2012) report stressed the importance of carers respecting people's dignity but rejected instituting compulsory staffing ratios in care homes (Lewis and West 2014). A report in 2014 on home care services, which are provided predominantly by private companies, found some elderly people were receiving care from up to fifty different members of staff per year (Koehler 2014). Another inquiry by the EHRC (2011) documented numerous instances of neglect and deprivation of dignity and of basic human rights. Both reports indicate the inadequacies of the current inspection bodies.

Limitations of current performance and quality management techniques

Electronic systems for recording data and performance management have many purposes, of which facilitating inter-professional working is only one. An equally important function is to increase managerial control and monitoring of social workers and other front-line professionals. More explicit procedures may be helpful for some social workers and may also promote greater equity between service users within and across local authorities. Such systems also focus on outcomes, encouraging strategic thinking and accountability for resource usage (Banks 2007). However, the methods of performance management introduced rely exclusively on quantitative measures, with a consequent focus on those aspects which *can* be measured, such as waiting times, calls logged, or the number and type of qualifications 'looked-after' children acquire, rather than the potentially more meaningful qualitative aspects of an individual's situation. Procedure therefore has been emphasized to the exclusion of professional judgement and has undermined trust (Banks 2007). Banks concludes: 'We are left with practitioners more akin to technicians rather than reflexive, creative and committed professionals . . . [I]n working for social justice . . . the care, passion and commitment of social professionals . . . is needed to moderate and enliven the policy-led technical-procedural drive for equity that is currently dominating much practice in Britain' (2007: 21). The Munro Report echoed this criticism of audit procedures relying on a relatively automated and impersonal approach to the task: 'The original form of audit was face-to-face; the auditor listened to an account of how work had been done. But pressures of cost and time have led to audit now being primarily an indirect check, focusing on scrutinising organizations' internal systems of control rather than making a direct examination of practice itself' (Munro 2011: 1.19).

One paradoxical consequence of the intensification of performance management for inter-agency working is that social workers working outside the local authority setting, for example in a hospital, may have two incompatible lines of managerial accountability. Social workers may come under pressure from a health manager to secure the discharge of an elderly patient from hospital to meet a target, but with adverse consequences for the patient's longer-term recovery and rehabilitation. The social worker, as a member of the hospital team, may be expected to meet hospital performance targets which conflict with ensuring the appropriate diagnosis and care of the patient, and which disregard their values and skills. Targets may also lead to 'gaming' – for example, medical staff in an A&E department at risk of breaching the 4–hour maximum wait passing an elderly patient with a 'social need' on to the hospital social worker, despite a medical assessment not having been completed (Harris and Unwin 2009).

Munro recommended that inspection should move away from assessing compliance with procedures to focusing on whether services do actually provide effective help for children's and families' needs, but the diversification of service providers for both adults and children, through the increased role of the private and voluntary sectors, has made this increasingly difficult for inspection bodies (and local authorities) (Ofsted 2013: 6). She also recommended that inspections should simultaneously examine all services relevant to children's well-being, including health, education, police and the justice system. After consultation and piloting of integrated multi-agency inspection, Ofsted concluded that this was impractical and burdensome. As an alternative, in 2015–16 it will pilot joint inspections targeted on specific areas of concern, such as the sexual exploitation of children and young people (Ofsted 2015).

The role of supervision

The shift in the focus of social work from casework to care management, alongside increased external auditing and inspection, based on various measures of performance, has had an important impact on the nature of supervision. Professional supervision has a number of different functions. It offers support with difficult and traumatizing issues, provides an opportunity for discussion and guidance on how to work with specific cases, and contributes to an individual's ongoing professional development. In recent years, such professional supervision has increasingly been displaced by supervision as a means to manage individual performance, by focusing on issues such as 'case closure, adhering to timescales and completion of written records' (Munro 2011: 115). Munro proposed a reduction in the degree of central prescription of social work practice to promote a 'learning culture' amongst child and family social workers. She also recommended that the career structure for social workers should not involve leaving practice, so that experienced social workers were not diverted into management but could provide expert professional supervision and guidance to develop less experienced workers' competence and expertise.

5.6 Austerity, local government cuts and pressures on social work

The financial crisis of 2008, and the election in 2010 of a Coalition government, committed to eliminating the public expenditure deficit over a single parliamentary term by drastically cutting public expenditure, had significant implications for social work. Local authorities lost 26% of their budget between 2010 and 2015. Although some areas invested in front-line social work posts, children's social care posts across the UK fell by 4% between 2010 and 2013. Inspection evidence from local authorities and children's homes showed the disruptive impact of using short-term staffing solutions, particularly when the annual staff turnover rate of care staff could be as high as 16% (Ofsted 2013: 6–8). The annual ADASS survey showed that, between 2010 and 2014, spending on social care fell by 12% while the population of those looking for support increased by 14% (ADASS 2014), with further cuts to public expenditure planned until at least 2020.

A number of factors continue to contribute to increasing demands on social services at the same time as there is a reduction in available resources:

- An *ageing population* means there are increasing numbers of elderly people requiring help to remain living independently in the community, and increased demand for residential services, including specialist dementia services. In 2012 there were 1.4 million people aged 85 and over in the UK, 40% with a severe disability that made it difficult to carry out daily activities. At least 670,000 people in England and Wales were estimated to be living with dementia (Joseph Rowntree Foundation 2013). By 2020 over 20% of the population will be over 65, and it is likely that adult social care will absorb more than 90% of local government expenditure (Lowndes and McCaughie 2013). Age UK found that the number of older adults receiving social care services in 2012–13 had fallen by more than 25% since 2005–6, at the same time as there had been a 30% increase in the population aged 85 and over. Tighter eligibility criteria mean that only those in the highest-risk categories receive any local authority-funded home care (Glendinning 2012; *Guardian*, 6 March 2014).
- *Changes to the welfare system*, including cuts to benefits for people of working age and restricted eligibility criteria for disability benefits, have resulted in increased financial pressure on poor families. This includes rising debts exacerbated by the introduction of changes to Housing Benefit whereby families with 'spare rooms' have been forced to move into smaller accommodation or cover the shortfall. From 2010/11 to 2014/15, those using the Trussell Trust's food banks (many in paid work) increased from about 62,000 to over 1 million (Trussell Trust 2015). A survey in 2014 by the mental health charity Mind found an increased demand for mental health services, as a result of unemployment, benefit cuts and poor housing, at the same time as support services were reduced (TCSW 2014).
- *Universal services*, such as Sure Start Children's Centres, were cut by local authorities forced to reduce expenditure.
- The high-profile media coverage of child deaths led to *an increase in referrals to children's services*. In 2012–13, there were almost 600,000 referrals of children to social care services in England, resulting in 440,000 initial assessments and 230,000 core assessments (DfE 2013a). In the same year, there were over 11,000

applications to receive children into local authority care in England, compared to just over 8,800 in 2009–10 (Child and Family Court Advisory and Support Service (Cafcass) 2014).

• Reductions in secondary healthcare provision for people with mental health problems culminated in *increased pressure on community mental health services* at the same time as resources were reduced. At least 1,711 psychiatric beds were closed between April 2011 and October 2013, most on acute adult wards, older people's wards and psychiatric intensive care units – a 9% reduction in in-patient provision (*Guardian*, 17 October 2013).

As part of the Coalition government's commitment to greater 'localism', the ring-fencing of some local authority funding ended, giving local authorities greater freedom to determine how their reduced budget was allocated, but this meant severe cuts to some services, such as Children's Centres, whose funding was previously ring-fenced, in some local authorities. A survey by the children's charity 4Children found that, while use of Children's Centres had increased and they were supporting an estimated two-thirds of the 500,000 most vulnerable families, spending on Children's Centres and Early Years services had been cut by 20 per cent between 2012/13 and 2014/15. In children's services, reduced local authority budgets meant a heightened focus on child protection, with fewer preventative and universal services for children and families. The focus on high-risk child protection cases has also led to sexually abused children, teenagers at risk of sexual exploitation, children with mentally ill parents and disabled children being overlooked (Martin et al. 2010). A reduction in the number of posts for qualified social workers in adult social care (Lymbery 2010) suggests much complex work is being allocated to unqualified workers.

Cuts to Early Years' provision were at odds with the Coalition government's commitment to an early intervention and prevention agenda, which was supported by reports that demonstrated that this minimizes long-term costs (Field 2010; Allen 2011). The combined effect of budget cuts in different areas of local authority funding can have particularly damaging effects for certain groups. Lowndes and McCaughie argue that curtailing services for families affected by DV has led to poor inter-agency co-ordination resulting in a 'seriously negative compound impact' (2013: 536), at a time when DV is increasing, in part because of the increased economic pressures on vulnerable families.

However, there is evidence (Hastings et al. 2012; *Guardian*, 16 October 2013; Lowndes and McCaughie 2013) that some local authorities have transformed services, taking a more strategic approach to budget reductions and devising new kinds of solutions. This has involved improved information sharing and better service integration, attempting to meet needs through working holistically and in an outcome-focused and needs-led, rather than service-led, way. Whilst economizing on senior salaries, almost half of all English local authorities have combined the roles of director of adults' and children's services, with some benefits for greater integration of services, such as mental health services, across age groups (*Guardian*, 16 October 2013). Some local authorities have also taken a client- or community-targeted approach, and focused resources on those geographical areas or neighbourhoods in greatest need. At the same time, Hastings et al., in their study of the early responses of local authorities in England to budget cuts, cited senior local government executives' concerns that the cumulative effect would '"tip" particular groups or places over vulnerability thresholds, leading to additional more intense problems or needs' (2012: 9).

5.7 Social work as a profession: education, training and professional regulation

There is a longstanding debate about what constitutes a profession, but social work has struggled to be accorded full professional recognition whatever criteria are used. The trait approach to professions, the most influential early sociological typology, claimed full professions such as medicine and law are characterized by a code of ethics, a regulatory body, high entry qualifications and approved university education/training, alongside control over their working practices and a dedicated body of knowledge (Johnson 1972). Social work has never possessed the status, extended education and high entry requirements, material rewards and discretion over its work that full professions have traditionally had. It has also continually struggled with its aims and purpose, boundaries, appropriate practice and academic location, knowledge base and methods/techniques (Parton 1996; Green 2006). Social work, therefore, was initially viewed as a bureau-profession and then later a semi- or mediated profession (Hugman 1991; Harris 1998; Harlow et al. 2013). Semi-professions are often funded by the state, which largely controls whom they work with and what they do, and social work's activities have been continually reshaped by changing and divergent political and welfare ideologies. Both these factors have restricted its autonomy and contributed to its continued low status.

While, originally, professions such as medicine and law were entirely self-regulating, professional regulation has increasingly involved professional bodies acting under some kind of state control. Many of the initiatives introduced in social work in recent years have been a response to the crisis for the profession precipitated by the deaths of children, most recently Victoria Climbié in 2000 and Peter Connelly in 2007. These cases prompted state reviews of social work's structures and systems, as the earlier part of this chapter has shown. They also influenced the systems for training and supervising social workers, for supporting and developing the profession, and for maintaining professional standards and accountability.

The qualification structure and professional regulation

The *Central Council for Education and Training in Social Work* (CCETSW) was set up in 1971 to fund and manage social work education in the UK. CCETSW oversaw the first unified generic qualification, the Certificate of Qualification in Social Work (CQSW). This was replaced over the next three decades by a number of other professional social work qualifications and a new organization, the General Social Care Council (GSCC), responsible for the development of the whole social care sector, including the education and training of social workers. In 2003 the minimum social work qualification became a Bachelor's or Master's degree, and 'social worker' became a 'protected title', requiring registration with the GSCC, which could discipline, suspend or strike off social workers for unprofessional conduct. The Social Care Institute for Excellence (SCIE) was set up in 2002 to improve standards in social care, counteract regional variations and synthesize current knowledge 'about what works in social care'.

Although these developments seemed to enhance social work's professional status, the government's primary focus was on producing a technically competent workforce, compliant with managerial demands, rather than a theoretically informed and critical profession (Rogowski 2010). Government ministers frequently reiterated social work was a practical 'common sense' profession not a theoretical one (Green 2006; Ferguson and Woodward 2009) and SCIE was more concerned with evidence-based practice (see chapter 6) than theory and wider understanding of complex issues.

Developments in the wake of the death of Peter Connelly

Soon after the first cohort of social work undergraduates qualified in 2006, the death of Peter Connelly led to a number of major reviews of social work practice and training. The government's Social Work Task Force (SWTF) found social workers stressed by many different aspects of their employment: insufficient preparation for practice from their training; high staff vacancies and caseloads; unfit IT systems; inadequate supervision; problematic performance management; disproportionate bureaucracy; and lack of a strong national voice guiding the profession. The Task Force recommended high-quality initial training and ongoing post-qualifying train-ing, and emphasized partnership, clearer career structures and professional roles, and workforce strategies that considered supply and demand. It also emphasized the importance of sufficient front-line practice resources, strong professional and gov-ernment leadership and more positive media representations of social work (SWTF 2009: 50). The recommendations are summarized in table 5.1.

The first report of the Munro Review (2010a), like the Task Force, uncovered heavy caseloads and a disproportionate amount of time spent complying with centrally pre-scribed procedures, timescales and targets. In her final report (2011), Munro stressed there should be greatly reduced central prescription and less emphasis on recording and compliance, and urged social work to re-engage with risk, relationship and pro-fessional judgement, re-focusing on 'doing the right thing' rather than 'doing things right [procedurally]'. Munro was, however, criticized for failing to situate social work within a broader framework which acknowledged how neoliberalism and mana-gerialism reduce children's lives to a narrowly defined case requiring resolution (Rajan-Rankin and Beresford 2011).

In 2012 the GSCC's responsibilities were transferred to the Health Professions Council (HPC), re-named the Health *and Care* Professionals Council (HCPC). The HCPC assumed overall responsibility for codes of conduct, standards of proficiency and the registration and regulation of social workers, including post-registration training, but once again social work was subsumed in a predominantly health-focused organization.

The College of Social Work (TCSW) was set up in 2012 to promote the profes-sional development of social work and act as a voice for the profession. It brought in qualification thresholds and a written test for entry and introduced a Professional Capabilities Framework (PCF) which set out expectations of social workers at each stage of their career, from initial education and training to later career development.

Table 5.1 Recommendations of the Social Work Task Force (2009)

Recommendation	
1 **Calibre of entrants**	Strengthen calibre of entrants to social work training
2 **Curriculum and delivery**	Overhaul content and delivery of social work degree courses
3 **Practice placements**	Better arrangements for quality, supervision and assessment of practice placements
4 **Assessed year in employment (ASYE)**	Introduction of ASYE as final stage in qualifying as social worker
5 **Regulation of social work education**	Better and more transparent regulation of social work education
6 **Standard for employers**	Clear national standard for support that social workers can expect from employers in order to do their job effectively
7 **Supervision**	Clear national requirements for supervision of social workers
8 **Front-line management**	Training and support for front-line managers
9 **Continuing professional development (CPD)**	More coherent and effective national framework for CPD and raised expectations of entitlement to ongoing learning and development
10 **National career structure**	A single nationally recognized career structure
11 **National College of Social Work**	An independent national College of Social Work, developed and led by social workers
12 **Public understanding**	Programme to increase public understanding of social work
13 **Licence to practise**	Introduction of a licence to practise system for social workers
14 **Social worker supply**	System for forecasting levels of supply and demand for social workers
15 **National reform programme**	National reform programme for social work

Source: adapted from the Social Work Task Force (2009:12).

Simultaneously, the HCPC published its own Standards of Proficiency (SOP) identifying its 'threshold standards, of what a social worker in England must know,
understand and be able to do following [qualification]' (Narey 2014: 5). A new curriculum was introduced, and between 2013 and 2015 all social work programmes had to
be rewritten and successfully accredited by the HCPC, and ideally also inspected and
approved by TCSW. Although the HCPC's Standards and TCSW's Capabilities have
been mapped onto one another, two sets of standards are indicative of a continuing
lack of coherence in defining the profession.

Two 'independent' reviews of social work education and training commissioned
by different government departments (Education and Health) were published in
2014 within a month of one another (Narey 2014; Croisdale-Appleby 2014). Their
findings and recommendations were rather different, although both were concerned
with raising standards. Narey stressed the importance of teaching students more
about 'practicalities', and less about 'irrelevant' political theory, accusing some social
work educators of indoctrinating impressionable young students with 'idealistic
left-wing' dogma which prevents appropriate intervention in child protection cases
because they inaccurately perceive parents as 'victims of social injustice'. He also
suggested social work should become a two tier profession with a new category of
social work assistants complementing graduate social workers. Given that unqualified social work assistants have always supported social workers and have sometimes
been disproportionately used to the detriment of service users' needs (Lymbery 2010)
as they lack the expertise and values required, this suggestion, if adopted, threatens
to weaken social work further. Croisdale-Appleby, by contrast, was more attuned to
the complexities of social work and the importance of nuanced and multi-disciplinary theory to guide understanding and action.

There was a continuing lack of clarity about which body represented the social
work profession. The British Association of Social Workers (BASW) was established
in 1971 as a professional association for social workers. Its relationship with TCSW,
whose role was 'to uphold the agreed professional standards and promote the profession and the benefits it brings to the general public, media and policy makers' (TCSW
website), was a difficult one. Attempts to merge the two organizations failed in 2012
when TCSW walked out of talks on the grounds that it would not take on representation of members in disputes with employers or disciplinary hearings because this
role could potentially conflict with upholding professional standards (*Community
Care* 28 September 2012). In June 2015 the newly elected Conservative government
cut the funding for the College, after it had failed to recruit the target of 31,000 fee-
paying members by 2015 and after Ministers rejected the College's proposal that it
take on additional revenue-generating functions, such as post-qualifying training,
forcing it to close after less than four years (*Community Care* 18 June 2015). A number
of TCSW's key functions and resources, including the PCF, CPD endorsement and
several publications, were transferred to the British Association of Social Workers
(BASW) as part of the closure process.

In a further institutional development, Munro's recommendation that a Chief
Social Worker should be appointed to 'advis[e] Government on social work practice' was accepted in 2013. The role was divided between two Chief Social Workers,
Isabelle Trowler (Children and Families) and Lyn Romeo (Adults). The role has
five key elements: (i) to support and challenge the profession to ensure that service

users receive the best possible help from social workers; (ii) to provide independent expert advice to ministers on social work reform and general policy implementation; (iii) to provide leadership and work with key people in social work to drive forward reform; (iv) to challenge weak practice to improve the quality of social work; and (v) to provide leadership to principal social workers to improve practice and influence national policy making and delivery (DfE 2013b). At the time of writing, it is unclear what effects these Chief Social Workers may have on the profession.

New routes to social work qualification

Two new routes to qualification, in addition to the two-year MA or three-year undergraduate programme, have been introduced since 2010. *Step Up to Social Work*, a 14-month intensive employer-based training course, is offered in partnership with a university, which provides the academic input. Students receive substantial bursaries. The aim of the course is to 'enable high-achieving graduates or career changers who have worked with children to train to become qualified social workers' (DfE 2013c). Four cohorts of around 300 students had been admitted by May 2015. The second route, *Frontline*, modelled on the 'high flier' route into teaching, *Teach First*, is a training programme for child and family social work, which offers qualification as a social worker in 13 months and, after a second year, a Master's degree. Frontline trainees are given a 5-week intensive summer training course and then start as employees in a local authority, supervised by an experienced social worker. Two pilots ran in 2014 and 2015, each with 100 students who will work in local authorities in Greater Manchester and Greater London. The programme has been extremely popular, with almost 6,000 people applying for 100 places in 2014 (Narey 2014).

In 2015 the Coalition government invited bids for a further initiative in social work training, 'teaching partnerships', in which initial social work training would be strongly embedded in statutory settings and would involve practitioners in teaching and research in collaboration with a partner university. The process of bidding and selection took place within a few weeks in February/March 2015, with successful partnerships expected to admit students to start training in September 2015 (DfE 2015). While the proposal to make such partnerships the principal means of providing social work training was welcomed by BASW, it expressed doubts about the feasibility of successful implementation in the context of financial cuts both in local authorities providing statutory services and in universities (BASW 2015b). Serious concerns were also expressed by the body representing universities involved in social work education about the short timescale, the introduction of yet another model of provision into social work education, the lack of attention to the relevance of international experience, a shift towards service-based specialization, and the exclusion of the private, voluntary and independent sectors from the proposal, despite their increasingly important role in employing social workers (Joint University Council Social Work Education Committee / Association of Professors of Social Work (JUCSWEC/APSW) 2015). At the time of writing it was unclear how the proposed teaching partnerships would evolve.

An assessed and supported first year in practice was instituted (ASYE), although social workers are allowed to register with HCPC before completing it, raising questions about how seriously it is taken, and dedicated funding for CPD remains uncertain.

A number of criticisms have been made of these recent developments. There is concern these new programmes are divisive for the profession, with Step Up and Frontline presented as 'elite' specialist child protection programmes, not providing students/trainees with a generic social work foundation, alongside anxiety that money will be diverted from traditional social work degree programmes into these schemes. The accelerated training inevitably reduces the academic input and risks trainees having an inadequate foundation for developing a critical understanding of the issues they are dealing with, and becoming part of 'a profession built on "know how" rather than "know why"' (Croisdale-Appleby 2014: 29). Some academics also claim that these new programmes are not being evaluated in a fair and impartial way *vis-à-vis* traditional university programmes (Schraer 2014).

There is also disquiet in the profession that little attention has been paid to earlier recommendations suggesting there should be less reliance on problematic ICT systems, rigid timescales and centralized performance indicators, and urging a return to professional judgement and more reflexive supervision. Clearly a reformed career structure, retaining experienced professionals in practice to support and supervise new practitioners, is a positive move but might be jeopardized by a continuing insistence on centralized control and prescription. Furthermore, there is little indication that social workers are being supported nationally to do their jobs effectively or that public opinion has become any more positive. No caps have been placed on caseload numbers and a survey of 1,000 social workers by BASW found 77 per cent reported unmanageable and ever-increasing caseloads and major problems with retention (2012b).

5.8 Conclusion

The establishment of social work as a single profession in the 1970s stemmed from the Seebohm Committee's identification of the need for a service which could work preventatively with families to address the underlying causes of their problems. However, within a short time there was a return to specialization within social work. This was partly in response to a series of inquiries into child protection failures in the 1970s and 1980s, which demonstrated the complexity of child protection work and the importance of cooperation with other agencies and deflected attention from Seebohm's vision of a holistic preventative approach to family problems.

Specialization was not reflected in major institutional reforms until 2004 when the inquiry into the death of Victoria Climbié pointed yet again to the problem of poor communication between the different agencies responsible for child protection. Child and family social work was combined with education to create new local authority Children's Services Departments, which made the final separation from adult social work.

By the end of the 1990s, the focus of policy was on promoting cooperation between agencies and professions working with a particular client group, rather than on bringing together those working to provide personal social services into a single professional and institutional setting. Inter-professional and inter-agency working raises new problems about maintaining professional identity while working in effective collaboration with others, and social work has struggled to assert its professional identity and status, particularly in relation to health and health professionals.

The 1980s saw a fundamental change in the role of social workers brought about by the marketization of welfare, under the influence of Thatcher's neoliberalism. With marketization, social workers became the enablers and managers of services that were increasingly provided by private or non-profit organizations. This change had major implications for the ethos of social work and the criteria against which performance was judged. Personal social services, like all other public services, have increasingly been held accountable for their performance against centrally specified targets and are subject to increasingly elaborate systems of audit and inspection by central government. Combined with the extended use of information technologies for record keeping and information sharing, this has resulted in social workers' time becoming more and more taken up with inputting data into electronic systems.

Scandals surrounding child deaths and an unrealistic assumption that they are all preventable have shaped the organization and development of social work to a disproportionate extent. Scandals about the abuse of elderly, disabled or mentally ill service users have never provoked the intensity of inquiry and subsequent reform to social work practice that child deaths have done. There is some indication in recent developments in social work training, such as the introduction of Frontline, that social work is becoming a specialized profession focused on child protection and policing vulnerable families. More generic and preventative forms of social work with both children and families and other service user groups have been eroded, particularly in the climate of financial austerity following the global financial crisis in 2008, leaving minimally qualified social care and health staff to struggle with the complex issues raised by poor disadvantaged families and a rapidly ageing population.

The major reviews of social work practice and training prompted by Peter Connelly's death in 2007 have recommended a return to valuing professional judgement, with less central prescription and much greater local autonomy, stressing the need to strengthen the profession, increase the calibre of recruits and improve public understanding of social work. However, there remain significant unresolved divisions and contradictions between some of the new bodies and training systems that have been set up. Social work has therefore not yet emerged from the crises of the first decade of the twenty-first century. It faces considerable challenges in delivering support to the most vulnerable and needy in the context of unprecedented cuts in public expenditure and the continual reviews of, and changes to, social work education and organizational functioning and structures.

Discussion questions

- What are the strengths and limitations of using private companies in competition with each other to provide welfare services, such as social care for older adults, drug and alcohol services, employment services or rehabilitation of offenders?
- Has the use of performance and quality management techniques, electronic systems and closer inter-agency and inter-professional working improved social work practice?

- Discuss the impact austerity measures and local government cuts have had on social work and social care since the 2008 financial crash.
- In what ways have changes in social work education and training been beneficial and in what ways have they constrained the development of the social work profession?

Further reading

Dickens, J. (2011) 'Social Work in England at a Watershed – As Always: From the Seebohm Report to the Social Work Task Force', *British Journal of Social Work*, 41, 22–39.

Harris, J. and White, V. (eds.) (2009) *Modernising Social Work: Critical Considerations*. Bristol: Policy Press.

Jordan, B. and Drakeford, M. (2012) *Social Work and Social Policy under Austerity*. Basingstoke: Palgrave Macmillan.

Rogowski, S. (2010) *Social Work: The Rise and Fall of a Profession?* Bristol: Policy Press, chs. 5, 6 and 7.

A note about devolution

In 1998 some powers which previously rested with the UK government in Westminster were devolved to newly established legislatures in Wales and Scotland. This chapter has focused on changes in the organization and governance of social work in England in the period after devolution. Policy and legislation in Scotland and Wales have diverged, to some extent, from the situation in England. Northern Ireland has had its own legislature for much longer, although its powers were taken back to Westminster during the Troubles (1974–98). We have not attempted to cover the details of the institutional arrangements for social work in Scotland, Wales and Northern Ireland, but the economic and ideological context for social policy and social work in all four constituent nations of the UK has been similar, as has the direction of policy change in relation to governance. This means that the general points made in this chapter and in the following one apply across the UK despite these differences in detail.

Students wishing to look in more detail at arrangements in Wales, Scotland and Northern Ireland should consult the following:

Wales
Williams, C. (ed.) (2011) *Social Policy for Social Welfare Practice in a Devolved Wales*, 2nd edn, Birmingham: Venture Press.

Scotland
Hothersall, S. and Bolger, J. (2010) *Social Policy for Social Work, Social Care and the Caring Professions: Scottish Perspectives*, Farnham: Ashgate.

Davis, R. and Gordon, J. (eds.) (2011) *Social Work and the Law in Scotland*, 2nd edn, Basingstoke: Palgrave Macmillan.

Northern Ireland

Heenan, D. and Birrell, D. (2011) *Social Work in Northern Ireland: Conflict and Change,* Bristol: Policy Press.

6 Social Work in Practice: The Interface between the Individual and the State

6.1 Introduction

Earlier chapters of this book have shown the importance of neoliberalism in shaping the role of the state in the organization, funding and delivery of welfare services since the late 1970s. There is currently a consensus across the main political parties in England that market competition improves the quality and efficiency of state-funded services, with the result that those using them have increasingly been conceptualized as 'consumers', rather than 'clients'. These changes have had important implications for citizens' access to social services and for the relationship between social workers and service users. Passive 'clients' have, at least in theory, been transformed into empowered individual consumers. Simultaneously, risk has replaced need as the basis of eligibility. As a result, state social workers nowadays largely assess risk and manage access to services for those judged eligible, with the services themselves mostly provided by the voluntary and private sectors.

This chapter examines the concepts of need and risk, and shows how risk assessment has become the dominant paradigm within social work, shifting the role of social worker from caseworker to care manager. The focus on risk and the attempts to manage it have led to a new emphasis on ensuring that social work practice is based on research evidence. This raises questions about what constitutes evidence and what it means to base practice on evidence. We look at the effects of the focus on risk for child and family social work, where child protection work has become highly proceduralized in the attempt to manage and control risk. For adult service users, the increased emphasis on their active role as empowered consumers has brought responsibilities as well as rights. We discuss what empowerment means for service users and the problems and benefits associated with the moves to personalize services. The final section of the chapter examines the impact of these various changes in practice on the relationship between service users and social workers.

6.2 Need and risk

'Need' is central to ideas about the role of the welfare state and social policy but is a notoriously difficult concept to define satisfactorily. Policy documents and the media frequently refer to 'children in need', the needs of older people, carers and people with disabilities, policies to meet needs, but who determines what these various needs are and how they should be met? The glossary in Dean's book *Understanding Human Need* (2010) contains thirty different terms containing the word need, such as 'absolute need', 'basic need' and 'inherent need', indicating the complexity of the concept and different understandings of it. Social policies that provide for education, housing, healthcare and various forms of social care are implicitly, if not explicitly, based on some notion of need, but arriving at an agreed definition is surprisingly difficult, given that the term is so widely used.

Needs are often contrasted with 'wants' or preferences, although this distinction is not always easy to maintain. A child may say that she 'needs' an ice cream, when actually she just *wants* an ice cream. But saying that you *need* something places some responsibility on the person addressed to respond and implies an unmet need results in some kind of harm, in a way that saying you *want* something does not (Spicker 1993). Children's awareness of the moral imperative that 'need' implies explains why they may say they 'need' something which adults dismiss as a 'want'. But what about someone who says they need a mobile phone or a computer? Are these real needs? It is increasingly difficult to function in contemporary Britain without a mobile phone or access to the internet, although twenty or thirty years ago the idea that someone might *need* these was absurd. Social and technological change renders items and services necessities, when they were once luxuries enjoyed by a few people, because those who lack them may be excluded from full social participation. Therefore, while some needs, defined at their most abstract, seem to be universal – all humans need food, clothing and some kind of shelter – when needs are specified at a more local and historically specific level, it becomes harder to identify precisely which are needs and which are wants or preferences. There is an extensive literature on needs, and we will not attempt here to do more than indicate some key issues which arise in trying to define and specify what human needs are. Useful discussions and further guidance on the literature are contained in Lister (2010: ch. 6) and Dean (2010).

Doyal and Gough, in their book *A Theory of Human Need*, argue for conceptualizing human needs as 'the universal pre-requisites for successful . . . participation in a social form of life' (1991, quoted in Lister 2010: 176). For Doyal and Gough these universal pre-requisites are physical health and autonomy. This specification of universal human needs is so general that it is not particularly helpful in identifying the social policies required to meet these needs. Doyal and Gough identify what they call 'intermediate needs' – the conditions required to achieve physical health and autonomy. These are: nutritional food and clean water; protective housing; a non-hazardous work and physical environment; appropriate healthcare; security in childhood; significant primary relationships; physical and economic security; appropriate education; safe birth control and child-bearing. How these needs are met varies with social, cultural and material conditions so that accepting that some human needs are universal does not imply these can be specified in a unique and definitive way. While there may be agreement about the most abstract specification of universal human needs, detailing what constitutes an adequate response to these 'intermediate needs' becomes more difficult. What is required for housing to be protective? What levels of crowding in accommodation mean that it is not sufficiently protective? If a house is damp or difficult to heat, is it sufficiently 'protective'? When it comes to specifying the conditions required to meet each of Doyal and Gough's intermediate needs, a consensus is difficult to reach, even if, at a more abstract level, there is agreement that some human needs are universal.

The recognition that human needs are historically and socially contingent raises the question of how they are identified within a particular society and by whom.

Bradshaw's (1972) typology of need clarifies the different ways in which needs may be identified. He distinguishes between:

- *Normative needs*: defined according to expert or professional standards or norms – for example, the identification of children's needs on the basis of the expertise of child psychologists, social workers or child health professionals.
- *Felt needs*: individuals or groups identify these themselves, such as a child feeling he or she needs a drink or a sleep.
- *Expressed needs*: the public articulation of felt needs by an individual or group – for example, parents telling the local authority that their children need a safe accessible playground.
- *Comparative needs*: the identification of need on the basis of a comparison of the characteristics of one group within a population relative to similar groups – for example, a local authority identifying an area within a city as in need of additional child health services because of a high level of infant mortality relative to other similar areas in the city.

Needs identified in these different ways may overlap but are unlikely to coincide completely. For example, a doctor may say that a child needs to have her temperature reduced by cool bathing, which may differ from what the child herself feels she needs, and perhaps with the parents' expressed need for the child to be prescribed antibiotics.

Social work and needs

Social work is centrally concerned with meeting needs, although a key problem it has faced throughout its history has been how to define and limit the needs to which it responds. In the nineteenth century, charitable organizations responded to this dilemma by differentiating between the deserving and the undeserving poor. With the creation of the welfare state in the post-war period, the scope of state social work extended but so did the number and types of needs which services had to respond to. The provision of services can itself uncover unmet needs as the early intervention and prevention policies introduced by the Sure Start programme illustrate. An early evaluation report found that levels of special needs had risen among children starting school in Sure Start areas – the authors concluded that this was probably because of unmet need being identified (*TES* 15 April 2005). Similarly, another evaluation report found a significant increase in section 47 referrals (for a child protection enquiry) and new registrations on the child protection register (now known as the child support plan), explained as possibly the result of better or earlier identification of families needing support (Barnes et al. 2006).

The BASW code of ethics states that 'Since its beginnings over a century ago, social work practice has focused on meeting human needs and developing human potential' (2012a: 5). But alongside this principle there is the intractable problem of limited resources, so that BASW states, four pages later: 'Social workers should ensure that resources at their disposal are distributed fairly, according to need' (2012a: 9). In social work, need has increasingly been equated with the risk of an adverse outcome if the need is not met. This slippage is illustrated in the extract below from a local authority website showing the eligibility criteria for adult social care, in which the assessment of need is expressed entirely in terms of the degree of risk to the individual:

> We will use the information gathered at your needs assessment to determine which of the four bands your needs fall in:
>
> **Critical**
> Your needs will be assessed as meeting the critical band if your circumstances mean that you are **at immediate risk** in your daily life. For example, you are unable to carry out any of your personal care routines. You are at significant risk of harm or neglect.
>
> **Substantial**
> You needs will be assessed as meeting the substantial band if your circumstances mean that there is a **risk of breakdown** of the present situation. For example, you need support to carry out most of your personal care.
>
> **Moderate**
> Your needs will be assessed as meeting the moderate band if your circumstances identify **moderate risk** in your daily life. For example, you have some difficulties with your personal care but this does not put you at risk.
>
> **Low**
> Your needs will be assessed as meeting the low band if your circumstances identify **minimal risk** in your daily life. For example:
> • You are able to carry out your personal care routine but with some difficulty
> • You have some difficulty in accessing activities in the community but this does not affect your daily life.
>
> Needs in the **moderate** and **low** bands will not qualify for help from [the] Council. However, we may talk to you about short-term support we can offer so you can live more independently. (taken from www.barnet.gov.uk/info/209/needs_assessment_by_social_services/396/needs_assessment_by_social_services)

Complex systems have developed since the mid-1990s for arriving at an 'objective' assessment of the risks to individuals in different circumstances, so that social work practice has become heavily dependent on protocols and procedures, which have considerably displaced professional judgement from the centre of social work practice (Webb 2006). This is justified by an appeal to evidence-based practice, which is discussed further in section 6.4. Here, we examine how risk has come to stand for need in contemporary social policy.

Risk and social welfare

Two sociologists, Beck (1992) and Giddens (1991, 1999), have written extensively about the emergence in the late twentieth century of the 'risk society'. They argue that the contemporary world is characterized by new risks produced by human activity, such as climate change, the risk of nuclear annihilation and the dangers of nuclear power, or international financial disasters such as the banking collapse of 2008. These pose new challenges for governments, which have increasingly sought to attempt to control and manage these risks through regulation at both the national and the supranational level (for example, through the EU, or through global institutions such as the WHO or the UN). Implicit within such attempts is the belief that, with enough knowledge, it is possible to predict and, by appropriate intervention, prevent adverse outcomes, and that where such adverse outcomes are not prevented someone can be blamed (Kemshall 2008).

The containment and management of risk has become an increasing preoccupation of social policy too. In health policy, for example, there is a strong emphasis on prevention and early intervention. Smoking, lack of exercise and obesity are all risk factors for coronary heart disease, diabetes, stroke and various forms of cancer. This has led to policies that aim to change individual behaviour, implying that those individuals who fail to make the recommended changes will be seen as responsible for their ill health and so less deserving of NHS healthcare. But a 'risk factor' is not the same as a cause, and there is no simple causal relationship between these risk factors and diseases. Environmental factors are also associated with cancer and diabetes. Environmental pollution is an important contributory factor in lung cancer; shift work is associated with an increased risk of diabetes. Stress, which may result from social conditions (such as debt, unemployment, marital breakdown) or environmental conditions (poor housing, overcrowding and noise), is associated with many diseases and illnesses.

There are many other examples of how social policy has become increasingly focused on the identification and management of risk. The Sure Start programme, introduced in 1998, drew on an analysis of the household and parental characteristics ('risk factors') associated with various poor outcomes for children. These focused on individual characteristics (such as maternal education or smoking) rather than structural ones, such as poverty, poor housing and environment. This led to interventions aimed at changing parental behaviours rather than some of the more intractable socio-economic problems which also contribute to the reproduction of disadvantage (Clarke 2006). A similar analysis underpins the Family Intervention Programmes (FIPs) introduced nationally in 2006 to address anti-social behaviour and youth offending by targeting 'families at risk' (Nixon and Parr 2009). The identification of families with characteristics associated with a range of social problems continued under the Coalition government's Troubled Families programme introduced after the riots of 2011 (Department for Communities and Local Government (DCLG) Troubled Families website). Both the FIPs and the Troubled Families programme identified 120,000 families whose characteristics constituted a 'risk' for future criminal and anti-social behaviour and other adverse outcomes. The 'risk factors' fall into five categories: family functioning, criminal or anti-social behaviour, problems at school, health problems, no adult member of the family in employment (DfE 2011). Looking at this list, it is difficult to identify which of these 'risk factors', associated with the problems of 'anti-social behaviour (ASB), youth crime, inter-generational disadvantage and worklessness', might be construed as cause and which as effect.

The rationale for the interventions is couched less in terms of the needs of the families, and more in terms of the potential financial cost to the state: for example, the costs of crime, poor mental and physical health, the need for children to be received into care, and poor educational outcomes leading to unemployment. The government website for the Troubled Families programme offers this brief definition of troubled families: 'those that have problems and cause problems to the community around them, putting high costs on the public sector'. It continues: 'Government data collected in October and November 2011 estimated that £9 billion is spent annually on troubled families – an average of £75,000 per family each year. Of this, an estimated £8 billion is spent reacting to the problems these families have and cause, with just £1 billion being spent on helping families to solve and prevent problems in the longer term' (DCLG Troubled Families website). Criteria for families to be included in the programme were originally that they should meet three of four conditions: be involved in youth crime or anti-social behaviour; have children who are regularly truanting; have an adult on out-of-work benefits; cost the public sector large sums in responding to their problems. In 2013 the scheme was expanded to cover up to 400,000 additional families between 2015 and 2020. The criteria for inclusion were extended to families with children under five; domestic violence; and poor mental or physical health (DCLG 2014).

The Troubled Families programme's aims are to reduce school exclusion, juvenile crime and anti-social behaviour and improve pathways to paid employment, and it employs a system of 'payment by results' under which the local authority receives funding only when it can successfully demonstrate achievement of at least some of the objectives set. The Coalition government claimed to have 'turned around' the lives of almost 53,000 families by May 2014 (DCLG press release August 2014). However, the National Audit Office (2013) pointed out the government's criteria for being 'turned around' related to just reducing one of the indicators of multiple problems, which might leave the other problems unaddressed. One danger of schemes such as this is that by focusing on 'high-risk' situations, funding is diverted from community-based initiatives dealing with children and families in need, increasing the likelihood that lower-risk children and families will encounter crisis situations later.

It is striking that social workers have had a very limited role in initiatives – such as Sure Start, the Family Intervention Programme and the Troubled Families programme – which aim to intervene with families identified as constituting a high risk for anti-social behaviour, school failure or long-term unemployment. Work of this kind was central to social work in the 1960s and 1970s. The term 'social work' was also absent from New Labour's discussion of preventative work with disadvantaged families (Butler and Drakeford 2001) and the work was allocated to voluntary and commercial organizations, with much carried out by relatively unqualified workers (Penna 2003). Prevention can mean a narrow surveillance and control approach which targets, tracks and monitors high-risk service users in relation to child abuse, crime or mental illness, or alternatively a broader approach, tackling issues such as poverty using wider community and societal measures. The Thatcher government adopted the former approach under the Children Act 1989 which resulted in resources being focused on high-risk child protection cases, generally disregarding wider family support, and this very limited preventative role for social work has continued under subsequent governments.

In the absence of an agreed theoretical model of how a particular adverse outcome is produced, actuarial techniques, analogous to those used in the insurance industry, are used to try to identify situations of highest risk and for deciding when intervention is needed (Webb 2006). Insurers are concerned with calculating the probability of a particular outcome for groups of individuals with common characteristics, so that they can determine an appropriate premium to insure against the risk of that outcome for those individuals. Different population groups have different risks, calculable from various sources of data. For example, data from the DVLA (Driver and

Vehicle Licensing Authority) and the police enable calculation of the probability that a woman aged over fifty and driving a car with an engine size below 1000cc will be involved in an accident over a period of 12 months. The more detailed the specification of the group, the more precisely the risk can be calculated, but something as complex as a motoring accident can never be predicted with absolute certainty for any one individual. Young men driving very powerful cars at night within 6 months of passing their test may be much more likely to have an accident than older women, but having those characteristics does not determine that a young man *will* have a car accident. Similarly, a child growing up in a family defined as 'troubled' will not automatically become a criminal, leave school without qualifications or spend their adult life claiming benefits, and children from much more privileged circumstances may commit crimes or end up unemployed. This preoccupation with risk and the belief that, with sufficient research and evidence, risks can be controlled have created a context for social work in which risk management is the dominant concern, with failures to prevent adverse outcomes attributed to failures by the professionals involved. The next section examines how the focus on risk has changed the nature of social work and the relationships between social workers and the people they work with.

6.3 Risk, intervention and social work

The clearest application of risk management in social work has occurred in child and family social work, in relation to child protection. An increasingly elaborate system of protocols and standardized assessment tools has been developed since the 1990s in an attempt to identify children 'at risk' of significant harm who may need to be removed from their home situation in order to protect them (Broadhurst et al. 2010a and b). However, despite these efforts to identify risk and thereby eliminate it, children continue to die at the hands of close family members (for example, Victoria Climbié 2000, Peter Connelly 2007, Daniel Pelka 2012). These rare but very high-profile events have led to regular inquiries to identify who or what was to blame for the failures in a system which is supposed to prevent such eventualities. The system of serious case reviews (SCRs) in England examines the circumstances where vulnerable children have died, been injured or been seriously put at risk, aiming to understand what has happened and to identify possible improvements in practice. However, it may not be possible to predict the danger to children in all circumstances. Munro argued that the model of causality which underpins these inquiries tends to 'push the system towards ascribing responsibility to individuals [producing] solutions aimed at controlling errant individuals' (2010b: 1140). Furthermore, an analysis of SCRs between 2003 and 2005 concluded that much child abuse could not have been predicted even if decision makers had had a complete picture of the situation (Brandon 2008, cited in MacDonald and MacDonald 2010). MacDonald and MacDonald point out that the causal pathway which results in the serious injury or death of a child is highly complex, rendering it impossible to predict with any certainty which circumstances will lead to harm and which ones will not. They argue 'risk' would be better characterized as 'uncertainty', encouraging a broader focus in social work on disadvantaged or neglected children, rather than on the prevention of serious injury or death, which cannot be accurately anticipated.

Broadhurst et al. (2010a) identify two different risk-assessment approaches: (i) actuarial, which is quantitative and generates an individual score which can be compared to some norm and used as the basis for predicting the likelihood of a particular outcome – for example, the likelihood of re-offending; and (ii) structured, which is intended to support professional judgements by providing a standard set of issues to be considered and so directs attention to ensure that particular risk factors are considered. Structured risk assessment, in the form of the *Framework for the Assessment of Children in Need and their Families* (DH 2000), is the principal approach in child protection social work. However, as MacDonald and MacDonald (2010) point out, decision making in social work generally takes place in situations of uncertainty rather than where the risk can be calculated with any degree of accuracy.

Broadhurst et al., in their ethnographic study of risk management and decision making in children and family social work teams, identified three key features of risk management in practice:

- risk management is a reflexive, tailored response to the particular circumstances of each case.
- risk assessment practices are embedded in social relations – both within the team and between the social worker and client. This means they are both unique to particular circumstances and also reflect habitual responses in the team.
- risk assessment is guided by multiple rationalities, including compassion, empathy and a sense of responsibility for others, as well as more instrumental concerns (2010a: 1052).

The requirements for completing the risk assessment protocol have to be accommodated within a social relationship between the social worker and the client in which maintaining mutual respect and trust is important for working effectively with a family. It may be difficult for a social worker to fulfil the requirements of a statutory home visit during which information on a whole range of circumstances has to be collected, including what food is in the fridge, what toys and books there are and the cleanliness of the home environment, at the same time as maintaining a good working relationship with the parent(s) as a means to help improve the family's circumstances. The way in which this was managed by the social workers in Broadhurst et al.'s study was unique to each family and social worker. But social workers felt that the specificity of the home visit protocol diverted them from the more therapeutic role which they had played historically, as this quote illustrates: 'Primarily it [the home visit] is just to check on the child's welfare. In terms of therapeutic intervention that is not something that we really do as social workers anymore just because of the way that our role has changed. We are more network coordinators and record keepers now than social workers I suppose' (2010a: 1058).

The assessment process became increasingly bureaucratized in the course of the 2000s, in response to inquiries into child deaths and in an attempt to reduce the scope for error by reducing individual autonomy. The use of information technology has also been increased in the belief that the in-built structure of the recording system will positively guide social workers' thinking. At the same time this increases the scope for surveillance of practice and leads to dangerous short cuts and excessive form filling alongside indiscriminate recording of information (see chapter 5). These developments, therefore, have devalued professional expertise and encouraged a culture of blame and fear, contributing to a defensive culture amongst social workers, whose practice, as Stanford argues, is ever more oriented 'towards managing and securing against risk as opposed to genuine attempts to respond to need', in order to avoid being blamed when things go wrong (2010: 1065). She points out that discussion of risk tends to be polarized between two alternative risk identities: being 'a risk' (to others because of the physical or emotional threat that someone represents) or 'at risk' (vulnerable in some way), obscuring the fact that individuals may be both simultaneously. Stanford argues that a preoccupation with risk tends to obscure any consideration of need, but her study of Australian social workers found that, in practice, despite their fears of being blamed or harmed if they failed to respond in the right way to risk, social workers were prepared to take risks themselves in the interests of their clients. They were not so constrained by the fears generated by the policy focus on risk that they subordinated all their professional ethical impulses to risk management.

The defensive culture of blame produced by these practices and systems has serious negative effects on working relationships within and between organizations as individuals seek to 'cover their backs', and this in turn threatens good co-operative working. The Munro Review identified reduced job satisfaction, high staff turnover and a reduction of the time available for children and families as consequences of the high level of proceduralization in child and family social work (2011: 1.23). A study by the Office of National Statistics (ONS) found that social workers, alongside police officers and health managers, were amongst Britain's most overworked and 'overemployed' workers (Inman 2014). A vicious circle can be set up in which poor morale leads to staff taking time off sick with the result that colleagues are put under increased pressure, with larger caseloads. Furthermore, Munro argued that highly specific protocols reducing professional autonomy ultimately lead to poorer outcomes for children, which further contribute to poor morale and high staff turnover (Munro 2011: appendix A).

Given these problems with the dominant risk-focused paradigm in child protection, what could be done to improve the system? Some argue for a less instrumental and mechanistic approach which examines the meaning, causes and effects of risk and addresses uncertainty about children's safety through the exercise of professional judgement rather than through increasingly specific protocols (e.g. Munro 2010a, 2011; France et al. 2010). This involves ensuring that social workers are adequately educated and receive appropriate reflexive and supportive, as opposed to bureaucratic, supervision, thereby requiring a different approach to knowledge and evidence, which moves away from the positivism that has informed risk management in the last two decades. It also involves accepting the inevitability of a degree of uncertainty in the complex circumstances that arise in families, with the consequence that it will never be possible to predict with absolute accuracy whether a child will suffer harm in the future.

6.4 Evidence-based practice

From the mid-1990s onwards, there was a growing emphasis on the importance of policy and practice in the public sector being *evidence-based*, to ensure that what was being done was 'worthwhile and being done in the best possible way' (Davies et al. 2000: 2). The evidence-based practice (EBP) movement originated in medicine and was subsequently extended to other areas, including social work. Davies et al. argue that a new emphasis on evidence occurred because of an increasingly educated and well-informed public; expanded availability of data of all kinds through developments in IT; a growth in the size and capacity of the research community; emphasis on the importance of productivity and competitiveness; and escalating governmental concern with scrutiny and accountability. While it would be difficult to disagree that practice should draw on evidence, deciding what kinds of interventions are effective in producing a desired outcome, what constitutes evidence, whose evidence is valid and how evidence should be combined with professional judgement in individual cases has been controversial and the subject of acrimonious debate (see, for example, Webb 2001; Sheldon 2001; Chalmers 2005; Hammersley 2005).

The medical origins of EBP are evident in the high value placed on evidence generated using methods associated with the natural sciences: systematic reviews of the literature and randomized controlled trials (RCTs) to establish the effectiveness of interventions. The principle underpinning RCTs is that the effect of an intervention can be isolated by creating two groups in which the only feature that differs systematically between the two is the intervention. Subjects are allocated randomly to the 'treatment' condition and the 'control' (either no or 'usual' intervention). On the assumption that the only difference between the groups is the intervention, any difference in outcomes between the two is attributed to the intervention. While these methods may be appropriate for establishing whether a new drug will effectively treat a particular medical condition in a high proportion of the population (but there may be problems even here with establishing causality), they are less useful for evaluating the effectiveness of a social intervention with a family, because of the difficulties of creating two comparable groups which differ only in whether or not they receive the intervention. Social interventions are complex, consist of multiple components whose effects cannot be individually evaluated, and take place in the real world where families cannot be insulated from other changes going on around them.

There are very few examples of the use of RCTs in social work research, particularly in the UK, and looking at an example of one helps to show why they may not be particularly appropriate to investigate questions relevant to social work practice. A study by Macdonald and Turner (2005) looked at the effectiveness of a parenting training programme for foster carers dealing with challenging behaviour. Carers who asked to take part in the programme were randomly allocated either to a parenting group or (as the control group) to a waiting list for a future programme. Random allocation in this way for carers who were strongly motivated to take part because of the problems they were experiencing reveals one of the first problems with the RCT method. A number of carers allocated to the study withdrew when they heard that they had been allocated to the control group (waiting list). This raises ethical questions about withholding a service which carers in difficult circumstances felt they needed. The study found no statistically significant difference in the children's behaviour at the end of the study between the intervention group and the control group – both had improved to some extent. The authors reported that some carers were working with very difficult children with little support from social workers, and that this therefore may have partly explained the lack of success of the intervention. But this also suggests that what was needed was a more individualized intervention with each family, directed at their particular circumstances and needs, rather than the kind of standardized programme that an RCT design requires. Dixon et al. (2014) provide a useful discussion of the practical difficulties of carrying out an RCT involving a more complex social work intervention.

As this example indicates, it is very difficult to meet the strict conditions that underpin RCT logic for social interventions. Furthermore, RCTs have limited explanatory power for social research, relying on observation of 'objective', measurable characteristics of people subject to an intervention, rather than exploration of subjective experience (see section 3.3 in chapter 3 on contrasting perspectives on social science). Human behaviour can only be understood by reference to meanings, intentions, ideas and beliefs, which are not observable in the way that blood pressure, body mass index and blood group are. Nor can interventions in social work be standardized in the way that medical treatment can be. An intervention with a family depends crucially on the nature of the relationship established between the social worker and the various family members in a way that an injection or surgical operation generally does not. The outcomes of an intervention also cannot be identified very precisely or measured very reliably (Hammersley 2005). Therefore, the 'hierarchy of evidence' used in medical interventions, which has adopted the RCT as the 'gold standard' for research evidence, is arguably neither appropriate nor practicable in relation to most social work interventions. This implies that a variety of research methods is required to establish what works, for whom, and under what circumstances, for interventions in social situations. Qualitative methods can provide insight into the meanings that are attributed to particular actions and situations and to the processes by which a given outcome is achieved.

In terms of the practicalities of implementing EBP in social work there are some further difficulties. The first is what Mullen et al. (2005) call the 'authority challenge'. The founding principle for evidence-based medicine, which provided the model for other fields, was that individual practitioners would identify and critically evaluate the appropriate evidence in their field for themselves, but is this a feasible and appropriate model for social work practitioners – in terms of the time and resources available to them? Mullen et al. suggest that an alternative might be the production of authoritative research-based guidelines by practitioners with research expertise, which could then be disseminated to practitioners more widely. This is the model adopted by NICE (the National Institute for Health and Care Excellence), which was originally set up to disseminate evidence on the clinical effectiveness of medical interventions, but since April 2013 has included social care within its remit.

The SCIE is often regarded as social work and social care's equivalent to NICE. It is very practice focused, describing its role as improving 'the lives of people who use care services by sharing knowledge' and putting knowledge into practice. It has numerous resources on its website, including research reviews of various types on different issues and regarding different service user groups and interventions; practice guidelines on key issues; videos; a publications database; and research and knowledge review guidelines.

In medicine, systematic reviews have been used as a way of assessing the current state of knowledge in a particular field. A systematic review involves a rigorous search of the empirical research literature according to predetermined inclusion and exclusion criteria (around words and concepts, dates and research methodology) and is normally framed around a question about 'what works'. Only the most rigorous studies are included (ideally RCTs) and their findings are synthesized as the basis for deciding on appropriate treatment. Qualitative research is traditionally ranked lower than expert opinion in the assessment of study quality in medicine. SCIE's approach has been more flexible, however. SCIE's recommendations (Rutter et al. 2010) allow the inclusion of qualitative studies and also stress the importance of additionally including stakeholder (practitioner, organizational, policy and service user / carer) knowledge. Nevertheless, systematic reviews have been criticized as too conceptually narrow and theoretically limited in terms of practitioner knowledge, if they are the only approach used to survey current knowledge (see Gray and McDonald 2006). This is because they fail to locate findings in a broader political and social context or critically examine relevant theoretical concepts and political debates.

There is also the question of whether there is sufficient evidence of the right kind available for the types of situations which social workers are dealing with. Empirical evidence linking an intervention to an outcome may not be the most useful kind of perspective from which to approach working with parents struggling to combine maintaining themselves in employment, dealing with their own relationship difficulties and caring for a child with a severe physical disability and two younger siblings. A theoretically informed perspective on family systems and dynamics may be more helpful in thinking creatively about possible ways of supporting a family with a disabled child, than empirical evidence on the outcomes of a particular intervention for families with disabled children, which may have been developed and implemented in a different social and cultural context.

A further difficulty arises in relation to the application of research evidence to practice. What does it mean to *base* practice on *evidence*? A crude interpretation might be that evidence from research should somehow determine practice by providing a formula about what to do in a particular circumstance. However, as Hammersley (2005) argues, practice ultimately relies on the judgement of a trained professional, drawing on different sources of information, about how best to act in the unique circumstances of a case.

More recently, there has been a move away from referring to evidence-*based* practice, in favour of talking about evidence-*informed* practice. This implies that research evidence is only one of several sources of useful information, and also arguably gives a greater role – implicitly, if not explicitly – to professional judgement:

> Evidence-based practice is sometimes used in a narrow sense to refer to using methods of helping service users that have research evidence of some degree of effectiveness in some places where the methods have been tried and evaluated. Here it is used in the broader sense of drawing on the best available evidence to *inform* practice at all stages of the work *and* of integrating that evidence with the social worker's own understanding of the child and family's circumstances and their values and preferences. It is not simply a case of taking an intervention off the shelf and applying it to a child and family. (Munro 2011: 92, emphasis added)

In contrast to some discussions of evidence-based practice in the late 1990s and early 2000s, which dogmatically asserted social workers needed to subordinate their practice to research evidence, recent discussion in social work seems less prescriptive, with more acknowledgement of the role of professional judgement in deciding on an appropriate course of action. The SWTF final report, for example, emphasized the importance of social work education developing students' skills in critically evaluating their actions and decisions. Although it urged the social work profession to 'use the best evidence to determine how it can be more effective' (2009: 6), it also warned that 'the profession is at risk of becoming too mechanised and de-skilled, through an over emphasis on compliance rather than judgment' (2009: 55).

6.5 Empowerment and personalization

Risk and the empowered citizen

The post-war welfare state was a collective response to external risk and aimed to meet universal needs, about which there was some social consensus, with relatively uniform services funded and provided by the state. The commodification of welfare in the 1980s resulted in need and risk becoming increasingly individualized by the 1990s (Kemshall 2008). The Thatcher governments of the 1980s rejected large-scale public services as inefficient and ineffective, replacing them with services ostensibly more tailored to individual needs, with variety provided through the market. This transformation, which involved the construction of those using public services as empowered individual consumers able to make informed choices between different services, is a corollary of neoliberal ideology. This is based on a highly individualized conceptualization of society and an associated belief that the market is the most effective and just system of distribution (see chapter 2). Individuals are assumed to be rational actors pursuing their own self-interest who will make choices that optimally promote their well-being. Sub-optimal choices are made only when the information individuals are given is poor or incorrect. The service user, empowered to make choices about which services to use or how to spend the money allocated to them to meet their needs, is thereby also made responsible for the consequences of the choices made (Clarke 2005; Kemshall 2010). There are many examples across the welfare state of how this empowerment has been put into practice. Parents have been given responsibility for choosing their child's secondary school, using published information about how pupils from different schools had performed in national tests to help them. In the health service, patients were offered a choice about which hospital and which consultant they were referred to by their GP. Performance data on schools, the health service, local authority departments or the police was supposed to empower individuals and make services more responsive and accountable, but such an approach fails to acknowledge structural factors which might mean that some individuals are far less able than others to understand and exercise the choices which this approach requires of them.

'Empowerment' to make choices between alternative services / service providers requires the time and resources to access information about those services and an appropriate level of education to make sense of it. Do the educational test results published for a school or the death rates for a medical procedure for a particular surgeon/hospital consider the socio-economic advantage/disadvantage of the pupils/patients or the complexity of their problems? Can police figures on clear-up rates for crime be trusted? To make sense fully of much of the information provided about public services requires a good deal of time and a critical understanding of the strengths and limitations of the data provided. While providing people with choice between services and service providers may appear to be a 'good thing', giving individuals greater control and autonomy, in reality there are huge inequalities in people's capacities to exercise those choices. The rhetoric of 'choice' places the responsibility for poor choices on the individual, but overlooks structural factors affecting these choices.

Child protection and mental health social work are predominantly concerned with high-risk cases and mandated (involuntary) service users, and it is difficult to make empowerment and partnership working a reality when the balance of power is so unequal. Holt and Kelly (2014) show that, although the rhetoric of service user involvement is included in policy with children and families, with provision for them to be legally represented in administrative proceedings dealing with a child's possible admission into care, parents may be afraid to engage with legal representatives because of their own vulnerability or difficulty in understanding procedural formalities. They may also see legal representation as part of the system that 'threatens' them and their families (2012: 163). There is no requirement for children to be separately represented, making it hard to see how they can meaningfully engage in the process. Furthermore, it is likely that local authorities will have access to more experienced and expert legal advice than parents. Cuts to the level of legal aid payable for this category of work mean that experienced advocates may be unable or unwilling to undertake the work. For people with mental health problems, the preoccupation with risk has led to policies to increase control and compulsion rather than empowerment. For example, people discharged from hospital after being compulsorily detained under a mental health section, can be made subject to a community treatment order (CTO), which requires them to take medication that they have been prescribed. This runs directly counter to policies of increasing choice and represents a failure to provide community mental health services that those with chronic mental health problems would choose to engage with (Lawton-Smith et al. 2008). For someone at risk of losing their liberty as the result of a mental health section or CTO, or who fears having their child removed by social workers, the language of choice and empowerment is meaningless and deceptive (Carey 2013).

Increasingly, where the risk is to the individual rather than to others, once eligibility for the limited state resources has been determined by a professional, the responsibility for making the arrangements is offered to the individual in the name of personalization, choice and empowerment. These three concepts are closely interlinked in current policies for social care provision. We examine how personalization has been interpreted in policies on social care for disabled and older adults.

Social care and steps towards personalization

There have been two fundamental shifts in adult social care policy since the early 1990s:

- a move from institutional care to community-based care, involving the creation of quasi-markets in care;
- an emphasis on giving the individual service user a greater role in identifying their needs, and more choice and control over how those needs are met.

These changes have taken place in the context of a rapidly increasing older population and attempts to contain or reduce public expenditure, and have entailed important changes in the role of social workers. The introduction of quasi-markets and the implications of this for the governance of social care were discussed in chapter 5. In this chapter we turn to the role of the individual service user and the implications, both for themselves and for the role of social workers, of their more active role in identifying and meeting their needs.

The move away from institutional care to community-based care brought about by the 1990 NHS and Community Care Act was a response to the rapidly rising cost to the state of paying for residential and nursing care for disabled and older adults. The intention was that the local authority would be responsible for making an assessment of an individual's needs, and appropriate services would then be provided from a 'care market' which would be stimulated into offering a wider range of services responsive to individual circumstances. The needs assessment was to be carried out by social workers, working closely with the person requiring community care. Social workers became the co-ordinators of services, in the form of a 'care package' that was increasingly provided by not-for-profit and for-profit organizations, rather than by the local authority itself.

Care services were commissioned by the local authority, and in order to achieve economies of scale this was often done on the basis of block contracts for 'set list' services, rather than purchasing a specific service to meet the needs of a particular individual. As funding constraints grew, domiciliary services were commissioned on a 'task and time' basis, which meant that service users were often provided with a visit of 30 minutes or less. This left insufficient time for proper care with little continuity of carers across visits (Lewis and West 2014: 5). The effect was that, despite the declared policy aim of ensuring that services were needs- or choice-led rather than service-led, the reality was a lack of choice or control for service users over their service provision.

In the context of limited resources and rising demands for care, social workers, in their role as care managers, found it difficult to separate out assessing need from their awareness of the limited resources available. Their role became increasingly one of rationing access to services and targeting them on those who represented the greatest risk – in the case of older adults, primarily the risk of needing (more expensive) residential care. Assessment itself had to be rationed, and this tended to be done on the basis of the type of services for which an individual might be eligible, with comprehensive needs assessment limited to those considered likely to qualify for services on the basis of an initial screening (Ellis et al. 1999: 270).

The separation of needs assessment from service provision meant that social workers were no longer able to engage in long-term work with older and disabled people, and this in turn profoundly affected their professional identity. The social worker's role became focused on the task of gathering information according to a predetermined format in order to determine eligibility for services, rather than on a continuing professional/client relationship (Ellis et al. 1999: 268). The official guidance on community care referred to assessments being carried out by a 'practitioner', representing a denial of the distinctive role of social work (Cheetham 1993, cited in Ellis and Davis 2001: 133). A study in two local authorities of the implementation of the 1990 legislation found that social workers were struggling to act in accordance with their conception of good social work, which consisted of activities such as: 'acting as an advocate, promoting self-determination, building relationships, exploring need qualitatively and developing responses which took account of the particular circumstances of individuals and households' (Ellis et al. 1999: 272).

In 1996, in a further extension of the marketization of care, the Conservative government introduced a discretionary system of *direct payments* (DPs) to disabled adults of working age to enable them to purchase their own care arrangements. This cash-for-care system was a first step towards a particular interpretation of *personalization* of care. Instead of a package of care services being funded by the local authority on the basis of a needs assessment, disabled people could decide for themselves who should provide them with what services and when. This greater control contributed to promoting independence and social inclusion, and was seen by the disability movement as an essential element in achieving the right to self-determination, in a rights-based model of the role of social work (Spandler 2004: 192).

The 1997 Labour government extended direct payments to older people, parents of disabled children, carers and young people aged sixteen and seventeen from 2000, and in 2003 *required* all local authorities in England to offer such payments to all eligible individuals who consented to and were able to manage them. The promotion of DPs and their extension to a much wider constituency of potential users was an expression of Third Way ideology (see chapter 2), with its commitment to active citizenship and its concept of the state as enabler rather than provider. The particular system adopted for cash-for-care payments in England placed the responsibility for accessing appropriate care services on the individual recipient of the direct payment, operating in a relatively unregulated market. This contrasts with the system adopted in Norway, where the local authority or a third-sector organization assumes responsibility for training and employing personal assistants (PAs), but the individual whom the PA supports manages them and determines what tasks are undertaken (Christensen and Pilling 2014).

Direct payments have most commonly been used to employ a PA who provides support closely tailored to the individual's requirements, including activities not included in conventional services, such as accompanying them on shopping trips or leisure activities. Research with users of direct payments found high levels of user satisfaction and well-being (Glendinning 2008: 452). However, the numbers of people taking up direct payments was low – in 2005–6 it was only 2.5 per cent of all those receiving community-based social care services. Younger physically disabled adults account for the majority of spending on DPs. In 2011–12 they accounted for 57 per cent of expenditure, while only 15 per cent went to those aged 65 and over, who are numerically the much larger group (Lewis and West 2014: 6).

Direct payments are unlikely to be appropriate for certain groups receiving social care services in the community. A person in receipt of direct payments has to recruit their PA, take on the responsibilities of an employer and account for how they have spent the money allocated. Frail elderly people or those with fluctuating medical conditions where the need for support varies unpredictably may feel unable or unwilling to take on these responsibilities. A number of studies have shown that many elderly people do not want the role of a 'rational economic decision maker in the social care market place'. They experience too much choice as highly stressful or do not have the appropriate information necessary to make an informed choice (Daly 2012: 182–3). People with learning difficulties or with dementia may not have sufficient insight into their situation to be able to weigh up alternative options (Glendinning 2008; Lewis and West 2014), while those with mental health problems may have difficulty in disentangling social care from healthcare needs (Audit Commission 2010: 40) and in countering assumptions by social workers that they will be unable to manage DPs appropriately (Taylor 2008). Furthermore, acting effectively to secure the services needed requires an individual to operate as a confident and well-informed consumer within the care 'market'. There is an assumption implicit in the policy that the market will respond to demand by offering the services that people want, but this may not be the case for highly specialist services, or in rural areas where population density means that it may not be profitable to provide a particular service for which there is insufficient demand (Spicker 2013).

A series of policy documents published by the Department of Health between 2005 and 2007 (DH 2005; DH 2006; Local Government Association (LGA) 2007) made personalization of services a central objective in the development of adult social care. Personalization was a wide-reaching policy, involving not only the development of personal budgets, which have come to dominate the personalization agenda, but also prevention and re-ablement (promoting independent living for those discharged from hospital), better access to universal services and the development of social capital (Needham and Glasby 2014). Personal budgets aimed to extend the benefits of DPs to a wider population and overcome some difficulties identified above. Under the system, individuals who are eligible for local authority-funded social care are told how much money is available to spend on meeting their needs. They can then choose how the money is spent and how much direct control they want to have over the money. The allocated budget can either be taken as a DP, or it can be managed on their behalf by the local authority or a third party (Glendinning 2012). If the funds are used to purchase services through a broker or from the local authority, the service user does not have to manage the budget personally, while retaining (some) choice and control over services. Personal budgets continued to be promoted by the Coalition government. By 2013, 76 per cent of those eligible had a personal budget, although two-thirds were *managed* personal budgets (Needham and Glasby 2014: 13).

2014 Care Act

The 2014 Care Act consolidates previous legislation on social care and provides a new framework for future provision. The Coalition government claimed that it: 'represents the most significant reform of care and support in more than 60 years, putting people and their carers in control of their care and support' (DH 2014). It gives all those eligible for community-based social care the legal right to a personal budget, with effect from April 2015. Furthermore, even where an individual is not eligible for local authority-funded social care, they are entitled to help from the local authority to assess their care needs, suggesting a potentially large increase in requests for care assessments, when this part of the legislation comes into force from April 2016. The Care Act also requires local authorities to establish information and advice services to inform everyone within their area about rights and entitlements under the Act and how they can access them. It gives local authorities a duty to facilitate a diverse and sustainable care market (SCIE 2014). Other important provisions are new entitlements for carers in order to help them continue in their caring role for longer, a strong emphasis on preventing or delaying the need for support, with a requirement to promote integration with the NHS and other services. The legislation requires local authorities to set up adult safeguarding boards and to conduct reviews in a similar way to LCSBs. These are demanding requirements to meet in the context of further projected cuts to local authority budgets in the period 2015–20.

Strengths and limitations of personalization

The proponents and opponents of the personalization agenda have been divided about its benefits and disadvantages, reflecting the different origins and aims of the policy – from the disability movement on the one hand, and neoliberalism on the other. These offer conflicting interpretations of what independence, choice and control, which are so central to the policy, mean (Needham and Glasby 2014: 15–16). While the independent living movement is a bottom-up movement of disabled people who seek to promote change and social justice through collective action, based on a social rather than a medical model of disability (Ferguson 2008, cited in Needham and Glasby 2014), neoliberalism is individualistic and primarily concerned to promote economy and efficiency through the market, reducing state spending on welfare. The five key claims advanced by the advocates of personalization are that it: (i) transforms people's lives for the better; (ii) saves money; (iii) reflects the way people live their lives; (iv) is universally applicable; and (v) makes appropriate use of people's expertise in relation to their own lives and needs (Needham 2011). These perceived benefits are consonant with the reframing of citizenship from a passive, dependent rights-based conception to an active model based on individual rational action and the individualization of responsibility (Taylor-Gooby 2008).

While some younger physically disabled adults have welcomed the empowerment which personal budgets and DPs have brought for them, they have proved more problematic for other groups. Glasby (2014) summarizes the concerns raised about direct payments and personal budgets as follows:

- they are being used to restrict government spending and promote a flawed view of consumerism in community care services;
- the success of direct payments and personal budgets relies too heavily on the attitudes and training of front-line workers;
- they are inadequately financed and do not allow the purchase of sufficient care;
- they introduce the possibility of a two-tier system, where those who continue to opt for direct services are disadvantaged, and the most persistent and articulate get better outcomes;
- they lead to greater exploitation of care workers;
- they expose service users to greater risk of abuse or significant harm;
- they may be used by authorities to distance themselves from service users labelled as troublemakers;
- the practicalities of managing them are prohibitive;
- recruiting staff presents an insurmountable barrier for some people.

Although it could be argued that the quasi-marketization inherent within personalization has brought greater rights and choices for clients as consumer-citizens, in contrast to their previous depiction as passive clients who had to accept whatever 'expert' professional social workers prescribed for them, these concerns suggest more negative consequences. Scourfield (2007) claims service users are increasingly caught between a proliferation of confusing and conflicting roles, including those of citizens, clients, consumers, managers and entrepreneurs. Combining consumerism with active citizenship neglects the values of equity and equality that were central to traditional notions of citizenship (see chapter 2), and gives precedence to the individualism implicit in consumerism (Powell and Doheny 2006) rather than the collectivism of the disability rights movement. The service users most social workers come into contact with are rarely articulate people who are aware of and able to argue and campaign for their rights. They could therefore be categorized as 'flawed consumers' (Bauman 2004). Consumerism and choice are only possible when someone has real and informed choices and can choose from a range of options, or alternatively elect not to make a choice. Personalization as it has been implemented in social care policies is appropriate for some individuals under some circumstances, but its current status as a panacea is not supported by the evidence – especially for some user groups.

Implications of care management, direct payments and personalization for social work

The changes to the organization and delivery of social care since the 1990 NHS and Community Care Act have had a major impact on the role of social workers with adults. The transformation of social workers into care managers involved an increase in the time spent on office-based bureaucratic paperwork, and a feeling that social work was becoming deskilled, with much less scope for engagement with individuals and the communities in which they lived. Needs assessment and provision of services was, in the context of inadequate resources, a system for rationing, with social workers suffering a loss of professional autonomy. They were only able to work as an emergency service with people judged to be at risk (Carey 2003; McDonald et al. 2008) and consequently felt demoralized (e.g. Balloch et al. 1999; Postle 2002). Furthermore, the adult social worker role was steadily eroded through stealth measures that slowly replaced qualified workers with unqualified social work assistants (Lymbery 2010). This was cheaper and politically expedient but tended to undermine social justice, because unqualified workers are less bound by professional values, have less expertise and tend to be more compliant with employers' demands (Butler and Drakeford 2001; Humphrey 2003).

Social workers' role as care managers has remained relatively unchanged with the advent of DPs and the more recent personalization agenda outlined above, but resources have become even more limited, because of budget cuts and a growing population of older people with increasing care needs. This in turn has resulted in a continuing crisis of identity and morale for social workers. SCIE commented: 'In the changing adult social care scene, social work has not always found it easy to define its distinctive role and professional contribution. In many local authorities, the stress on personalisation has left social workers uncertain about what they have to offer' (2013: 12). The SCIE report commented on employers' failure to appreciate the skills and knowledge that social workers have and their possible contribution to addressing the multiple problems of large numbers of disabled adults and older people. In view of these various factors, it is perhaps unsurprising that adult social work remains in something of a crisis.

6.6 The changing relationship between the social worker and the client/service user

From the 1940s to the 1980s, social workers were depicted as enabling 'professional' experts who worked with vulnerable and passive 'clients' in the context of a psycho-dynamically influenced casework relationship (Evans and Harris 2004; Scourfield 2007). Educated and trained 'professional' experts defined, and decided paternal-istically on the best way to meet, vulnerable people's needs. Social workers after the Second World War adopted a psychosocial therapeutic approach in which they advised and supported individuals who had significant needs, although little atten-tion was paid to the wider structural context. Social work retained the individual casework method inherited from the COS but tried to avoid its moralism, adopting a more apparently neutral, knowledge-based approach. This drew heavily from psy-choanalysis and psychology and focused on normal and abnormal development, although even then some social workers were scathing about this 'psychiatric deluge' which they thought obscured the important social context (Wooton 1959; Heraud 1970). Harris (2008) argues that this continuing individualized ethos was based on the assumption that, with the advent of the welfare state, poverty would be abolished and that any remaining problems were increasingly likely to be linked to individual or family dysfunction rather than structural inequalities. An alternative interpretation is that social work entered into an implicit bargain with the state, in order to become officially accredited as a bureau-profession, with a guaranteed service user base and state-funded education, in return for relinquishing any commitment to radically changing society (Hugman 1991; Jones 2001).

In the 1970s, social work practice began to move away from a psychosocial individualized model towards more complex, systems-based theories (e.g. Pincus and Minahan 1973). Although systems theories did not attribute clients' prob-lems to structural issues, they acknowledged inadequacies in systems and their interconnected relationships. However, at the same time, more focused – but still individualistic – theories, such as crisis intervention, task-centred casework and various cognitive behavioural therapies, came into vogue. The radical Marxist-oriented social work practice movement also emerged in the 1970s (Bailey and Brake 1975; Corrigan and Leonard 1978) but was more in evidence in universities than at grassroots level, possibly because it presented social workers unequivocally as control agents of an oppressive state, which gave them little scope for making a positive contribution as state-funded professionals. Some softer and less 'radical' but community-orientated forms of social work practice were, however, being practised at the time and were advocated in the 1982 Barclay Report.

The changes to the welfare state in the 1980s, discussed in chapter 5, in particular the influence of NPM in the public sector, transformed ideas about the relationship between welfare professionals and their clients. The managerialist model removed many of the 'social' and relational aspects that had previously characterized social work practice and tried to replace the uncertain and ambiguous elements of social work with standardized procedures and systems of performance management (White et al. 2009). Passive 'clients' became 'service users' who were to be seen as the consumers of services (Farrell 2010), and these consumers have more recently been conceptualized as 'experts through experience' (see chapter 4). As we have seen, social workers, particularly those working with adults, became care and budget managers in the 1990s. The notion of an ongoing and therapeutic, or at least support-ive, personal relationship between social worker and service user was largely erased, with the possible exception of high-risk child protection and mental health cases (although in these cases control was often more prominent than care or support). The importance of interpersonal skills and establishing trust was discounted (Smith 2001). Although the emphasis of child and family social work has oscillated since its inception between preventative, relational-based work and the surveillance and monitoring of 'problem' families with children 'at risk', there was never a 'golden age' when social workers were allowed the time or resources to do long-term community-based work with disadvantaged families (Parton 2011). The emphasis has always been weighted towards surveillance and high-risk child protection cases, despite the introduction in more recent policy of the language of 'safeguarding' (in relation to both children and adults), which arguably allows for ways of working which are more holistic and focused on general well-being rather than exclusively addressing statu-tory work.

Concepts such as 'empowerment' and 'partnership working' which emerged in the 1990s promised more than they could deliver, as did anti-oppressive and anti-discriminatory approaches to social work (examined in chapter 4) which first appeared in the late 1980s. They ignored the considerable institutional power social workers had over service users and the fact that many service users only became involved with social workers in the first place because they were extremely vulnera-ble, or were involved involuntarily. The relationship-based nature of child and family work has been further threatened by the discontinuities created by institutions, so that children and families are continually moved between 'intake, assessment, children in need, child protection, looked-after children and leaving care teams, all determined by changing service and legal definitions of the child' (Jones 2014: 496). For those who are the subject of a child protection investigation or a mental health assessment, either of which could lead to compulsory state intervention, the profes-sional / service user relationship is often mandatory or a last resort on the part of the service users. Their construction as consumers who have rights (of choice, complaint and redress, or exit – at least in the abstract) does not reflect the reality of their situ-ation. Such a construction may suit some client groups, such as adults with learning disabilities, who might prefer to see themselves as customers paying for a service, with all the consumer protection this potentially brings, but not all will have the capa-bility to act safely and effectively in this role. As Fyson and Kitson's research (2010) has shown, many professionals have over-privileged the choices given to adults with learning disabilities and not counterbalanced these with adequate consideration of their vulnerability and limited capacity, which has led to many being bullied, har-assed and sometimes even killed within their community.

Electronic recording, tick-box and time-limited assessments, a narrow form of 'evidence based' practice and the use of performance indicators as a management tool have undermined professional autonomy, discretion and risk-taking. Nevertheless, a small-scale study of the exercise of discretion by social workers and managers found that, although some managers attempted to control and direct practice, many prac-titioners still exercised considerable discretion (Evans 2011, 2013). IT systems and formal procedures were less constraining of individuals than has sometimes been claimed. These procedures often created more, rather than less, discretion in practice, because they were so cumbersome and detailed. It was consequently impossible to adhere to them completely, so social workers chose what to follow and what to ignore. Most of the managers saw themselves not as rule-bound administrators but primarily as social work professionals there to support more junior colleagues and uphold professional values which enabled client needs to be met. Assessments of needs and risk also inevitably involved professional judgements, and discretion was always present when a choice had to be made amongst a number of different possible courses of action. Therefore, for the most part, Evans' social workers and managers did not see their role as solely concerned with performance indicators and rationing. Carey and Foster (2011) in their study of statutory adult and child social workers also uncovered numerous individual acts of covert resistance or subversion. Examples ranged from making assessments that exaggerated needs to ensure service users would receive services, to attempts by a small minority of social workers to support service users in confronting unfair policies. The practitioners' motivations for 'deviancy' varied considerably and were not necessarily, or even often, political. They ranged from alleviating boredom, to trying to get the 'best deal' for already disadvantaged service users, to challenging social injustice, although most interviewees explained their behaviour at a general level in terms of supporting and empowering service users. Fine and Teram's Canadian study showed social workers took both overt and covert actions against perceived organizational justices impacting on their service users. Although they acknowledge in some situations covert resistance may be the best response, they exhort social workers to consider 'more systematically avenues for overt actions . . . as basic social values can paradoxically be found even in the logics of dominantly neoliberal organizations' (2013: 1312).

6.7 Conclusion

This chapter has shown how need has increasingly been replaced by risk as the determinant of the circumstances under which an individual or family will have access to state resources, with important consequences for social work practice. Social workers have become responsible for assessing risk using standardized procedures and this has undermined their professional autonomy to a considerable degree. The preoccupation with risk and the search for rational, technical solutions to the problems of uncertainty have given a central role to the use of specific kinds of research evidence to guide policy and practice. But a recognition of the complexity of evaluating the effects of social interventions means that evidence from research, using a variety of methods, both quantitative and qualitative, as well as wider conceptual and theoretical knowledge and ethical considerations, are important. These all need to be combined and used to inform the exercise of professional judgement, rather than judgement being replaced by proceduralism and a narrow form of EBP.

Neoliberalism, with the central place it gives to the individual consumer operating in a free market, has also resulted in important changes in the relationship of social workers to those they work with. Since the mid-1980s, the passive client of welfare services has been replaced in policy discourse, by active, empowered individual consumers / users of services, who are responsible for identifying their needs and purchasing their own services to meet them. While the questioning of professional authority that this involves has undoubtedly brought significant benefits to some groups, such as younger physically disabled people, there are important limitations to the applicability of this model of personalization to the different situations that social workers are called on to deal with. In particular, frail older people and people with learning disabilities may not have the capacity or the will to act as consumers in a care market. It is also hard to see how personalization and empowerment are applicable to people subject to compulsory social work interventions, such as care proceedings, or mental health sections, where their power to 'exit' the situation is severely limited. Furthermore, the rhetoric of personalization and empowerment is currently not supported by the resources necessary to make this a reality. Severely limited local authority budgets mean that access to funded social care is largely restricted to the highest category of 'risk'. The 2014 Care Act imposed new duties on local authorities to promote well-being, to provide everyone who wants one with a needs assessment, to promote a healthy market in care services, and to provide information and advice to those who do not qualify for local authority-funded services. This potentially opens up a substantial increase in demands for assessment, information and advice, without the prospect of any additional resources. Similarly, policies to engage and work with parents and children have resource implications which current local authority budgets cannot meet. In both cases the policy aims are laudable, but the lack of resources calls into question how serious the commitment really is.

This change towards the provision of highly rationed, risk-oriented social services, in which social workers' actions are closely scrutinized and performance-managed, has had a significant impact on the role of social workers, their relationship to the recipients of social services, and the way they work. Although there have been recent attempts to reverse the increasing bureaucratization and proceduralization of social work, and to reinstate the centrality of relationship work and professional judgement, particularly in work with children and families, the policies of the last thirty years have affected social workers' professional standing and self-confidence, and it will require time and resources to restore these.

Discussion questions

- Discuss and account for the transition from need to risk in social work. Outline the potential consequences for service users and for social workers operating in different areas or specialisms.
- What sources of knowledge and 'evidence' should social workers take into account when making an assessment or evaluating possible ways of intervening?
- What are the strengths and weaknesses of the personalization agenda? Should all service users be treated as empowered citizen consumers?
- How has the relationship between the social worker and service user changed over time and has this change been to the benefit of either the social worker or the service user?

Further reading

Lister, R. (2010) *Understanding Theories and Concepts in Social Policy*, Bristol: Policy Press, ch. 6.

Kemshall, H. (2008) *Risk, Social Policy and Welfare*, 2nd edn, Buckingham: Open University Press.

McLaughlin, H. (2009) 'What's in a Name: "Client", "Patient", "Customer", "Consumer", "Expert by Experience", "Service User" – What's Next?' *British Journal of Social Work*, 39, 1101–17.

Spicker, P. (2013) 'Personalisation Falls Short', *British Journal of Social Work*, 43, 1259–75.

Webb, S. (2006) *Social Work in a Risk Society*. Basingstoke: Palgrave Macmillan.

7 Social Work and Globalization

7.1 Introduction

This book has so far focused on social policy in the UK and the implications of recent policy developments in England for social work, but national social policy is increasingly shaped by institutions and events beyond the nation state. This has occurred partly as a consequence of economic globalization and its social and cultural effects, and partly because of the development of a whole variety of supranational institutions, from regional bodies such as the EU to global ones, such as the UN or the IMF, which affect policies in individual nations. This chapter looks at globalization as a phenomenon and its implications for social policy and social work in Britain, and for social work as a global profession.

7.2 What is globalization?

Globalization is a contested concept but the term is used to refer broadly to the effects of the interaction of developments in a number of different spheres: technological, cultural and social, political and economic (Lorenz 2006). The interaction of these developments has resulted in

> a dense, extensive network of interconnections and interdependencies that routinely transcends national borders . . . These interconnections are expressed in ways that appear to 'bring together' geographically distant localities around the world, and events happening in one part of the world are able to quickly reach and produce effects in other parts of it. It is this *enmeshment* which gives rise to consciousness of the world as a shared place. (Yeates 2012: 194, emphasis added)

This enmeshment has three dimensions: (i) events and activities occur over a very wide geographical area (extensity); (ii) the degree and regularity of interconnectedness have increased (intensity); and (iii) these global interactions and processes take place far more quickly than in the past (velocity) (Yeates 2012: 195).

For example, the development of the internet and of social media has made it possible for individuals around the world (extensity) to communicate with each other frequently and copiously (intensity) and almost instantly (velocity). This in turn has had important social and political consequences. The results are evident in new methods of organizing social movements, as recent pro-democracy social protests in Hong Kong (2014) and Egypt (2012) showed. It has become possible to mobilize large numbers of people very quickly over a wide geographical area, in a way that would not previously have been possible. Developments in communications technologies have had other very important effects at a whole variety of levels, from enabling families and friends to stay in touch across continents to facilitating business transactions around the world at all times of the day and night. These technologies have also brought immediate and vivid access to events around the world through news media, and have made people in different countries much more aware of events such as natural disasters, wars, disease or famine in distant parts of the world. Another consequence of advances in communication technologies has been to create much greater possibilities for exposure to other cultures, and this, combined with the dominance of a small number of global corporations such as Coca-Cola, McDonald's, Nike, SKY and Apple, has resulted in a degree of cultural convergence across the world.

In the economic sphere, globalization refers to the practices of large corporations which organize their production across the globe, siting factories in countries with low labour costs and relatively lower levels of labour protection, and producing goods to be sold throughout the world. If conditions change, these corporations can move production to another part of the globe, with major economic and social implications for the countries that they move away from or into. Lorenz (2006) argues that globalization has produced *transnational* as opposed to multinational corporations, which constitute an economic network that has freed itself from a link to a distinct geographical location as a 'base', in order to achieve maximum flexibility of the production process. The power of transnational corporations to affect the economies of the countries where they operate gives the interests of big business considerable influence over economic and social policies in those countries. This has contributed to the ideological dominance of neoliberalism around the world, with the priority this gives to the free operation of the market and minimal state interference. It has also reduced the power of individual nation states to introduce social policies which might increase labour costs, or reduce corporate profits. Corporations are able to locate themselves in the country whose tax regime is most advantageous to them, which may not be the place where their profits are made. Such tax avoidance reduces state revenue in those countries which have less 'corporation-friendly' tax policies, and therefore, amongst other things, the resources available to fund welfare services. Recent examples include Amazon, which has made its European base in Luxembourg to minimize the tax paid on its profits, despite the revenue from its business in Luxembourg representing a tiny fraction of its total sales in Europe (*Guardian*, 8 October 2014). Similarly, Apple channelled its European business through Dublin, to take advantage of lower corporation tax in the Republic of Ireland (*BBC News* 29 September 2014).

Global financial markets, using the power of information and communications technologies, are able to shift enormous amounts of capital around the world within moments, with dramatic effects on the economies of individual countries, as was apparent in the 2008 financial crash, and more recently in Russia, with the devaluation of the rouble in December 2014. These economic effects have major implications for the living conditions and social policies of individual nations, and are the results of actions by institutions which can operate beyond the control of national governments.

The power and autonomy of nation states has also been challenged by the growth in the number of supranational institutions whose treaties, regulations, directives and rulings impinge on what national governments do. These institutions may also be influenced by powerful transnational businesses. At a regional level, nation states have grouped together, often primarily for economic reasons, but with consequences for other aspects of national policy for the members of the group. In Europe, the EU promotes the free internal movement of capital and labour, but has also introduced a range of social policies that are binding on its members, as one means of creating a 'level playing field' amongst them. Thus, gender equality legislation is a requirement of EU membership, including rights to maternity, paternity and parental leave, and equality within national social security systems. New supranational institutions, such as the European Commission or the European Court of Justice, have been created by the EU to develop policies and enforce legislation across its member states. Similar groupings exist around the world – for example, in Africa, the Southern African Development Community; in South America, the Mercado Comun del Sur; and in South East Asia, the Association of South East Asian Nations.

At a global level, inter-governmental organizations, such as the IMF, are able to exercise considerable power over the policies of individual states. For example, when Greece had to borrow from the IMF in the wake of the 2008 financial crisis to avoid defaulting on its loans, the IMF made it a condition that public expenditure was drastically cut and state assets sold, with impoverishing effects on a significant proportion of the population. Similarly, when the UK government had to borrow from the IMF in the 1970s, the loan was conditional on cutting public expenditure and this heralded the end of Keynesian policies which aimed to minimize unemployment (see chapter 1). Other global inter-governmental organizations include the World Bank, the UN, the World Trade Organization (WTO) and the Organisation for Economic Co-operation and Development (OECD). The policies of these organizations exercise considerable influence in a variety of ways over the countries that are members.

The expansion in the number of inter-governmental organizations is matched by a growth in international non-governmental organizations representing transnational social movements or advocacy networks, which lobby on social policy issues and are involved in the delivery of social policy (Yeates 2012). Yeates provides a helpful summary of the different kinds of entities to which globalization has given rise and their motivations (see table 7.1).

As a consequence of globalization, the power of nation states has been 'hollowed out', with 'state powers and capacities . . . moved upwards, downwards and sideways' (Jessop 2000, cited in Lorenz 2006). International interdependence has increased because 'events and decisions in one country or region can have far-reaching effects on the populations of apparently or formally unrelated countries' (Lyons 2006: 367). This means that to understand social policy in a given nation it is necessary to look beyond national borders and consider the ways in which these different entities affect national policies and their implementation.

Social work and globalization

While it is clear that the developments outlined above are important for understanding the pressures and constraints on national social policy, how far are they relevant to social work? Opinions on this are divided. Webb argues that 'social work has at best a minimal role to play within any new global order, should such an order exist' (2003: 191) and 'any notion of global or trans-national social work is little more than a vanity' (2003: 202). However, for others, while they agree that social work is mainly

Table 7.1 Typology of transnational entities

Type	Definition	Motivation	Examples
Epistemic communities	Experts in different countries linked through production and dissemination of knowledge	Scientific ideas	Think tanks, research institutes, e.g. International Federation of Social Workers (IFSW); International Association of Schools of Social Work (IASSW)
Transnational advocacy networks, transnational social movements	Individuals in different countries linked through a common concern	Moral ideas	Human rights, health and welfare, gender justice, environmental movements, e.g. International Council on Social Welfare (ICSW); International Red Cross; Save the Children; Médecins sans Frontières; Greenpeace
Transnational corporations	Economic entities in different countries linked through the pursuit of economic gain	Profit	Coca-Cola (drinks), McDonald's (fast food), Nike (sportswear), Apple (computers and phones)
Transnational criminal networks			Trafficking and smuggling of humans and commodities such as drugs and tobacco
Transnational professions	Professionals in different countries linked through knowledge and expertise that is not owned by any single society	Technical expertise	Medicine, nursing, law, engineering, social work
Transnational governmental networks	Governmental actors in different countries linked through a common issue or concern	Common public mandates	IMF; EU Council of Ministers; OECD; WTO

Source: adapted from Yeates 2014: 4. Reproduced by permission of Polity Press.

concerned with local practice, the fact that many of the social problems that they deal with have their origins, directly or indirectly, in global or regional events means that it is important to have an understanding of this and to develop responses that address them regionally or globally. Furthermore, since welfare policy is subject to regional, international and global influence, social workers need to understand this and the implications for practice developments and 'must now think in terms of trans-national as well as trans-cultural social work' (Lyons 2006: 378).

The influence of neoliberalism through global policy forums such as the OECD, and the more local effects of EU membership and the closer exchange of policy ideas which this has brought, has resulted in some degree of policy convergence within Europe and across OECD members. At the same time, local conditions and cultural practices continue to play a significant role in shaping the way in which policy is implemented, and local 'bottom up' responses are important in modifying global social policies, a process which Harris and Chou (2001), in their study of community care policy in the UK and Taiwan, call 'glocalization'. Across Europe, for example, national policy is converging on 'cash-for-care' systems, with increasing marketi-zation of care services and, arguably, a reduction in social solidarity and collective responses to care needs. However, the ways in which this policy is implemented in different countries differ according to the nature of the welfare regime (see chapters 2 and 6), with important implications for the character of the market in care that has been introduced (see, for example, Winkelmann et al. 2014). This points to the impor-tance of social workers having an awareness of global pressures, combined with an understanding of their own local and national institutions.

Social work has always been an international profession, although international issues have rarely assumed much significance on UK curricula or programmes (Lyons 2006; Powell and Robison 2007). Early social work pioneers worked and lived across national borders and many were politically active. A concern with interna-tional social justice issues such as poverty, famine, women's rights and world peace brought these pioneers together and 'through scholarship and advocacy, organi-zational leadership and international travel and direct cultural borrowing [they] contributed to [international] diffusion of social work knowledge' (Hegar 2008: 722). Globalization makes such international cooperation and the exchange of ideas and experience across national boundaries even more important for contemporary social work.

The following sections look in further detail at how globalization gives rise to new kinds of social problems for social work in Britain, at the role of supranational governmental and non-governmental bodies in creating and responding to social problems, and finally at internationalism within social work as a profession.

7.3 Social problems arising from economic globalization

Migration

One of the consequences of economic globalization has been an increase in migra-tion around the world. Extreme poverty and conflict in the Global South have resulted in flows of economic migrants to Europe, and a rise in the numbers of refugees and asylum seekers. Forced migration from non-Western countries is increasingly becoming a major socio-political issue for many Western countries that have tried to stop the inflow of migrants searching for better living conditions (Jönsson 2014). Attempts to restrict immigration through increasingly strict border controls have in turn created the conditions for a global criminal business in people trafficking, with migrants subjected to forced labour in a variety of industries and forced into criminal activities. Women and girls are particularly vulnerable to sexual exploitation and trafficking (US Department of State 2014). Membership of the EU has also resulted in significant population movement between EU member states. All of these developments have important consequences for social work.

Although there is a long history of immigration to the UK, including drawing on the population of British colonies to meet labour shortages in the UK in the 1950s and 1960s, globalization has resulted in immigration from a wider range of countries, over a much shorter period of time, resulting in much greater cultural and ethnic diversity. According to the 2011 Census, 13 per cent of UK residents (7.5 million people) were born outside the UK, an increase of over 3 million people since the previous census in 2001. In London the proportion of the population born outside the UK rose to 37 per cent, making it the most diverse city in the UK, with only 44 per cent of people in London in 2011 describing themselves as 'White British' (*BBC News* 11 December 2012).

As Williams and Graham point out (2014), migration is driven not only by economic motivation but also, increasingly, by transnational networks involving family and community ties. Contemporary migration patterns are more likely than in the past to involve stretching families across space, creating 'global chains of care' (Hochschild, cited in Garrett 2006: 323). Another characteristic of more recent migration patterns, associated with globalization, is migration as a temporary rather than a permanent phenomenon. This applies particularly to younger workers migrating within the EU, and to the higher education sector, where students may come for a limited period of study and then return to their home country or move to a third country. These different patterns of migration amongst different groups and for different purposes point to the importance of resisting the homogenization of migrants to the negative stereotype commonly found in the media, where migrants are portrayed as scroungers or a drain on welfare systems, overlooking their diversity and the positive contributions which they make.

Immigrants from some ethnic minorities tend to be over-represented among those who are poor – partly because of discrimination – and to suffer associated problems of poor health and disability, and are therefore more likely to come into contact with social services. Anti-immigration sentiment, whipped up by media-scaremongering about immigrants 'swamping' the UK and representing a drain on the welfare state, has resulted in new rules that seek to exclude various categories of migrants from access to welfare services. Consequently, the policing of eligibility has increasingly become entwined with managing national borders as refugees, migrants and aliens become identified with 'benefit tourism' and taking advantage of the welfare system (Garrett 2006: 322). This hostile discourse around immigration makes immigrants particularly vulnerable to discrimination and abuse.

Williams and Graham (2014) argue that policies of multiculturalism which prevailed in the 1980s have been replaced by a focus on integration, in which cultural and language differences are seen as problematic and underpin a deficit model

adopted in working with immigrants (see also chapter 4). They point to the importance of acknowledging processes of intergenerational change, with second- and
third-generation immigrants differing very significantly from their parents and
grandparents. This underlines the importance of not constructing all migrants
and their descendants as 'other', and so failing to acknowledge the ways in which
communities adapt and change over time.

Migration raises important issues for social workers in relation to kinship care,
an example of the global chains of care referred to above. Kinship care refers to the
care of children, whose immediate family is unable to care for them, by members of
the extended family or, in some cases, friends within the same community. The 1989
Children Act proposed this as the preferred option, and in the context of a shortage
of foster carers and the desire to find culturally appropriate care it has received more
attention recently (Lyons 2006). For migrant families, this may mean that children
are left in, or sent from the UK to, another country to be cared for by members of the
extended family. This in turn may involve social workers in working internationally
to ensure children are safe, requiring that social workers familiarize themselves with
aspects of the welfare system and immigration legislation in the host country. Lyons
gives the example of children, whose mother was unable to care for them in London,
being sent to live with their aunt and her husband in Paris. Social workers had to
travel to Paris to visit the family and discuss the arrangements with them through an
interpreter. Conversely, children may be sent to the UK to be cared for by members
of the extended family if their parents are unable to care for them or because they
believe that this will be in the child's best interests. The case of Victoria Climbié, sent
from Ivory Coast to London to live with her great-aunt (see chapter 4), illustrates the
difficulties that social workers and other professionals faced in disentangling respect
for cultural difference from the obligation to ensure a child's safety and well-being.

'Illegal' migrants

Policies in the UK and elsewhere in Europe to restrict immigration have contributed
to the growth in international criminal gangs trafficking those who are unable to gain
legitimate entry. Once in the UK, their undocumented status makes these migrants
vulnerable to continuing exploitation by those who trafficked them and by unscru-
pulous employers. Women are particularly vulnerable to labour market exploitation,
human trafficking and sexual violence. A Swedish study examining social workers' interactions with undocumented workers found that social workers tended to
see these migrants either as 'victims' in need of education and development, or as
'illegal' and therefore not entitled to any form of support. These perceptions were
gendered, with women and children more likely to be seen as victims, while men
were more often seen as responsible for their situation and the difficult position in
which this placed them and their families. However, social workers found themselves
in a dilemma in responding to 'illegal' migrants, between their obligations to someone in need, and following national law and rules (Jönsson 2014). The problem in
Sweden has been 'offloaded' onto the NGOs which have taken principal responsibility for responding to the needs of undocumented migrants. Social workers' responses
to the dilemmas which these migrants posed fell into three categories: *conformists*
framed the problem in individual terms, as one of poor individual choices, which

they bore no responsibility to solve; those who adopted a *critical* position saw illegal migration as a product of neoliberal globalization. They were committed to resisting pressures for a managerialist approach to social work, and saw their role as committing them to fighting for social justice. They used their discretion to find ways round the rules of social work practice in the interests of those they were working with. The third group, the *legalistic improvers*, looked for ways in which they could exploit legal loopholes to secure provision for undocumented migrants, for instance by using the Convention on the Rights of the Child.

Similar dilemmas exist in the UK, where social workers may face conflict between their safeguarding duties and immigration policy. They may find themselves simultaneously acting as 'agents of control' and 'gatekeepers to services' while struggling to protect vulnerable adults and children (Ottosdottir and Evans 2014). This in turn makes it hard to retain the principles of social justice and care central to social work ethics. The annual US Department of State country-by-country report on trafficking and slavery identifies some of the difficulties that social workers may face in negotiating between law enforcement and meeting needs. The report's recommendations for the UK include:

- Balancing law enforcement with a victim-centred response to protect trafficking victims
- Ensuring that a greater number of victims of trafficking are identified and provided access to necessary services regardless of immigration status
- Providing victims with access to services before they have to engage with immigration and police officers
- Ensuring child victims' needs are assessed and met
- Ensuring child age assessments are completed in safe and suitable settings and children are not awaiting care in detention facilities. (2014: 394)

Refugees and asylum seekers

Asylum seekers are a distinct category of migrants, who have been forced to leave their country of origin because of the threat to their safety from war or political or religious persecution or natural disasters, and who are seeking permission to remain in the country where they have sought refuge. Refugees are asylum seekers who have been granted such 'leave to remain'. Until this legal status is granted, asylum seekers in the UK have very limited entitlements to financial support and to social care, and have to live with the fear that their asylum claim will be turned down and they will be deported. Asylum seekers are not allowed to take up paid employment and the level of welfare benefits they receive is substantially below the level of Income Support. They are not entitled to any additional benefits for disability. A high proportion of child asylum seekers have suffered trauma of some kind and there are high levels of mental and physical ill health within this population (Children's Society 2012).

Children may arrive as unaccompanied minors, who have experienced trauma and loss, but whose need for care may be subordinated to the demands of the immigration service to establish their age in order to determine their legal status and their rights. Where the UK Border Agency does not accept a young person's claim to be a minor, they are treated as an adult until their age can be established. There were 1,400 age disputes in 2008, and procedures for assessing age are a matter of concern to the professionals involved. In 2008, approximately 6 per cent of children in public care were unaccompanied asylum seekers (Wade 2011b). Assessment of unaccompanied children and young people presents considerable challenges to social workers, who may be dealing with children who have been traumatized and may be wary about revealing information about themselves because of uncertainty about how it will be used. Wade's study found that social workers were sympathetic towards the accounts given by the young people they worked with, but fewer than half the assessments were rated adequate or better by the researchers. The initial assessment tended to focus only on the most basic facts and Wade therefore argued that young people's accounts of their experiences needed to be returned to throughout their placement, in order to provide them with opportunities to re-tell their story.

Where social workers were able to find placements for the young people which provided the opportunity to build new attachments, resume education and construct networks of social support, this had protective effects in terms of the mental health and resilience of the young people. However, both social workers and the young people had to cope with a high degree of uncertainty about the future. The majority of unaccompanied minors are only given temporary leave to remain in the UK and are expected to return to their country of origin when they reach adulthood. Most young people would prefer to stay in the UK. This means that social workers need to be pre-pared to work with young people to help them face this difficult future and to plan for the uncertainties of potentially returning to their country of origin, with which they may no longer be familiar and where they may have few family or social connections.

Williams and Graham (2014) argue that the effectiveness of current social work approaches to working with all categories of migrants is limited by four inter-related processes:

- *decontextualization*: social workers' failure to understand the situation of the migrant in the contexts both of global neoliberal economic doctrine and of the co-ordinated attempts to exclude migrants and asylum seekers;
- *disaggregation*: individualization and separation of needs, resulting in a lack of understanding of the complexities and intersections of migrants' situation;
- *culturalization*: a focus on cultural or language issues as problematic – this consti-tutes migrants as 'other' and fails to see them as rights bearing;
- the replacement of multiculturalism by policies of integration. This leads to social workers adopting *ambivalent assimilationalism*. The ambivalence resides in social work's ethical commitment to social justice, care, user involvement, part-nership and empowerment. Assimilation threatens to devalue cultural difference and impose a mythical unitary 'British culture' (see also chapter 4).

Contributions of migrants to social care

As we have seen (chapter 6), there is growing demand for social care because of an ageing population, high levels of female employment and greater survival of people with long-term ill health and disabilities. The social care market is increasingly dependent on workers recruited from abroad to provide personal care in both resi-dential settings and individuals' homes. Jobs in the care sector are generally female dominated, poorly paid, involve demanding work and have low status, and this means that the indigenous population may be reluctant to take them. Yeates (2009) argues that there is a new *international* division of reproductive labour – of which social care work is a part, and which governments condone and even encourage – that involves the export of female labour. Women migrants' work as care assistants in the UK not only helps meet domestic demand, but also helps families and communities in their country of origin through the remittances which they send back, as part of a 'global care chain', involving women from the Global South working in the Global North to support children left in the care of female relatives (Williams 2010).

While stricter immigration legislation has recently made it very much more difficult for new migrants to enter the UK from outside the EU to undertake this kind of low-paid work, migration within the EU from Central and Eastern Europe remains an important source of labour for care work (Williams 2010; Hussein et al. 2011). In Hussein et al.'s study (2011), employers and Human Resources (HR) managers characterized migrants as hard-working, honest and reliable, often in contrast to UK workers. Migrants were also felt to have a more respectful attitude to older people and to care genuinely about those they worked with. Many migrants were better qualified than care workers recruited locally, and in some cases saw care work as a good point of entry that would eventually lead to better-paid work more consistent with their level of qualification.

Williams (2010) argues that a new transnational political economy of care has come into existence. This has four dimensions: the *transnational movement of care labour*; the *transnational dynamics of care commitments*, involving care at a distance, substitute care or a lack of care because of migration; the *transnational movement of care capital*, referring to the rapid growth of commodified care as big business; and finally the *transnational influence of care discourses and policies* manifest, for example, in the widespread adoption by European welfare states of cash payments to enable individuals to purchase their own care (see chapter 6).

Transnational care capital

The marketization of social care services, discussed in chapter 5, has opened up new commercial opportunities for private companies selling care services. In the UK, this has resulted in a number of international private equity firms entering the market for residential care. Three-quarters of residential care for older people is provided by private, for-profit companies (Brennan et al. 2012), which, because of the increasing elderly population, see this as a good investment. Four large internationally owned companies control almost a quarter of the 'market' (Scourfield 2012). Because these companies are motivated principally by profit rather than a service ethos, when they encounter commercial failure the consequences for residents have been very serious. Southern Cross was a US-based private equity firm which by 2011 owned over 750 care homes, representing more than 10 per cent of the 'beds' in the UK (Scourfield 2012). In 2011 it ran into serious financial difficulties, and frail, elderly residents, and their families, experienced a period of uncertainty and distress about whether they would have to move elsewhere. In the end another company took over responsibility for many of the homes, but the crisis demonstrated the problems associated with ownership of such services by companies controlled from outside the UK and with little interest in the business other than the potential profit that it offers.

7.4 Supranational institutions and governance

Supranational institutions play an increasingly important part in influencing national social policy. This influence is exercised in a variety of ways and at a variety of levels. At a regional level, the EU plays an important part in distributing resources between member states and directly and indirectly shaping social policy, through its regulations, recommendations and directives. Individual countries in breach of the rules can be held accountable through bodies such as the European Court of Justice. The governance of the EU has created forums which encourage the exchange of ideas and promote the development and evaluation of social policies at a European level. For example, the European Social Policy Network (ESPN) is funded by the EU to 'ensure expertise and provide rigorous assessments of European and national social policies and to foster a high-quality debate on innovative policy solutions'. It describes itself as 'a tool to assist the European Commission in the formulation of evidence-based social policies [that] will contribute in particular to the assessment of the National Reform Programmes and the National Social Reports' (ESPN website).

Beyond the EU, Conventions agreed at a European level, and the institutions created to enforce them, such as the European Convention on Human Rights and the European Court of Human Rights, provide important common benchmarks and standards across signatory countries, which influence policy and practice at a national level. We saw in chapter 4 how the Convention and the decisions of the Court have been important in the interpretation of human rights in relation to religious expression in individual European countries.

At a global level the policies of IGOs such as the UN, the IMF and the World Bank play an important part in directing resources to individual nations and shaping policy through the conditions which they attach to them. Many IGOs are seen as operating in the interests of the Global North, promoting neoliberal policies which give a residual role to social policy and encourage the growth of commodified welfare for those who are better off (Yeates 2012: 204). Global treaties, while not directly enforceable, express the common commitment of signatories to the aims set out in them. The UN Convention on the Rights of the Child (UNCRC), for example, to which the UK became a signatory in 1989, requires a report every five years on how each signatory has implemented the articles of the Convention. This in turn can be a valuable source of pressure on national governments to address particular policy problems identified by the UN Committee on the Convention on the basis of the national report, such as the treatment of young people in custody, asylum-seeking children and child poverty (UNCRC 2008). The Convention arguably gave impetus to providing greater recognition of children's rights, which was incorporated into the 1989 Children Act in the form of rights to independent representation of children in legal proceedings.

Other IGOs, such as the OECD, play an important role in bringing about policy convergence between their members through the exchange of information and ideas which they promote. Bringing together comparative information on aspects of the welfare systems of OECD members can act as a stimulus to policy convergence and provides an important channel for dissemination of dominant ideological perspectives.

Globalization has resulted in a proliferation of IGOs with increasing influence, and there has been a corresponding growth in international non-governmental organizations (INGOs). INGOs include a wide range of different kinds of organizations, including trade unions and professional associations, consumer groups and third-sector organizations, such as Oxfam or the Red Cross, that work on international problems of poverty, poor health, humanitarian aid, the environment, etc. These organizations may be involved both in formulating or lobbying for particular policies and delivering services as agents of IGOs such as the World Bank or the UN (Yeates 2012).

Social work, IGOs and INGOs

Historically, social workers have had an involvement both in IGOs such as the UN, and in INGOs. However, this involvement has declined over time as these agencies have focused on humanitarian action and social development while social work in the Global North has become increasingly individualistic and apolitical (Hugman 2010). One study found 37 per cent of the workforce of twenty INGOs were social work-qualified, although most worked in just four organizations, predominantly as programme directors, suggesting that social work's potential contribution to other areas, such as development, service management and consultation, was neglected (Claireborne 2004). Six organizations did not see social work as relevant to their mission, although they were concerned with many issues relevant to social work, such as human rights, community and leadership development, education and reducing poverty. Most INGOS did not advertise for social workers *per se* but recruited from many professions, including law, healthcare and teaching, despite some of their key tasks, such as working with survivors of conflicts and disasters, being eminently suited to social workers. It is, however, unclear whether the relative absence of social workers from these INGOs is because they apply for posts but are rejected because they are seen as apolitical micro counsellors, or whether few apply. Social work, however, may be missing valuable opportunities internationally in relation to its broader global social justice and human rights mission, as there is clearly a professional gap.

The work of UNICEF, which is concerned with the well-being of children, whether they have been trafficked, orphaned by pandemics, or are street children or child soldiers, is of particular relevance to social work. Most of its work is conducted in the Global South. UNICEF has employed a number of 'barefoot' social workers in remote areas, particularly in relation to child protection. This involves recruiting local women and giving them basic short courses in social work methods and concepts. Social workers are also involved with the UNHCR (United Nations High Commissioner for Refugees), primarily dealing with resettlement, repatriation and psychosocial issues relating to asylum seekers, refugees and forced migrants, for whom rape is a major issue.

There are a number of INGOs with a more specific focus on social work. The International Council on Social Welfare (ICSW) has members from more than seventy countries around the world. It works at local, regional and international levels, 'to advance social welfare, social development and social justice' (ICSW website), conducting research, disseminating information and lobbying at a variety of governmental levels, working with IGOs and other INGOs. Its wide remit, including social development, means that it has 'General Category' consultative status with the Economic and Social Council of the United Nations (ECOSOC). This means it can contribute to discussions about international economic and social issues and be involved in the formulation of policy recommendations. Two other social work INGOs, the International Association of Schools of Social Work (IASSW) and the International Federation of Social Workers (IFSW), are mainly concerned with social work education and with promoting international social work practice (see section 7.5). Their principal focus on social work as a profession means that they are less involved in international policy making of a broader kind, although both organizations have 'Special Category' consultative status with the UN (Healy 2008).

7.5 Professional networks and epistemic communities

Social work as an international profession

The first international conference of social work was held in 1928, led by affluent North American and European women, reflecting the gender and class characteristics of social work at that time (Eilers 2003). The conference was attended by over 5,000 delegates representing forty-two countries. Three international social work organizations were established out of subsequent conferences: the IASSW, the ICSW and the IFSW, which, in different ways, have worked to promote the development of the profession (IASSW and IFSW) and the advancement of social welfare (ICSW).

The journal *International Social Work* started publication in 1958, through the joint efforts of the ICSW and the IASSW. It initially acted as a source of information for the profession on the work of the UN and of international professional associations, only becoming a more academic publication from the 1970s onwards (Healy and Thomas 2007). The definition of international social work has been contested (Haug 2005; Dominelli 2010; Trygged 2010) with some using the broader term 'the social professions' rather than 'social work' because of differences in the nature of the work and the professions involved in different countries (Powell and Robison 2007; see also chapter 2). Early definitions in the 1930s and 1940s included working across borders and through international bodies, such as the League of Nations, and international assistance and exchange of ideas through conferences and publications. In the 1970s and 1980s, the focus of international social work shifted to narrower conceptions of comparative social work and cross-cultural awareness (Healy and Thomas 2007; Powell and Robison 2007). More recent definitions draw attention to the importance of international professional action with an acknowledgement of 'interdependence within a globalising world' and the use of cross-national comparisons and international perspectives to look at local practice, as well as participation in cross-national or supranational policy and practice activities (Lyons 1999: 12).

A global definition of social work and global minimum standards for the profession were agreed by the IASSW and the IFSW in 2001. The process of arriving at a definition presented significant challenges due to different worldviews (Hare 2004; Sewpaul 2006). Some standards or values put forward were challenged as ethnocentric and/ or colonial, while conversely there was concern that an uncritical acceptance of all normative cultural customs might condone harmful or abusive practices (Trygged 2010). The most recent global definition of social work adopted by the IASSW and IFSW in July 2014 states:

> Social work is a practice-based profession and an academic discipline that promotes social change and development, social cohesion, and the empowerment and liberation of people. Principles of social justice, human rights, collective responsibility and respect for diversities are central to social work. Underpinned by theories of social work, social sciences, humanities and indigenous knowledge, social work engages people and structures to address life challenges and enhance wellbeing.

Although some people have argued that human rights discourse is an unwelcome Western imposition, it complements a social justice and needs model because it is entitlement based (Skegg 2005).

Global standards for education and training were drawn up in 2004 (IASSW 2005). These are concerned with protecting service users, encouraging relationships between educational establishments globally, the cross-national movement of social workers and supporting the development of social work education globally. Debates, however, surround the standards' viability as 'what is valued academically, epistemologically and ontologically varies between countries and cultures' (Payne and Askeland 2008: 60), and the Global North has tended to dominate the various international professional associations. Different countries have different criteria for what counts as valued knowledge or evidence, what is ethically or culturally important and what constitutes social work. The IFSW and ICSW presidencies have historically been located in the North, but in 2004 the IASSW elected an Ethiopian, Professor Abye Tasse, as its first president from the South, followed by Professor Angie Yuen from Hong Kong. This could be regarded as a major achievement as it shifted preconceptions about who could lead international social work organizations (Lyons 2006).

In some poorer countries, access to money, books, computers and the internet may be difficult, making it hard for social workers to read relevant literature and attend international conferences to exchange ideas. The IFSW and IASSW have subsidized conference fees and travel costs for poorer countries (Hugman 2010), but this is only one barrier. Both organizations are English-speaking. In countries where English is not the first language, exchange is difficult, and even in European countries there may be language and cultural difficulties, despite similar social and political systems and reasonably widespread fluency in English as a second language (Green 1999). The dominance of the Global North in the discussion of social work education at an international level is partly because social work has a longer history in this part of the world, while it is a relatively new and underfunded profession in many countries in the Global South. The main issues of contention are whether the intellectual and political dominance of the Global North means it is foisting inappropriate values, methods and forms of social work on other countries in an ethnocentric imperialist manner, being unprepared to engage with them as equals and perhaps also learn from them.

Recruitment of social workers from overseas

Many social workers in the UK originate from other countries. High vacancy levels in the UK have resulted in social workers being recruited from overseas (e.g. Ahmed 2007), either arriving in the UK with qualifications gained abroad or gaining a social work qualification after arriving in the UK. Overseas social workers are generally reported being as 'hard working' by recruitment agencies, although little research exists examining service users', employers' and colleagues' perceptions of them (Hussein et al. 2010).

Different sources categorize social workers in different ways, making statistics hard to compare. Some sources categorize them by where they qualified, while others group them according to their ethnic/'racial' origin, and others according to nationality. In 2007, 6,400 registered social workers had qualified overseas (8% of the total); by 2010 this had increased to 6,700 (Carson 2010). Others may have not registered because they could not afford to, or had taken a different career path or their qualification could not be verified as equivalent. One survey showed 19% of social workers registering in 2008–9 were from a non-White ethnic background (GSCC 2010, cited in Laird 2014). There is great regional variation in the concentration of foreign-born social workers, with 48% of the total practising in London and 21% in the West Midlands. Almost one in five of those born outside the UK are European, mostly Irish, with a similar proportion from Australasia and 33% from sub-Saharan Africa (ONS 2006). As mentioned earlier, many immigrants from Eastern Europe and developing nations are employed within the privatized social care sector (Experian 2006), often at a level below their qualifications and skills (Cuban 2008), but this employment may act as a stepping stone to a social work qualification. A high proportion of Black African men who train as social workers initially worked within social care upon arriving in the UK (Evaluation of the Social Work Degree Qualification in England Team 2008).

The push and pull factors for social workers vary according to where they originate from. Social workers from countries with similar welfare systems, such as New Zealand and Australia, fall into two groups: those who come to work in the UK temporarily, early in their careers, and another older, more diverse group with more family commitments and professional experience who often settle in the UK permanently (Evans et al. 2006). One small-scale survey of health and welfare professionals, including ten social workers, found motives for relocation included better pay, anticipated knowledge and skill accumulation which would benefit their career if they returned home, and different travel and professional opportunities (Moran et al. 2005). In another study, social workers, predominantly from South Africa and Zimbabwe, reported smaller caseloads and better wages as key incentives (Sale 2002). Conversely, there are examples of disillusioned overseas social workers with unrealistic expectations of living standards in the UK, one being totally dismayed that he had been placed in social housing (Sale 2002). Another study reported social workers, mostly from Australia, expressing concern about the poor public image of social workers in the UK (Eden et al. 2002). Some overseas social workers also report lowered professional confidence because of different policy, legislation and care systems cross-nationally (Firth 2004).

The number of social workers recruited from outside the UK is relatively small by comparison with the overseas recruitment of health workers (Hussein et al. 2010). Agencies reported that employers preferred applicants from countries similar to the UK. Nevertheless, they recruited from many countries – Africa, Eastern Europe, the Caribbean, Australia, the USA and mainland Europe – but were more reluctant to accept applicants from developing countries because of the brain and skills drain this would constitute for their country of origin. Some barriers associated with employing overseas-trained staff are related to cultural knowledge, norms and sensitivity. These issues render skills transferability more problematic for social work, which requires better interpersonal and communications skills and greater cultural awareness than, for example, professions such as engineering and accountancy. However, the experience of someone who has travelled and been educated across different countries may be particularly useful if they are able to consider cultural and professional differences between contexts self-critically and reflexively, and integrate and synthesize their knowledge to work in a sensitive and informed manner across different situations (Yan 2005, cited in Hugman 2010).

Even though there are now global standards for social work and European legislation standardizing the practice of a number of professions and introducing reciprocal recognition of national qualifications, there may be significant gaps or 'black holes' (Faulconbridge and Muzio 2011). A number of commentators have therefore suggested that the employment of social workers who have trained overseas requires rigorous induction and ongoing supervision (Brown et al. 2007; Skills for Care South West 2007). Obtaining visas and procuring up-to-date police checks and overseas references present practical obstacles to their employment and, from a professional perspective, different interpretations of codes of ethics are also a potential problem.

UK social workers working elsewhere in the world

The movement of social workers internationally is two-way. One international recruitment agency reported receiving over 400 expressions of interest from UK social workers considering emigrating for a variety of reasons, including better work–life balance or just a sense of adventure (Carson 2010). Outward migration by social workers from the UK is mostly to English-speaking countries in the Global North such as Australia. For UK social workers working overseas, a number of issues are important. Some work in English-language countries in the Global North but with indigenous peoples, such as Native American Indians in the USA, Aboriginals in Australia, Maori people in New Zealand, and First Nations (Aboriginal) and Inuit people in Canada. European settlers exploited, stigmatized and marginalized these groups and in some countries continue to do so. Some social workers are also engaged in projects in the Global South where cultural norms and languages are very different. Because of this it has been suggested imposition of European social work techniques and practices is inappropriate. *Indigenization* involves adapting existing models and practices to a new cultural climate, but, due to claims this was an imperialist approach, others propose *authentization, authentication* or *recontextualization*. This involves constructing a model of social work which is consistent with the political, economic, social and cultural characteristics of a particular country or culture (Walton and El Nasr 1988; Tsang et al. 2008). It may therefore involve a community social development approach which incorporates some religious or spiritual aspect. In some countries or communities, centuries of aggressive colonization have undermined the capacity of the indigenous peoples to recognize, address or campaign for their own rights and needs, which suggests serious rebuilding, identity, confidence and capacity work is required (Green and Baldry 2008). Yip (2004) also argues that some social work values such as confidentiality, empowerment, self-determination and autonomy, are Eurocentric and individualistic. They are therefore problematic to implement in the Global South where other values, such as harmony, family stability and responsibility, predominate.

Hugman (2010) compares Yip's analysis of a Chinese male/female DV scenario with a similar case examined by Healy (2007) involving a Vietnamese immigrant settled in the USA. Both Yip and Healy concur that DV is morally wrong. Yip asserts the way to persuade the Chinese woman to leave her husband is to focus *not* on her needs/rights or the wrongness of his actions but on the welfare of her daughter, as this is consistent with Chinese values. Healy conversely is more concerned with cultural values being misappropriated to elevate one person's human rights and deny another's, and indeed norms of family harmony and societal stability would seem to be an anathema, if they are conditional on colluding with or indirectly condoning domestic abuse. Infanticide often occurs in very poor societies because of limited access to contraception or terminations together with insufficient resources to feed and care for all children born (see Scheper-Hughes 1992). This may be compounded by patriarchal ideologies which exacerbate female infanticide by culturally subordinating girl children, as occurs in China and India (Green and Taylor 2010). Some abusive cultural practices therefore need to be located within wider social justice arguments which factor in cultural understandings and deprivation, disadvantage and poverty which may corrupt and corrode cultural practices.

Cross-national collaborations and exchanges

In the UK most collaborations and exchanges between social workers since the 1970s have been at a European, regional level as opposed to a global level, mainly funded by dedicated European monies. These often include cross-national comparative research projects on specific issues such as the balance between therapeutic support and legal intervention with regard to child sexual abuse (e.g. Green 1999), and practitioner and education exchange visits, exemplified by the ERASMUS and TEMPUS programmes. These projects have, however, tended to be concerned with comparisons of policy and practice at the micro and meso level, across small numbers of countries, with relatively little focus on structural or wider global issues.

Practitioners and academics can learn much from published cross-national research and debate, now included not only in dedicated regional and global journals such as *International Social Work* and the *European Journal of Social Work*, but also in *Social Work Education*, which is subtitled an 'international journal', and British-based journals such as *BJSW* and *Child and Family Social Work*. These regularly publish articles from overseas scholars and/or refer to research conducted in other countries as a comparator to UK research. Despite this, few articles refer to the interconnected and interdependent global context and/or to social development. Most students mainly draw on literature concerned with the UK, and very occasionally the European context, because their education, training and practice encourage this. However, international social work research, hitherto under-utilized, can help practitioners learn from and adapt other countries' policies and practices (Hokenstad and Midgely 2004). Such research includes: (i) *supranational* research, conducted in one country but drawing on literature from others; (ii) *intra-national* research, primarily associated with studying immigrants, asylum seekers and refugees; and (iii) *transnational* research, comparing different countries (Jung and Tripodi 2007). The study of different countries' welfare regimes (see chapter 2) and Humphreys and Absler's analysis of social work responses to DV across nations, time and history (see chapter 3) are two good examples of transnational research.

7.6 Conclusion

Globalization, understood as the complex interactions between economic, technological, cultural and social forces across the world, has reduced the power of individual nation states to control economic and social policy and has given rise to new social problems which in turn have important implications for social work. Greater population mobility across the globe, prompted by global inequality, conflict and natural disasters, combined with attempts to restrict immigration in the countries of the Global North, have drawn social workers into the policing of national borders – for example, through their involvement in age assessment of child asylum seekers. Such developments raise new ethical dilemmas for the profession about how to balance legal duties with social justice and a humanitarian response to need. More restrictive immigration legislation, introduced as a response to increased global population mobility, has given rise to new criminal trafficking networks which expose those trafficked to abuse and exploitation. This again raises questions about balancing the care and protection of victims of trafficking with the enforcement of immigration legislation. Victims may be deterred from seeking help from social workers, amongst others, because they feel caught between two equally undesirable alternatives: continued exploitation or deportation.

Global care chains link migrants working in the UK to extended families living in other parts of the world, who are dependent on them for financial support. Many of these migrants are carrying out care work in the UK which elderly and disabled people depend on for their well-being. Social workers need to have an awareness of the complex interdependencies which affect the care and support of others, both in the UK and elsewhere in the world. The Global North tends to benefit from these care chains at the expense of the Global South, with skilled labour, such as nurses, attracted to the UK to meet labour shortages. Although remittances make an important contribution to the home countries of many migrants, these countries also lose both the skills and the unpaid caring which these migrants would otherwise contribute in their country of origin.

Although social work has a long history of international exchange of ideas, which has been promoted through various international bodies since the late 1920s, a global definition of social work and global standards for the education and training of social workers were only introduced at the beginning of the twenty-first century. The creation of new supranational governmental and non-governmental institutions in response to economic globalization has made it increasingly important for social workers across the globe to speak with one voice, and to have a means of making representations to IGOs and INGOs. The process of arriving at such global definitions and standards is a difficult one, which has necessarily involved recognizing and accommodating cultural and resource differences between the countries of the Global North and those of the South. Similar issues of cultural adjustment and responsiveness arise when social workers go to work abroad, whether this is coming to work in the UK or going from the UK to other parts of the globe.

Discussion questions

- Discuss, using relevant examples, why an understanding of globalization and the wider international context is important for social workers operating in one specific locality or nation.
- What tensions and dilemmas currently confront social workers working with asylum seekers and illegal immigrants? Can these be resolved or managed? If so, how?
- How might the ability to engage with European and international human rights legislation help social workers to practise in a way more congruent with upholding key professional values and ethical mandates?
- Outline and discuss the ways in which globalization has impacted upon both the social work and social care labour force in the UK and on the changing service user population.

Further reading

British Journal of Social Work (2014) 'Special Issue, "A World on the Move": Migration, Mobilities and Social Work', 44 (supplement 1).

Hugman, R. (2010) *Understanding International Social Work: A Critical Analysis*, Basingstoke: Palgrave Macmillan.

Lyons, K. (2006) 'Globalization and Social Work: International and Local Implications', *British Journal of Social Work*, 36, 365–80.

Yeates, N. (2012) 'Global Social Policy', in J. Baldock, L. Mitton, N. Manning and S. Vickerstaff (eds.) *Social Policy*, 4th edn, Oxford: Oxford University Press.

8 Conclusion and Bringing it All Together

The development of social work in the UK since the Second World War has been shaped by more general developments in social policy during this period. These have transformed the role of the state in terms of how, to what extent and under what conditions it provides for the welfare of its citizens. Understanding social work within this broader context helps to explain the changes which have taken place in the role of social workers, in the status, education and training of the profession, in the organization and delivery of services, and in the relationship between social workers and service users. Developments in social policy and in social work over this period are the outcome of political debate about which issues require state intervention and the appropriate role of the state in relation to its citizens, which raises questions about what citizenship means. Examining these issues in historical and comparative perspective enables us to see that current policies are only one possible response to contemporary problems, and that how these problems are framed plays a very important part in shaping responses to them. All of this underlines the political nature of social work. We hope that this book has given social work students a better understanding of this which will help them in future to find a way to carry out their role in accordance with their commitments to professional values and social justice.

The election in 1979 of a Conservative government committed to a neoliberal ideology resulted in some fundamental shifts in the role and organization of the welfare state. Neoliberalism has continued to be the dominant ideological framework shaping many of the social policies of subsequent governments. It is therefore important to see how some of its key principles have shaped welfare provision generally and social work in particular. The key changes that we have discussed in this book are the marketization of services and the increasing residualization of state-funded services, with eligibility determined by risk. Marketization has produced new problems of service fragmentation, requiring policies to promote closer working relationships between different agencies and professions. It has also changed the relationship between service users and those providing services, so that service users are increasingly conceptualized as empowered (and responsible) consumers, rather than passive clients. This is a concept much harder to apply to those whose engagement with social workers is compulsory, such as families subject to child protection proceedings or individuals who are detained under mental health legislation, or to those with lower mental capacity, such as people with learning disabilities. Here, we draw together our conclusions about the implications of marketization and residualization for social work.

For social work, marketization has meant that services once provided by social workers, or more generally by local authority social services departments, are now largely provided by a variety of private and not-for-profit agencies, while continuing to be paid for by the state. The role of social workers has, in many cases, become one of care management, determining eligibility for services and helping to assemble an appropriate package from different sources. Such outsourcing of services raises new issues about how the quality of such services is to be monitored and controlled. Services provided by the state were historically governed by an ethos of public service, and similar considerations often apply to not-for-profit organizations. Private providers are necessarily motivated by profit and this may conflict with providing appropriate training and supervision and fair pay and conditions for staff employed, in order that they can provide a good service. This is particularly true in the context of cuts to the budgets of local authorities who want to commission maximum services for the least possible cost from agencies competing for contracts. New centralized regimes of audit and inspection have been established to try to ensure that minimum standards of service quality are maintained. With some groups, such as elderly people in residential care, a very light touch has increasingly been adopted, in the hope that quality control by the profit-making organizations themselves will suffice. With other groups, such as families where there are child protection concerns, high social work staff turnover, increasing caseloads and rigid timescales, generic forms and new electronic systems, which are often unfit for purpose, increase the likelihood of poor and 'back covering' practice. Here, the paradox is that the attempt to ensure and monitor quality has actually created more problems and in some ways has reduced rather than enhanced quality.

The Thatcher/Major governments were determined to 'roll back the state', in terms both of the areas of society in which the state was involved, and of the cost to the state of its activities. Market competition was one strategy for keeping costs down, but another was to limit eligibility for services to those with no other means of obtaining them. 'Residualization' of services in this way goes against the social democratic principles which informed the post-war welfare state, and which saw state services as a collective response to need, regardless of means. This collectivist commitment is exemplified most clearly in the universal provision of free healthcare by the NHS, which is paid for out of general taxation. The success of neoliberal objections to taxation as an illegitimate interference with the liberty of individuals has made the question of increasing direct taxation almost politically impossible to voice in the UK and other neoliberal welfare regimes, such as those in Australia and the United States. In comparison, the Scandinavian countries have much higher tax regimes and more universal health, education and welfare services, which are generally supported by most of the population and lead to higher levels of interpersonal and governmental trust and less inequality.

A rapidly growing elderly population has increased the need for many forms of social care, without an associated increase in resources to meet that need, and indeed there have been substantial cuts imposed since 2010. Means testing has become increasingly widespread in the provision of adult social care. Those whose needs are deemed critical and who are unable to afford to pay for care themselves receive some limited resources. Those whose needs are deemed less critical, but who do not have the means to pay for care services which will allow them to live a life 'worth living', often do not. By contrast, those who are financially well off are generally able to buy whatever care services they choose in the private marketplace.

In both adult and children's services, risk rather than need has become the criterion for eligibility for services. In services for older adults, the risks that are prioritized are, at least partly, the risks of requiring more expensive institutional care, if support is not provided in the community. In children and family social work, limited resources have led to services being targeted almost exclusively on child protection, and the assessment of risk to children. Other issues which were, in the past, the province of social work, such as early intervention and support for families with a variety of intra-familial problems, are now provided by other agencies. They also tend to be delivered by either differently qualified or less highly qualified staff, often using standardized intervention programmes (for example, the nurse–family partnership or the Webster-Stratton parenting programmes).

Another consequence of the neoliberal belief in the market as the means to ensure the maximum economy, efficiency and effectiveness of services, was the introduction of methods of management used in the private sector. New public management was presented as an alternative to hierarchical bureaucracy (characterized as a 'command and control' model), which would promote innovation and dynamism. This has involved central government specifying performance targets for services, but leaving it to service providers at a local level to determine how to achieve these, although it is debatable how much local-level discretion and innovation are possible, given the central prescription of timescales, IT systems, forms and procedures. NPM was supposed to promote another central government policy objective – greater cooperation and partnership between agencies whose responsibilities are inter-related and overlapping. The problems faced by individuals and families with whom social workers engage inevitably involve many other services and agencies – for example, education, health, housing, the police and the justice system. If they are able to work together to resolve problems, this is likely to result in more effective and longer-lasting solutions. However, the different priorities of these agencies, combined with their distinct perspectives on the overlapping problems which they work with, create obstacles to such cooperation, which managerialist performance management can compound. Managerialism has resulted in a proliferation of systems for monitoring and measuring performance at a local level, which have introduced new time-consuming administrative burdens for front-line social workers and reduced the time they can spend working directly with service users.

One powerful criticism of social work in the post-war welfare state was that it was paternalist. Social workers used their professional expertise to make what they judged to be the most appropriate arrangements for their clients, with clients given little voice or choice about what services they received. Clients had to fit in with the services offered, rather than those services being shaped by the needs they themselves identified. Criticism of this came from both left-wing and right-wing political perspectives and from social movements representing different groups of service users. The neoliberal response to demands that the views of service users should be listened to was to transform clients into consumers, on the assumption that the new welfare service markets which were being created would have to respond to individual consumer demand in order to stay in business. Initially, this was done by social workers acting as purchasers on behalf of clients, which limited the extent to which service users could directly express their market preferences. More recently, the introduction of personal budgets, which under the 2014 Care Act are a right for all eligible social care users, has tried to give much greater direct control to individual service users. Personal budgets managed directly by service users have been empowering for many disabled adults, allowing them to make arrangements for personal care that enable much fuller social participation. However, for frail elderly adults, who constitute the majority of social care users, the responsibilities that direct management of a personal budget brings may be too difficult to exercise under conditions of fluctuating or declining health. Greater consideration needs to be given to other ways of listening to what service users want and making services responsive to individual circumstances.

Social workers work predominantly with poor individuals and families, and residualization has emphasized this. Poor families are a very diverse population, whose diversity has increased as globalization has brought about increased migration precipitated by both economic inequality and conflict across the globe. We have seen how individuals are often positioned at the intersection of several different social divisions such as 'race'/ethnicity, gender and religion, and this can result in some people suffering multiple oppression. Acknowledging the structural causes of disadvantage and exclusion suggests that social workers need to be prepared to address these as well as addressing the individual circumstances of the people with whom they work. A commitment to social justice may also mean sometimes having to challenge policies which are at odds with that professional commitment.

Social work emerged in England and Wales as a generic profession in 1970. It came out of the disparate welfare services provided by staff with a variety of levels and types of qualification, working in different departments of local government and the health service. The staff and services were brought together in a single local authority social services department. But the political and policy environment in which this new profession worked was transformed within a very short time. With this shift, the scope and nature of the work that social workers do have also undergone significant change. Repeated child protection scandals, amplified by the media into campaigns of vilification of social work, combined with the effects of neoliberal social policy and, most recently, substantial cuts in public expenditure, have precipitated repeated reforms in social work services and in professional training. This has divided practising social workers into different specialisms often located in different departments within or outside local government, changed the nature of the work undertaken and undermined the idea of social work as a single generic profession. Areas such as family support, in which social work was once the lead profession, are now no longer part of the work that social workers do. In social care, the policy pressure to work more closely with health services is in danger of subordinating social work to healthcare. This is reflected in the professional regulation of social work being taken over by the Health Professions Council, renamed the Health and Care Professions Council (HCPC). Many social work education departments, originally based within wider social science faculties in universities, are now increasingly being relocated in larger Health and Nursing departments. Within these departments, social work education often has little power because of its smaller size and disadvantaged clientele. Furthermore, it arguably has little in common with professions such as nursing, other than the fact they are both vocational professions. The appointment of two Chief Social Workers has given social work a new voice nearer to central government, but it remains to be seen how effective this will be in ensuring that social work remains a single profession with a single university-based generic professional qualification.

8.1 What can social workers do?

Seeing social work as one part of the welfare state, and thinking critically about how the problems social workers engage with come to be identified as problems, provides a wider perspective, from which it may be easier to see how social workers can convincingly assert what they have to offer. In recent years, social workers have felt they and their profession have been consistently undermined by repeated media scandals in which they have unfairly shouldered all blame. The solutions advocated by central government, such as marketization, with its claim of offering greater consumer voice and choice, higher entry standards for social work training, greater collaboration with other professions and agencies, evidence-based practice, closer auditing against centrally set performance targets, alongside a narrow focus on risk and reduced eligibility, have not resolved the problems. Furthermore, such changes have left many social workers feeling deskilled, demoralized and relatively powerless. Current practice under-uses social workers' skills and knowledge, encourages narrow, individualistic and defensive forms of working, and dissuades social workers from viewing or reflecting on their work within a wider historical, political and comparative context. Working with individuals or families always has been and should continue to be part of a social worker's role. However, even to work effectively at a micro or individual level, social workers need to be aware of how distinct political and philosophical viewpoints lead to contrasting welfare ideologies and social policies; of how social problems are differentially constructed and framed, and how this in turn results in alternative responses; of divergent understandings and responses to questions of social justice, rights, equality and difference; and finally of the importance of history and the international context which has been profoundly affected by globalization. These understandings may lead to social workers evaluating and responding to the problems they encounter and the tasks they are asked to carry out in more informed ways, which place a higher value on combating inequalities and therefore on social justice and human and citizenship rights. They need to understand that the rhetoric of 'consumer choice and voice' and of 'safeguarding' vulnerable individuals does not match the reality in terms of practice and resources, and that concepts like social justice, empowerment, and equality and difference are complex, multifaceted and contested constructs.

A good understanding of all these issues may then result in social workers being prepared to work in different ways with individuals, groups of service users and other groups – at micro, meso and macro levels – at different times. This may be done as a lone worker, as part of a professional group or in tandem with other professional groups, or may involve forming coalitions with service users or alliances with specific pressure or single issue groups, depending on the circumstances. A social worker may choose to subvert a particular guideline or policy to enhance the welfare of one or many service users, although this can never ultimately resolve resource issues in the long term. In another situation, a group of social workers may elect to challenge harmful or unfair organizational policies or practices if they can be shown to contravene certain notions of social justice or citizenship or human rights. At a more macro level, social workers could, ideally in conjunction with others, challenge the way in which a particular social problem is constructed and the solutions advocated to resolve it – for example, the inadequate resources allocated to care for the elderly and the way intergenerational conflict over resources is being encouraged in order to justify these decisions. Whether social workers originally came into the profession to do 'good work' with vulnerable or marginalized individuals or had wider aspirations of combating social injustice, and whether or not their viewpoints change during the course of their careers, they need to have the skills and knowledge to understand social work within a wider historical and global multi-level context. Social workers are, after all, 'social' workers, not teachers or healthcare workers, so they need to understand the social and the political. The international commitment in social work to human rights, social justice and working with the individual at the interface with their environment sets it apart from these other professions. These are valuable principles which social work needs to reclaim actively and defend vigorously in order to be a profession worth fighting for. The years ahead look likely to be challenging ones for social work, requiring a good critical understanding of the role of the profession within the broader welfare state, as a basis for standing up for its professional principles.

Bibliography

4Children (2014) *Sure Start Children's Centre Census 2014*, London: 4Children

Abel-Smith, B. and Townsend, P. (1965) *The Poor and the Poorest*, London: Bell

ADASS (Association of Directors of Adult Social Services) (2014) *ADASS Budget Survey Report* 2014, London: ADASS

Adler, N. (2013) 'Health Disparities: Taking on the Challenge', *Perspectives on Psychological Science*, 8: 679–681

Ahmed, M. (2007) 'Social Workers Drafted in from US to Tackle Birmingham Shortage', *Community Care*, www.communitycare.co.uk/Articles/2007/09/28/105944/social-workers-drafted-in-from-us-to-tackle-birmingham.htm

Ahmed, S. (2014) 'Widespread Sexual Abuse in Rotherham Has Caused Outrage – but Little Action', *The Guardian*, 6 October

Alcock, P. (2006) *Understanding Poverty*, Basingstoke: Palgrave Macmillan

Aldgate, J. and Tunstill, J. (1995) *Making Sense of Section 17*, London: HMSO

Alibhai-Brown, Y. (2001) *Mixed Feelings: The Complex Lives of Mixed-Race Britons*, London: The Women's Press

All Party Parliamentary Group (APPG) on Social Work (2013) *Inquiry into the State of Social Work Report*, London: BASW

Allen, G. (2011) *Early Intervention: The Next Steps*, London: Cabinet Office

Andenaes, A. (2005) 'Neutral Claims – Gendered Meanings: Parenthood and Developmental Psychology in a Modern Welfare State', *Feminism and Psychology*, 15(2): 209–26

Anderson, E. (1999) 'What is the Point of Equality?' *Ethics*, 109: 287–337

Annesley, C., Gains, F. and Rummery, K. (2007) *Women and New Labour*, Bristol: Policy Press

Anthias, F. (2014) 'The Intersection of Class, Gender, Sexuality and "Race": The Political Economy of Gendered Violence', *International Journal of Politics, Culture and Society*, 27(2): 153–71

Arendt, H. (1963) *Eichmann in Jerusalem: A Report on the Banality of Evil*, London: Penguin

Arts, W. and Gelissen, J. (2002) 'Three Worlds of Welfare Capitalism or More? A State-of-the-Art Report', *Journal of European Social Policy*, 12(2): 137–58

Ash, A. (2013) 'A Cognitive Mask? Camouflaging Dilemmas in Street Level Policy Implementation to Safeguard Older People from Abuse', *British Journal of Social Work*, 43: 99–115

Back, L. (1996) *New Ethnicities and Urban Culture: Racism and Multiculture in Young Lives*, London: UCL Press

Bailey, D. and Liyanage, L. (2012) 'The Role of the Mental Health Social Worker: Political Pawns in the Reconfiguration of Adult Health and Social Care', *British Journal of Social Work*, 42: 1113–31

Bailey, R. and Brake, M. (eds.) (1975) *Radical Social Work*, London: Edward Arnold

Baldock, J., Mitton, L., Manning, N. and Vickerstaff, S. (eds.) (2012) *Social Policy*, 4th edition, Oxford: Oxford University Press

Balloch, S., McLean, R. and Fisher, M. (1999) *Social Services: Working under Pressure*, Bristol: Policy Press

Bambra, C., Netuveli, G. and Eikemo, T. A. (2010) 'Welfare State Regime Life Courses: The Development of Western European Welfare State Regimes and Age Related Patterns of Educational Inequalities in Self-Reported Health', *International Journal of Health Services*, 40(3): 399–420

Banks, S. (2007) 'Between Equity and Empathy: Social Professions and the New Accountability', *Social Work and Society*, Festschrift Walter Lorenz: 11–22

175

Barclay, P. (1982) *Social Workers: Their Roles and Tasks,* London: Bedford Square Press

Barnes, H., Green, L. and Hopton, J. (2007) 'Social Work Theory, Research, Policy and Practice – Challenges and Opportunities in Health and Social Care Integration in the UK', *Health and Social Care in the Community*, 15(3): 191–4

Barnes, J., Cheng, H., Howden, B., et al. (2006) *Changes in the Characteristics of SSLP Areas between 2000/01 and 2003/04*, NESS/2006/SF/016, London: DfES

BASW (2012a) *The Code of Ethics for Social Work: Statement of Principles*, Birmingham: BASW

BASW (2012b) *The State of Social Work 2012*, May, http://cdn.basw.co.uk/upload/basw_112311-8.pdf

BASW (2015a) 'TCSW Announces its Decision Regarding the Transfer of Resources, including Professional Capabilities Framework, to BASW', press release, 21 August, https://www.basw.co.uk/news/article/?id=1014

BASW (2015b) *Implementation Proposals for Teaching Partnerships: BASW England Views*, http://cdn.basw.co.uk/upload/basw_123206-5.pdf

Batson, C. D., Polycarpou, M. P., Harmon-Jones, E., Inhoff, H. J., Mitchener, E. C., Bednar, L. L., Klein, T. R. and Highberger, L. (1997) 'Empathy and Attitudes: Can Feeling for a Member of a Stigmatized Group Improve Feelings towards the Group?' *Journal of Personality and Social Psychology*, 72: 105–18

Bauman, Z. (1989) *Modernity and the Holocaust*. Ithaca, NY: Cornell University Press

Bauman, Z. (2004) *Work, Consumerism and the New Poor*, 2nd edition, Maidenhead: Open University Press

Baynes, P. and Holland, S. (2012) 'Social Work with Violent Men: A Child Protection File Study in an English Local Authority', *Child Abuse Review*, 21(1): 53–65

Beck, U. (1992) *Risk Society: Towards a New Modernity*, London: Sage

Becker, H. (1963) *Outsiders: Studies on the Sociology of Deviance*, New York: Free Press

Beckett, K. (1996) 'Culture and the Case of Child Sexual Abuse', *Social Problems*, 43: 57–76

Beresford, P. and Croft, S. (2004) 'Service Users and Practitioners Reunited: The Key Component for Social Work Reform', *British Journal of Social Work*, 34(1): 53–68

Berger, P. and Luckmann, T. (1967) *The Social Construction of Reality*, New York: Anchor

Bernard, C. and Campbell, J. (2014) 'Racism, Sectarianism and Social Work' in C. Cocker and T. Hafford-Letchfield (eds.) *Rethinking Anti-Discriminatory and Anti-Oppressive Theories for Social Work Practice,* Basingstoke: Palgrave Macmillan

Best, J. (1995) 'Constructionism in Context' in J. Best (ed.) *Images of Issues: Typifying Contemporary Social Problems*, 2nd edition, New York: Aldine de Gruyter

Best, J. and Harris, S. R. (eds.) (2012) *Making Sense of Social Problems: New Images, New Issues*, Boulder, CO: Lynne Rienner Publishers

Beveridge, W. (1942) *Report of the Inter-departmental Committee on Social Insurance and Allied Services*, London: HMSO

Bilton, K. (1979) 'Origins, Progress and Future' in J. Cypher (ed.) *Seebohm across Three Decades.* Birmingham: BASW Publications

Birmingham Safeguarding Children Board (2013) *Serious Case Review in Respect of the Death of Keanu Williams*, www.lscbbirmingham.org.uk/images/BSCB2010-11-4.pdf

Birrell, D. (2006) 'The Disintegration of Local Authority Social Services Departments', *Local Government Studies*, 32(2): 139–51

Blackburn, R. M. (1999) 'Understanding Social Inequality', *International Journal of Sociology and Social Policy*, 19(9–11): 1–21

Bloch, A., Neal, S. and Solomos, J. (2013) *Race, Multiculture and Social Policy,* Basingstoke: Palgrave Macmillan

Blum, K. (2004) 'Stereotypes and Stereotyping: A Moral Analysis', *Philosophical Papers*, 35(3): 251–289

Bochel, H. (2012) 'The Conservative Tradition' in P. Alcock, M. May and S. Wright (eds.) *The Student's Companion to Social Policy*, 4th edition, Chichester: John Wiley & Sons

Bochel, H., Bochel, C., Page, R. and Sykes, R. (2009) *Social Policy: Themes, Issues and Debates*, 2nd edition, Harlow: Pearson

Boddy, J. (2013) 'European Perspectives on Parenting and Family Support' in J. McCarthy, J. Ribbens, C-A. Hooper and V. Gillies (eds.) *Family Troubles? Exploring Changes and Challenges in the Family Lives of Children and Young People*, Bristol: Policy Press

Boddy, J. and Statham, J. (2009) *European Perspectives on Social Work: Models of Education and Professional Roles*, London: Thomas Coram Research Unit

Boesten, J. (2010) 'Inequality, Normative Violence and Liveable Life: Judith Butler and Peruvian Reality', POLIS working paper 1 (2010), University of Leeds, www.polis.leeds.ac.uk/assets/files/research/working-papers/working-paper-no1-2010.pdf

Bourdieu, P. (1986) 'The Forms of Capital' in J. Richardson (ed.) *Handbook of Theory and Research for the Sociology of Education*, New York: Greenwood

Bradshaw, J. (1972) 'The Taxonomy of Social Need' in G. McLachlan (ed.) *Problems and Progress in Medical Care*, Oxford: Oxford University Press

Bradshaw, J. (2012) 'Child Well-being in the 2000s', in Child Poverty Action Group (ed.) *Ending Child Poverty by 2020: Progress Made and Lessons Learned,* London: CPAG

Bradshaw, J., Ditch, J., Holmes, H. and Whiteford, P. (1993) *Support for Children: A Comparison of Arrangements in Fifteen Countries*, Department of Social Security Research Report 21, London: HMSO

Brennan, D., Cass, B., Himmelweit, S. and Szebehely, M. (2012) 'The Marketization of Care: rationales and consequences in Nordic and liberal care regimes', *Journal of European Social Policy*, 22(4): 377–91

Brewer, C. and Lait, J. (1980) *Can Social Work Survive?* Michigan: Temple Smith

Broadhurst, K., Hall, C., Wastell, D., White, S. and Pithouse, A. (2010a) 'Risk, Instrumentalism and the Humane Project in Social Work: Identifying the Informal Logics of Risk Management in Children's Statutory Services', *British Journal of Social Work*, 40,: 1046–64

Broadhurst, K., Wastell, D., White, S., Hall, C., Peckover, S., Thompson, K., Pithouse, A. and Davey, D. (2010b) '"Performing Initial Assessment": Identifying the Latent Conditions for Error at the Front-Door of Local Authority Children's Services', *British Journal of Social Work*, 40: 352–79

Brodie, J. M. (2007) 'Reforming Social Justice in Neoliberal Times', *Studies in Social Justice*, 1: 93–107

Brown, H. and Stein, J. (1998) 'Implementing Adult Protection Procedures in Kent and East Sussex', *Journal of Social Policy*, 27(3): 371–96

Brown, K., Bates, N. and Keen, S. (2007) *Supporting the Continuing Professional Development Needs of Internationally Qualified Social Workers*, Leeds: Skills for Care

Brunsma, D. L. and Rockquemore, K. A. (2002) 'What Does "Black" Mean? Exploring the Epistemological Stranglehold of Racial Categorization', *Critical Sociology*, 28(1): 101–21

Burchardt, T. and Hills, J. (1999) 'Public Expenditure and the Public/Private Mix' in M. Powell (ed.) *New Labour, New Welfare State*, Bristol: Policy Press

Butler, I. and Drakeford, M. (2001) 'Which Blair Project? Communitarianism, Social Authoritarianism and Social Work', *Journal of Social Work*, 1(1): 7–19

Byrne, B. (2012) 'A Local Welcome? Narrations of Nation and Belonging in Citizenship Ceremonies', *Citizenship Studies,* 16(3–4): 531–44

Cafcass (2014) 'Care Applications in January 2014', https://www.cafcass.gov.uk/news/2014/february/january-2014-care-demand-statistics.aspx

Calhoun, C. (2003) 'Belonging in the Cosmopolitan Imaginary', *Ethnicities*, 3(4): 531–53

Campbell, B. (1988) *Unofficial Secrets: Child Abuse – the Cleveland Case*, London: Virago

Canvin, K., Jones, C., Marttila, A., Burström, B. and Whitehead, M. (2007) 'Can I Risk Using Public Services? Perceived Consequences of Seeking Help and Health Care among Households Living in Poverty: Qualitative Study', *Journal of Epidemiology and Community Health*, 61(11): 984–89

Carey, M. (2003) 'Anatomy of a Care Manager', *Work, Employment and Society*, 17(1): 121–35

Carey, M. (2008) 'Everything Must Go? The Privatisation of State Social Work', *British Journal of Social Work*, 38(5): 918–35

Carey, M. (2010) 'Critical Commentary: Happy Shopper? The Problem with Service User and Carer Participation', *British Journal of Social Work*, 39: 179–88

Carey, M. (2013) '"More Than This?" Some Ethical Doubts and Possibilities Regarding Service User and Carer Participation in Social Work' in M. Carey and L. Green (eds.) *Practical Social Work Ethics: Complex Dilemmas Within Applied Social Care*, Farnham: Ashgate

Carey, M. and Foster, V. (2011) 'Introducing "Deviant" Social Work: Contextualising the Limits of Radical Social Work whilst Understanding (Fragmented) Resistance within the Social Work Labour Process', *British Journal of Social Work*, 41: 576–93

Carr, S. (2014) 'Critical Perspectives on Intersectionality' in C. Cocker and T. Hafford-Letchfield (eds.) *Rethinking Anti-Discriminatory and Anti-Oppressive Theories for Social Work Practice*, Basingstoke: Palgrave Macmillan

Carson, G. (2010) 'Social Work Jobs Overseas and How to Get Them', *Community Care*, 3 September

Carvel, J. (2007) 'Public Sector Targets to be Scrapped', *The Guardian*, 18 July

Castles, F. G., Leibfried, S., Lewis, J., Obinger, H. and Pierson, C. (eds.) (2010) *The Oxford Handbook of the Welfare State*, Oxford: Oxford University Press

CCETSW (Central Council for Education and Training in Social Work) (1989) *Rules and Requirements for the Diploma in Social Work (Paper 30)*, London: CCETSW

CCETSW (Central Council for Education and Training in Social Work) (1991) *One Step Towards Racial Justice (the Teaching of Anti-racist Social Work in Diploma in Social Work Programmes)*, London: CCETSW.

Centre for Social Justice (2006) *The State of the Nation Report: Fractured Families*, London: Centre for Social Justice

Chalmers, I. (2005) 'If Evidence-informed Policy Works in Practice Does it Matter if it Doesn't Work in Theory?' *Evidence and Policy*, 1(2): 227–42

Chambliss, W. J. (1973) 'The Saints and the Roughnecks', *Society*, 11(1): (Nov./Dec.): 24–31

Charles, N. and Mackay, F. (2013) 'Feminist Politics and Framing Contests: Domestic Violence Policy in Scotland and Wales', *Critical Social Policy*, 33(4): 593–615

Charlton, J. I. (1998) *Nothing About Us without Us: Disability, Oppression and Empowerment*, Berkeley: University of California Press

Chief Secretary to the Treasury (2003) *Every Child Matters*, Cm. 5860, Norwich: TSO

Children's Society (2012) *A Briefing from The Children's Society Highlighting the Gap between Asylum Support and Mainstream Benefits*, www.childrenssociety.org.uk/sites/default/files/tcs/a_brief ing_from_the_childrens_society_on_asylum_support.pdf

Christensen, K. and Pilling, D. (2014) 'Policies of Personalisation in Norway and England: On the Impact of Political Context', *Journal of Social Policy*, 43(3): 479–96

Churchill, H. (2013) 'Retrenchment and Restructuring: Family Support and Children's Services under the Coalition', *Journal of Children's Services*, 8(3): 209–22

Claireborne, N. (2004) 'Presence of Social Workers in Nongovernment Organizations', *Social Work*, 49(2): 207–18

Clapton, G., Cree, V. and Smith, M. (2013) 'Critical Commentary: Moral Panics, Claims-Making and Child Protection in the UK', *British Journal of Social Work*, 43: 803–12

Clarke, J. (2004) 'Dissolving the Public Realm? The Logics and Limits of Neo-Liberalism', *Journal of Social Policy*, 33(1): 27–48

Clarke, J. (2005) 'New Labour's Citizens: Activated, Empowered, Responsibilised, Abandoned?' *Critical Social Policy*, 25(4): 227–463

Clarke, J. and Newman, J. (1993) 'The Right to Manage: A Second Managerial Revolution', *Cultural Studies*, 7: 427–41

Clarke, J. and Newman, J. (1997) *The Managerial State*, London: Sage

Clarke, J. and Newman, J. (2012) 'The Alchemy of Austerity', *Critical Social Policy*, 32(3): 299–319

Clarke, K. (2006) 'Childhood, Parenting and Early Intervention: A Critical Examination of the Sure Start National Programme', *Critical Social Policy*, 26(4): 699–721

Clinard, M. B. and Quinney, R. (1967) *Criminal Behavior Systems: A Typology*, New York: Rinehart Winston

Cocker, C. and Hafford-Letchfield, T. (eds.) (2014) *Rethinking Anti-Discriminatory and Anti-Oppressive Theories for Social Work Practice*, Basingstoke: Palgrave Macmillan

Cohen, G. A. (2000) *If You're an Egalitarian, How Come You're So Rich?* Cambridge, MA: Harvard University Press

Cohen, S. (1972) *Folk Devils and Moral Panics*, St Albans: Paladin

Cohen, S. (2002) *Folk Devils and Moral Panics*, 30th Anniversary edition, London: Routledge

Coleman, J. S. (1988) 'Social Capital in the Creation of Human Capital', *American Journal of Sociology*, 94(Supplement: Organizations and Institutions): s95–s120

Collins, S. and Wilkie, L. (2010) 'Anti-oppressive Practice and Social Work Students' Portfolios in Scotland', *Social Work Education*, 27 (7): 760–77

Commission on Dignity in Care (2012) *Delivering Dignity*, London: LGA, NHS Confederation and Age UK

Community Care (2004) 'Increase in Overseas Social Workers Poses Ethical Questions for Councils', www.communitycare.co.uk/2004/02/05/increase-in-overseas-social-workers-poses-ethical-questions-for-councils

Corbett, S. and Walker, A. (2013) 'The Big Society: Rediscovery of "the Social" or Rhetorical Fig-Leaf for Neo-Liberalism?', *Critical Social Policy*, 33(3): 451–72

Corrigan, P. and Leonard, P. (1978) *Social Work Practice under Capitalism: A Marxist Approach*, London: Macmillan

Cousins, M. (2005) *European Welfare States: Comparative Perspectives*, London: Sage

CQC (Care Quality Commission) (2012) *The State of Health Care and Adult Social Care in England in 2011/2012*, London: The Stationery Office

CQC (Care Quality Commission) (2013a) *Time to Listen: In Care Homes – Dignity and Nutrition Inspection Programme – National Overview*, London: CQC

CQC (Care Quality Commission) (2013b) *Not Just a Number, Home Care Inspection Programme, National Overview*, London: CQC

Cree, V. E. (2008) 'Social Work and Society' in M. Davies (ed.) *The Blackwell Companion to Social Work*, 3rd edition, Oxford: Blackwell

Cressey, D. R. (1978) 'A Theory of Differential Association' in E. H Sutherland and D. R. Cressey *Criminology*, 10th edition, Philadelphia: Lippincott

Croisdale-Appleby, D. (2014) *Re-visioning Social Work Education: An Independent Review*, https://www.gov.uk/government/publications/social-work-education-review

Cuban, S. (2008) 'Home/Work: The Roles of Education, Literacy, and Learning in the Networks and Mobility of Professional Women Migrant Carers in Cumbria', *Ethnography and Education*, 3(1): 81–96

Cunningham, S. and Tomlinson, J. (2005) 'Starve Them Out: Does Every Child Really Matter? A Commentary on Section 9 of the Asylum and Immigration (Treatment of Claimants etc.) Act, 2004', *Critical Social Policy*, 25(2): 235–75

Dalrymple, J. and Burke, B. (2006) *Anti Oppressive Practice, Social Care and the Law*, 2nd edition, Maidenhead: McGraw Hill / Open University Press

Daly, G. (2012) 'Citizenship, Choice and Care: An Examination of the Promotion of Choice in the Provision of Adult Social Care', *Research, Policy and Planning*, 29(3): 179–89

Daniel, B., Featherstone, B., Hooper, C. A. and Scourfield, J. (2005) 'Why Gender Matters for *Every Child Matters*', *British Journal of Social Work*, 35(8): 1343–55

Dannefer, D. (2003) 'Cumulative Advantage/Disadvantage and the Life Course: Cross-Fertilizing Age and Social Science Theory', *The Journals of Gerontology*, 58(6): S327

Davies, H., Nutley, S. and Smith, P. (eds.) (2000) *What Works? Evidence-based Policy and Practice in Public Services*, Bristol: Policy Press

Davis, A. (2008) *Celebrating 100 Years of Social Work*, Birmingham: University of Birmingham, www.birmingham.ac.uk/Documents/college-socialsciences/social-policy/IASS/100-years-of-social-work.pdf

DCLG (2014) *Troubled Families Leadership Statement 2014*, London: Public Health England

DCLG Troubled Families website, https://www.gov.uk/government/policies/helping-troubled-families-turn-their-lives-around

Dean, H. (2010) *Understanding Human Need*, Bristol: Policy Press

Dean, H. (2012) 'Socialist Perspectives' in P. Alcock, M. May and S. Wright (eds.) *The Student's Companion to Social Policy*, 4th edition, Chichester: John Wiley & Sons

Deeming, C. and Hayes, D. (2012) 'Worlds of Welfare Capitalism and Wellbeing: A Multilevel Analysis', *Journal of Social Policy*, 41(4): 811–29

Deliovsky, K. and Kitossa, T. (2013) 'Beyond Black and White: When Going Beyond May Take us Out of Bounds', *Journal of Black Studies*, 44(2): 158–81

Denney, D. (1998) *Social Policy and Social Work*, Oxford: Oxford University Press

Department for Education and Skills (DfES) (2004) *Every Child Matters: Change for Children*, Nottingham: DfES

Department of Health (DH) (1998) *Quality Protects: A Framework for Action*, Wetherby: DH

Department of Health (DH) (2000) *Framework for the Assessment of Children in Need and their Families*, London: The Stationery Office

Department of Health (DH) (2002) *Requirements for Social Work Training*, London: TSO

Department of Health (DH) (2005) *Independence, Well-being and Choice*, Cm 6499, London: TSO

Department of Health (DH) (2006) *Our Health, Our Care, Our Say: A New Direction for Community Services*, Cm 6737, London: TSO

Department of Health (DH) (2011) *Enabling Excellence: Autonomy and Accountability for Healthcare Workers, Social Workers and Social Care Workers*, Cm 8008, London: The Stationery Office

Department of Health (DH) (2014) 'Care Bill becomes Care Act', speech by Norman Lamb, https://www.gov.uk/government/speeches/care-bill-becomes-care-act-2014

Department of Health and Social Security (DHSS) (1988) *Working Together: A Guide to Inter-Agency Co-operation for the Protection of Children from Abuse*, London: HMSO

Deutsch, M. (2006).'A Framework for Thinking about Oppression and its Change', *Social Justice Research*, 19(1): 7–41

DfE (2011) *Monitoring and Evaluation of Family Intervention Services and Projects between February 2007 and March 2011*, Research Brief DFE-RB174, London: DfE, https://www.gov.uk/government/uploads/system/uploads/attachment_data/file/198144/DfE-RB174.pdf

DfE (2013a) 'Characteristics of Children in Need in England', statistical release, https://www.gov.uk/government/uploads/system/uploads/attachment_data/file/254084/SFR45-2013_Text.pdf

DfE (2013b) 'Office of Chief Social Worker: New Appointees Start', press release 13 October, https://www.gov.uk/government/news/office-of-the-chief-social-worker-new-appointees-start

DfE (2013c) 'Supporting Social Workers to Provide Help and Protection to Children', https://www.gov.uk/government/policies/supporting-social-workers-to-provide-help-and-protection-to-children/supporting-pages/canparent-trial

DfE (2015) *Teaching Partnerships 2015–16: Invitation to Express Interest*, London: DfE Social Work Reform Unit

Dickens, J. (2010) *Social Work and Social Policy: An Introduction*, London: Routledge

Dickens, J. (2011) 'Social Work in England at a Watershed – As Always: From the Seebohm Report to the Social Work Task Force', *British Journal of Social Work*, 41(2): 22–39

Digby, A. (1989) *British Welfare Policy: Workhouse to Workfare*, London: Faber and Faber

Dingwall, R., Eekelaar, J. M. and Murray, T. (1984) 'Childhood as a Social Problem: A Survey of the History of Legal Regulation', *Journal of Law and Society*, 11(2): 207–32

Dixon, J., Biehal, N., Green, J., Sinclair, I., Kay, C. and Parry E. (2014) 'Trials and Tribulations: Challenges and Prospects for Randomised Controlled Trials of Social Work with Children', *British Journal of Social Work*, 44: 1563–81

Dominelli, D. (2010) *Social Work in a Globalizing World*, Cambridge: Polity

Dominelli, L. (2002) *Anti-oppressive Social Work Theory and Practice*, Basingstoke: Palgrave Macmillan

Donzelot, J. (1980) *The Policing of Families*, London: Hutchison

Dorkenoo, E., Morison, L. and MacFarlane, A. (2007) *A Statistical Study to Estimate the Prevalence of Female Genital Mutilation in England and Wales*, London: FORWARD

Dowling, G., Powell, M. and Glendinning, C. (2004) 'Conceptualising Successful Partnerships', *Health and Social Care in the Community*, 12(4): 309–317

Driver, S. and Martell, L. (2000) 'Left, Right and the Third Way', *Policy & Politics* 28(2): 147–61

Duncan, S. (2007) 'What's the Problem with Teenage Parents? And What's the Problem with Policy?' *Critical Social Policy*, 27(3): 307–34

Dunleavy, P., Gamble, A., Heffernan, R. and Peele, G. (eds.) (2003) *Developments in British Politics 7*, Basingstoke: Palgrave Macmillan

Dunleavy, P., Margetts, H., Bastow, S. and Tinkler, J. (2006) 'New Public Management Is Dead–Long Live Digital-Era Governance', *Journal of Public Administration Research and Theory*, 16(3): 467–94

Dworkin, R. (1985) *A Matter of Principle*, Cambridge, MA: Harvard University Press

Dworkin, R. (2000) *Sovereign Virtue: The Theory and Practice of Equality*, Cambridge, MA: Harvard University Press

Dwyer, P. (2010) *Understanding Social Citizenship*, 2nd edition, Bristol: Policy Press

The Economist (2014) 'Employment Law: Faith in the Workplace', 12 April, www.economist.com/news/business/21600694-managers-are-having-accommodate-workers-religious-beliefs-while-taking-care-expressing

Eden, L., Bowdler, D. and Thorpe, R. (2002) 'Fertile work', *Community Care*, 1415: 38–9

Eilers, K. (2003) 'Social Policy and Social Work in 1928' in S. Hering and B. Waaldijk (eds.) *History of Social Work in Europe (1900–1960): Female Pioneers and their Influence on the Development of International Social Work Organizations*, Opladen: Leske and Budricj

Elliot, L. (2008) 'Up Up Up: Child Poverty, Pensioner Poverty, Inequality', *The Guardian*, 11 June

Ellis, K. and Davis, A. (2001) 'Managing the Body: Competing Approaches to Risk Assessment in Community Care' in R. Edwards and J. Glover (eds.) *Risk and Citizenship: Key Issues in Welfare*, London: Routledge

Ellis, K., Davis, A. and Rummery, K. (1999) 'Needs Assessment, Street-level Bureaucracy and the New Community Care', *Social Policy and Administration*, 33(3): 252–80

Ellison, N. (2012) 'Neo-liberalism' in P. Alcock, M. May and S. Wright (eds.) *The Student's Companion to Social Policy*, 4th edition, Chichester: John Wiley & Sons

Elston, T. (2014) 'Not So "Arm's Length": Reinterpreting Agencies in UK Central Government', *Public Administration*, 92(2): 458–76

Engebrigsten, A. (2003) 'The Child's – or the State's – Best Interests? An Examination of the Ways Immigration Officials Work with Unaccompanied Asylum Seeking Minors in England and Norway', *Child and Family Social Work*, 8(3): 191–200

EHRC (Equality and Human Rights Commission) (2011) *Close to Home: An Inquiry into Older People and Human Rights in Home Care*, London: EHRC

EHRC (Equality and Human Rights Commission) (2012) *Making Fair Financial Decisions: An Assessment of HM Treasury's 2010 Spending Review Conducted Under Section 31 of the 2006 Equality Act*, www.equalityhumanrights.com/sites/default/files/documents/Inquiries/s31_final.pdf

Esping-Andersen, G. (1990) *The Three Worlds of Welfare Capitalism*, Princeton, NJ: Princeton University Press

Esping-Andersen, G. and Myles, J. (2011) 'Economic Inequality and the Welfare State' in B. Nolan., W. Salverda and T. M. Smeeding (eds.) *The Oxford Handbook of Economic Inequality*, Oxford: Oxford University Press

Etzioni, A. (1998) *The Essential Communitarian Reader*, Lanham, MD: Rowman and Littlefield

Evaluation of the Social Work Degree Qualification in England Team (2008) *Evaluation of the New Social Work Degree Qualification in England*, Final Report to the Department of Health, Glasgow School of Social Work, Sharpe Research and Social Care Workforce Research Unit, King's College London, www.dh.gov.uk/en/Publicationsandstatistics/Publications/Publications PolicyAndGuidance/DH_086079

Evans, S., Huxley, P. and Munroe, M. (2006) 'International Recruitment of Social Care Workers and Social Workers: Illustrations from the UK', *Hong Kong Journal of Social Work*, 40(1–2): 93–110

Evans, T. (2011) 'Professionals, Managers and Discretion: Critiquing Street Level Bureaucracy', *British Journal of Social Work*, 41: 368–86

Evans, T. (2013) 'Organizational Rules and Discretion in Adult Social Work', *British Journal of Social Work*, 43: 739–58

Evans, T. and Hardy, M. (2010) *Evidence and Knowledge for Practice*, Cambridge: Polity

Evans, T. and Harris, J. (2004) 'Street-Level Bureaucracy, Social Work and the (Exaggerated) Death of Discretion', *British Journal of Social Work*, 34: 871–95

Experian (2006) *Attracting Talent: Final Report, Multi Client Study*, London: Experian

Farrell, C. M. (2010) 'Citizen and Consumer Involvement in UK Public Services', *International Journal of Consumer Services*, 34: 503–7

Faulconbridge, J. R. and Muzio, D. (2012) 'Professions in a Globalizing World: Towards a Transnational Sociology of the Professions', *International Sociology*, 27(1): 136–52

Featherstone, B. and Fraser, C. (2012) 'Working with Fathers around Domestic Violence: Contemporary Debates', *Child Abuse Review*, 21(4): 255–63

Featherstone, B., Broadhurst, K. and Holt, K. (2012) 'Thinking Systemically, Thinking Politically: Building Strong Partnerships with Children and Their Families in the Context of Rising Inequality', *British Journal of Social Work*, 42: 618–33

Featherstone, B., White, S. and Morris, K. (2014) *Re-Imagining Child Protection: Towards Humane Social Work with Families*, Bristol: Policy Press

Ferguson, H. (2007) 'Abused and Looked After Children as "Moral Dirt": Child Abuse and Institutional Care in Historical Perspective', *Journal of Social Policy*, 38(1): 18–33

Ferguson, H. (2011) *Child Protection Practice*, Basingstoke: Palgrave Macmillan

Ferguson, I. (2008) *Reclaiming Social Work: Challenging Neo-liberalism and Promoting Social Justice*, London: Sage

Ferguson, I. and Woodward, R. (2009) *Radical Social Work in Practice: Making a Difference*, Bristol: Policy Press

Field, F. (2010) *The Foundation Years: Preventing Poor Children Becoming Poor Adults*, London: Cabinet Office

Fine, M. and Teram, E. (2013) 'Overt and Covert Ways of Responding to Moral Injustices in Social Work Practice: Heroes and Mild-Mannered Social Work Bipeds', *British Journal of Social Work*, 43: 1312–129

Fink, J. and Lomax, H. (2012) 'Inequalities, Images and Insights for Policy and Research', *Critical Social Policy*, 32(1): 3–10

Firth, R. (2004) 'Enabling Social Workers to Work Abroad', paper presented at the IASSW/IFSW Conference, Adelaide, Australia

Fish, J. (2008) 'Far from Mundane: Theorising Heterosexism for Social Work Practice', *Social Work Education*, 27(2): 182–93

Flavin, P., Pacek, A. C. and Radcliff, B. (2011) 'State Intervention and Subjective Well-Being in Advanced Industrial Democracies', *Politics and Policy*, 39(2): 251–69

Forsythe, B. and Jordan, B. (2002) 'The Victorian Ethical Foundations of Social Work in England: Continuity and Contradiction', *British Journal of Social Work*, 32: 847–62

Foster, P. and Wilding, P. (2000) 'Whither Welfare Professionalism', *Social Policy and Administration*, 34(2): 143–59

France, A., Freiberg, K. and Homel, R. (2010) 'Beyond Risk Factors: Towards a Holistic Prevention Paradigm for Children and Young People', *British Journal of Social Work*, 40: 1192–210

Fraser, N. (2008) *Scales of Justice: Reimagining Political Space in a Globalizing World*, Cambridge: Polity

Fraser, N. and Honneth, A. (2003) *Redistribution or Recognition: A Political–Philosophical Exchange*, London: Verso

Freire, P. (2000) *Pedagogy of the Oppressed*, 30th anniversary edition, New York: Continuum International Publishing Group

Frost, P. and Hoggett, P. (2008) 'Human Agency and Social Suffering', *Critical Social Policy*, 28(4): 438–60

Fuller, R. C. and Myers, R. (1941) 'Some Aspects of a Theory of Social Problems', *American Sociological Review*, 24–32

Fyson, R. and Kitson, D. (2010) 'Human Rights and Social Wrongs: Issues in Safeguarding Adults with Learning Disabilities', *Practice: Social Work in Action*, 22(5): 309–20

Gaine, C. and Gaylard, D. (2010) 'Equality, Difference and Diversity' in C. Gaine (ed.) *Equality and Diversity in Social Work Practice*, Exeter: Learning Matters

Garfinkel, H. (1967) *Studies in Ethnomethodology*, Englewood Cliffs, NJ: Prentice Hall

Garrett, P. M. (1998) 'Notes from the Diaspora: Anti-Discriminatory Social Work Practice, Irish People and the Practice Curriculum', *Social Work Education*, 17(4): 435–48

Garrett, P. M. (2005) '"Social Work's Electronic Turn": Notes on the Deployment of Information and Communication Technologies in Social Work with Children and Families', *Critical Social Policy*, 35(4): 529–53

Garrett, P. M. (2006) 'Protecting Children in a Globalized World: '"Race" and "Place" in the Laming Report on the Death of Victoria Climbié', *Journal of Social Work*, 6(3): 315–36

Gentleman, A. (2009) 'Majority of Poor Children Have at Least One Parent in Work, says Study', *The Guardian*, 18 February

George, V. and Page, R. (eds.) (1995) *Modern Thinkers on Welfare*, Hemel Hempstead: Prentice Hall / Harvester Wheatsheaf

George, V. and Wilding, P. (1994) *Welfare and Ideology*, Hemel Hempstead: Harvester Wheatsheaf

Giddens, A. (1991) *Modernity and Self-Identity: Self and Society in the Late Modern Age*, Cambridge: Polity

Giddens, A. (1998) *The Third Way: The Renewal of Social Democracy*, Cambridge: Polity

Giddens, A. (1999) 'Risk and Responsibility', *Modern Law Review*, 62(1): 1–10

Gilligan, P. (2007) 'Well Motivated Reformists or Nascent Radicals: How Do Applicants to the Degree in Social Work See Social Problems, Their Origins and Solutions?' *British Journal of Social Work*, 37: 735–60

Glasby, J. (2014) 'The Controversies of Choice and Control: Why Some People Might Be Hostile to English Social Care Reforms', *British Journal of Social Work*, 44(2): 252–66

Glendinning, C. (2008) 'Increasing Choice and Control for Older and Disabled People: A Critical Review of New Developments in England', *Social Policy and Administration*, 42(5): 451–69

Glendinning, C. (2012) 'Home Care in England: Markets in the Context of Under-funding', *Health and Social Care in the Community*, 20(3): 292–99

Goldson, B. (2002) 'New Labour, Social Justice and Children: Political Calculation and the Deserving-Undeserving Schism', *The British Journal of Social Work*, 32(6): 683–95

Goodin, R., Headey, B., Muffels, R. and Dirven, H.-J. (1999) *The Real Worlds of Welfare Capitalism*, Cambridge: Cambridge University Press

Gove, W. R. (1975) 'The Labelling Theory of Mental Illness: A Reply to Scheff', *American Sociological Review*, 40(2): 242–8

Graham, M. and Schiele, J. H. (2010) 'Equality-of-Oppressions and Anti-Discriminatory Models in Social Work: Reflections from the USA and UK', *European Journal of Social Work*, 13(2): 231–44

Gray, M. and McDonald, C. (2006) 'Pursuing Good Practice: The Limits of Evidence Based Practice', *Journal of Social Work*, 6(1): 7–20

Green, L. (1999) *Getting the Balance Right: A Cross Comparative Analysis of the Balance between Legal Intervention and Therapeutic Support Systems in Relation to Responses to Child Sexual Abuse in England, The Netherlands and Belgium*, A Report prepared for the European Commission, November 1999, under the Daphne Initiative, project 98/205

Green, L. (2005) 'Theorising Sexuality, Sexual Abuse and Residential Children's Homes: Adding Gender to the Equation', *British Journal of Social Work*, 35(4): 453–81

Green, L. (2006) 'Pariah Profession, Debased Discipline: An Analysis of Social Work's Low Academic Status and the Possibilities for Change', *Social Work Education*, 25(3): 245–64

Green, L. and Featherstone, B. (2014) 'Judith Butler, Power and Social Work' in C. Cocker and T. Hafford-Letchfield (eds.) *Rethinking Anti-Discriminatory and Anti-Oppressive Theories for Social Work Practice*, Basingstoke: Palgrave Macmillan

Green, L. and Grant, V. (2008) 'Gagged Grief and Beleaguered Bereavements? An Analysis of

Multidisciplinary Theory Relating to Same Sex Partnership Bereavement', *Sexualities*, 11(3): 275–300

Green, L. and Masson, H. (2002) 'Peer Sexual Abuse in Residential Care: Issues of Risk and Vulnerability', *British Journal of Social Work*, 32(2): 149–68

Green, L. and Taylor, J. (2010) 'Exploring the Relationship Between Gender and Child Health: A Comparative Analysis of High and Low Economic Resource Countries' in B. Featherstone., C. A. Hooper., J. Scourfield and J. Taylor (eds.) *Gender and Child Welfare in Society*, Chichester: Wiley

Green S. and Baldry E. (2008) 'Building Indigenous Australian Social Work', *Australian Social Work*, 61(4): 389–402

Gusfield, J. R. (1967) 'Moral Passage', *Social Problems*, 15(2): 175–8

Hacking, I. (1991) 'The Making and Molding of Child Abuse', *Critical Inquiry*, 17(2): 253–88

Hall, P. (1976) *Reforming the Welfare: The Politics of Change in the Personal Social Services*, London: Heinemann

Hall, S., Critcher, C., Jefferson, T., Clarke, J. and Roberts, B. (eds.) (1978) *Policing the Crisis: Mugging, the State and Law and Order*, London: Macmillan

Hammersley, M. (2005) 'Is the Evidence-based Practice Movement Doing More Good than Harm? Reflections on Iain Chalmers' Case for Research-based Policy Making and Practice', *Evidence and Policy*, 1(1): 85–100

Hare, I. (2004). 'Defining Social Work for the 21st Century: The International Federation of Social Workers' Revised Definition of Social Work', *International Social Work*, 47: 407–24

Harlow, E., Berg, E., Barry, J. and Chandler, J. (2013) 'Neoliberalism, Managerialism and the Reconfiguring of Social Work in Sweden and the United Kingdom', *Organization*, 20(4): 534–50

Harris, B. (2004) *The Origins of the British Welfare State: Social Welfare in England and Wales 1800–1945*, Basingstoke: Palgrave

Harris, C. (2001) 'Beyond Multiculturalism? Difference, Recognition and Social Justice', *Patterns of Prejudice*, 35(1): 13–34

Harris, J. (1998) 'Scientific Management, Bureau-Professionalism, New Managerialism: The Labour Process of State Social Work', *British Journal of Social Work*, 28: 839–862

Harris, J. (2007) 'Looking Backward, Looking Forward: Current Trends in Human Services Management' in J. Aldgate, L. Healy, B. Malcolm, B. Pine, W. Rose and J. Seden (eds.) *Enhancing Social Work Management*, London: Jessica Kingsley

Harris, J. (2008) 'State Social Work: Constructing the Present from Moments in the Past', *British Journal of Social Work*, 38: 662–79

Harris, J. and Chou, Y.-C. (2001) 'Globalization or Glocalization? Community care in Taiwan and Britain', *European Journal of Social Work*, 4(2): 161–72

Harris, J. and Unwin, P. (2009) 'Performance Management in Modernised Social Work' in J. Harris and V. White (eds.) *Modernising Social Work: Critical Considerations*, Bristol: Policy Press

Hastings, A., Bramley, G., Bailey, N. and Watkins, D. (2012) *Serving Deprived Communities in a Recession*, York: JRF

Haug, E. (2005) 'Critical Reflections on the Emerging Discourse of International Social Work', *International Social Work*, 48(2): 126–35

Hayek, F. (1944) *The Road to Serfdom*, London: Routledge

HCPC (2013) *Consultation on Service User Involvement in Education and Training Programmes Approved by the Health and Care Professions Council (HCPC): Summary of Responses to the Consultation and our Decisions as a Result*, www.hcpcuk.org/assets/documents/10004110Consultationonserviceuserinvolvementineducationandtrainingprogrammes

Healy, K. (2014) 'Modern Critical Social Work: From Radical to Anti-Oppressive Practice' in K. Healy *Social Work Theories in Context: Creating Frameworks for Practice*, 2nd edition, Basingstoke: Palgrave Macmillan

Healy, K. and Hampshire, A. (2002) 'Social Capital: A Useful Concept for Social Work', *Australian Social Work*, 51(3): 227–31

Healy, L. M. (2007) 'Universalism and Cultural Relativism in Social Work Ethics', *International Social Work*, 50(1): 11–26

Healy, L. M. (2008) *International Social Work: Professional Action in an Interdependent World*, 2nd edition, Oxford: Oxford University Press

Healy, L. M. and Thomas, R. L. (2007) 'International Social Work: A Retrospective in the 50th Year', *International Social Work*, 50(5): 581–96

Hechter, M. and Horne, C. (2003) *Theories of Social Order: A Reader*, Stanford: Stanford University Press

Heenan, D. (2005) 'Challenging Stereotypes Surrounding Disability and Promoting Anti-Oppressive Practice: Some Reflections on Teaching Social Work Students in Northern Ireland', *Social Work Education*, 24(5): 495–510

Hegar, R. (2008) 'Transatlantic Transfers in Social Work: Contributions of Three Pioneers', *British Journal of Social Work*, 38: 716–33

Hendrick, H. (2003) *Child Welfare: Historical Dimensions, Contemporary Debate*, Bristol: Policy Press

Heraud, B. (1970) *Sociology and Social Work: Perspectives and Problems*, Oxford: Pergamon Press

Hester, M. (2011) 'The Three Planet Model: Towards an Understanding of Contradictions in Approaches to Women and Children's Safety in Contexts of Domestic Violence', *British Journal of Social Work*, 41(5): 837–53

Heywood, A. (2012) *Political Ideologies: An Introduction*, 5th edition, Basingstoke: Palgrave Macmillan

Hicks, S. (2011) *Lesbian, Gay and Queer Parenting: Families, Intimacies, Genealogies*, Basingstoke: Palgrave Macmillan

Hicks, S. (2014) 'Deconstructing the Family' in C. Cocker and T. Hafford-Letchfield (eds.) *Rethinking Anti-Discriminatory and Anti-Oppressive Theories for Social Work Practice*, Basingstoke: Palgrave Macmillan

Hier, P. (2011) 'Tightening the Focus: Moral Panic, Moral Regulation and Liberal Government', *British Journal of Sociology*, 62(3): 524–41

Higham, P. (2006) *Social Work: Introducing Professional Practice*, London: Sage

Hill Green, Y., Harris, B. and Morrow, J. (1986) *Lectures on the Principles of Political Obligation and Other Writings*, Cambridge: Cambridge University Press

Hills, J. (2013) *Labour's Record on Cash Transfers, Poverty, Inequality and the Life Cycle, 1997–2010*, Social Policy in a Cold Climate Working Paper 5, London: LSE, CASE

Hills, J. (2014) *Good Times, Bad Times: The Welfare Myth of Them and Us*, Bristol: Policy Press

Hills, J., Brewer, M., Jenkins, S., et al. (2010) *An Anatomy of Economic Inequalities in the UK: Report of the National Equality Panel*, London: Government Equalities Office

HM Government (2006) *Working Together to Safeguard Children: A Guide to Interagency Working to Safeguard and Promote the Welfare of Children*, London: The Stationery Office

HM Treasury (1991) *Competing for Quality*, Cm 1730, London: HMSO

Hodkinson, S., Watt, P. and Mooney, G. (2013) 'Introduction to Neoliberal Housing Policy: Time for a Critical Re-appraisal', *Critical Social Policy*, 33(1): 3–16

Hokenstad, M. C. and Midgely, J. (2004) 'Lessons from Other Countries: Current Benefits and Future Opportunities' in M. C. Hokenstad and J. Midgely (eds.) *Lessons from Abroad: Adapting International Social Welfare Innovations*, Washington, DC: NASW Press

Hollinsworth, D. (2013) 'Forget Cultural Competence: Ask For an Autobiography', *Social Work Education*, 32(8): 1048–60

Holt, K. and Kelly, N. (2014) 'Administrative Decision Making in Child-Care Work: Exploring Issues of Judgement and Decision Making in the Context of Human Rights, and its Relevance for Social Workers and Managers', *British Journal of Social Work*, 44(4): 1011–26

Home Office (2013) 'Domestic Violence Disclosure Scheme Guidance', https://www.gov.uk/government/uploads/system/uploads/attachment_data/file/224877/DV_Disclosure_Scheme_Guidance_-_REVISED_W.pdf

Hong, P. Y. and Song, H. (2010) 'Glocalisation of Social Work Practice: Global and Local Response to Globalization', *International Social Work*, 53(5): 656–70

Hopton, J. (2013) 'Ethical Contradictions in Critiques of Psychiatry' in M. Carey and L. Green (eds.) *Practical Social Work Ethics: Complex Dilemmas Within Applied Social Care*, Farnham: Ashgate

Hopwood, O., Pharoah, R. and Hannon, C. (2012) *Families on the Front Line? Local Spending on Children's Services in Austerity*, London: Family and Parenting Institute

Horwath, E., Stimpson, L., Barran, D. and Robinson, A. (2009) *Safety in Numbers: A Multi-Site Evaluation of Domestic Violence Advisor Services*, London: The Henry Smith Charity

Horwath, J. (2011) 'See the Practitioner, See the Child: The Framework for the Assessment of Children in Need and their Families Ten Years On', *British Journal of Social Work*, 41: 1070–87

Horwath, J. and Morrison, T. (2011) 'Effective Inter-agency Collaboration to Safeguard Children: Rising to the Challenge through Collective Development', *Children and Youth Services Review*, 33: 368–75

House of Commons (2011) *Annual Accountability Hearing with the Care Quality Commission, Ninth Report of Session 2010-2012*, London: The Stationery Office

Howe, D. (2009) *A Brief Introduction to Social Work Theory*, Basingstoke: Palgrave Macmillan

Hughes, D. (2011) 'Do Challenges to Students' Beliefs, Values and Behaviour have an Impact on their Sense of Wellbeing?' *Social Work Education*, 30(6): 686–99

Hughes, G. (1998) '"Picking over the Remains": The Welfare State Settlements of the Post-Second World War UK' in G. Hughes and G. Lewis (eds.) *Unsettling Welfare: The Reconstruction of Social Policy*, London: Routledge

Hugman, R. (1991) *Power in Caring Professions*, Basingstoke: Macmillan

Hugman, R. (2009) 'But is it Social Work? Some Reflections on Mistaken Identities', *British Journal of Social Work*, 39: 1138–53

Hugman, R. (2010) *Understanding International Social Work: A Critical Analysis*, Basingstoke: Palgrave Macmillan

Humphrey, J. C. (2003) 'New Labour and the Regulatory Reform of Social Care', *Critical Social Policy*, 23(1): 5–24

Humphreys, C. and Absler, D. (2011) 'History Repeating: Child Protection Responses to Domestic Violence', *Child and Family Social Work*, 16: 464–73

Humphries, B. (2004) 'An Unacceptable Role for Social Work: Implementing Immigration Policy', *British Journal of Social Work*, 34: 93–107

Hussein, S., Manthorpe, J. and Stevens, M. (2010) 'People in Places: A Qualitative Exploration of Recruitment Agencies' Perspectives on the Employment of International Social Workers in the UK', *British Journal of Social Work*, 40: 1000–1016

Hussein, S., Stevens, M. and Manthorpe, J. (2011) 'What Drives the Recruitment of Migrants to Work in Social Care in England?', *Social Policy and Society*, 10(3): 285–98

IASSW (2005) *Global Standards for the Education and Training of the Social Work Profession*, http://cdn.ifsw.org/assets/ifsw_65044-3.pdf

Inman, P. (2014) 'Public Sector Bosses Want to Cut their Hours', *The Guardian*, 26 November

Jay, A. (2014) *Independent Inquiry into Child Sexual Exploitation in Rotherham 1997-2013*. Rotherham: Rotherham Metropolitan Borough Council

Jeffs, T. and Smith, M. (eds.) (1983) *Youth Work*, Basingstoke: Macmillan Education

Jeyasingham, D. (2014) 'Open Spaces, Supple Bodies? Considering the Impact of Agile Working on Social Work Office Practices', *Child and Family Social Work,* advance access

Johnson, F. (2012) 'Problems with the Term and Concept of "Abuse": Critical Reflections on the Scottish Adult Support and Protection Study', *British Journal of Social Work*, 42: 833–50

Johnson, N. (1999) 'The Personal Social Services and Community Care' in M. Powell (ed.) *New Labour, New Welfare State? The 'Third Way' in British Social Policy*, Bristol: Policy Press

Johnson, P. and Kossykh, Y. (2008) *Early Years, Life Chances and Equality: A Literature Review*, Research Report 7, Manchester: Equality and Human Rights Commission

Johnson, T. (1972) *Professions and Power*, Basingstoke: Macmillan

Jones, C. (1983) *State Social Work and the Working Class*, Basingstoke: Macmillan

Jones, C. (2001) 'Voices from the Front Line: State Social Workers and New Labour', *British Journal of Social Work*, 31(4): 547–62

Jones, R. (2014) 'The Best of Times, the Worst of Times: Social Work and Its Moment', *British Journal of Social Work*, 44: 485–502

Jones, R., Bhanbhro, S., Grant, R. and Hood R. (2013) 'The Definition and Deployment of Differential

Core Professional Competencies and Characteristics in Multiprofessional Health and Social Care Teams', *Health and Social Care in the Community*, 21(1): 47–58

Jönsson, J. (2014) 'Local Reactions to Global Problems: Undocumented Immigrants and Social Work', *British Journal of Social Work*, 44 (Supplement 1): i35–i52

Jordan, B. and Drakeford, M. (2012) *Social Work and Social Policy under Austerity*, Basingstoke: Palgrave Macmillan

Joseph Rowntree Foundation (2013) *A Better Life: Valuing our Later Years*, York: JRF

JUCSWEC/APSW (2015) *APSW/JUCSWEC Response to the Implementation Proposals for Teaching Partnerships*, www.apsw.org.uk/wp-content/uploads/2015/02/jointapswjucswecresponsetoteaching partnershipfinal.pdf

Jung, S. Y. and Tripodi, T. (2007) 'Brief Note: Trends in International Social Work Research', *International Social Work*, 50(5): 691–8

Katz, I. and Hetherington, R. (2006) 'Co-operating and Communicating: A European Perspective on Integrating Services for Children', *Child Abuse Review*, 15(6): 429–39

Keeling, J. and van Wormer, K. (2012) 'Social Work Interventions in Situations of Domestic Violence: What We Can Learn from Survivors' Personal Narratives', *British Journal of Social Work*, 42(7): 1354–70

Kempe, C. H. (1968) *The Battered Child*, Chicago: University of Chicago Press

Kemshall, H. (2008) *Risk, Social Policy and Welfare*, Buckingham: Open University Press

Kemshall, H. (2010) 'Risk Rationalities in Contemporary Social Work Policy and Practice', *British Journal of Social Work*, 40(4): 1247–62

Kenway, P. (2013) *Working Families Receiving Benefits*, London: New Poverty Institute

Kitchener, M., Kirkpatrick, I. and Whipp, W. (2003) 'Supervising Professional Work under New Public Management: Evidence from an "Invisible Trade"' in J. Reynolds, J. Henderson, J. Seden, J. Charlesworth and A. Bullman (eds.), *The Managing Care Reader*, London: Routledge

Koehler, I. (2014) *Key to Care: Report of the Burstow Commission on the Future of the Home Care Workforce*, LGIU: The Local Democracy Thinktank, www.lgiu.org.uk/wp-content/uploads/2014/12/KeyToCare.pdf

Kvist, J., Fritzel, J., Hvinden, B. and Kangas, O. (eds.) (2012) *Changing Social Equality: The Nordic Welfare Model in the 21st Century*, Bristol: Policy Press

Laird, S. (2008) 'Social Work Practices to Support Survival Strategies in Sub-Saharan Africa', *British Journal of Social Work*, 38(1): 135–51

Laird, S. (2014) 'The Law, Professional Ethics and Anti-Oppressive Social Work' in C. Cocker and T. Hafford-Letchfield (eds.) *Rethinking Anti-Discriminatory and Anti-Oppressive Theories for Social Work Practice*, Basingstoke: Palgrave Macmillan

Laming, H. (2003) *The Victoria Climbié Inquiry*, London: The Stationery Office

Laming, H. (2009) *The Protection of Children in England: A Progress Report*, London: The Stationery Office

Langan, M. (1993) 'New Directions in Social Work' in J. Clarke (ed.) *A Crisis in Care? Challenges in Social Work*, London: Sage

Langan, M. and Clarke, J. (1994) 'Managing the Mixed Economy of Care' in J. Clarke, A. Cochrane and E. McLaughlin (eds.) *Managing Social Policy*, London: Sage

Lavalette, M. (2104) 'Social Work is about Complex Lives, Not Gove's Tick Box Solution', *The Guardian*, 18 February, www.theguardian.com/society/2014/feb/18/theory-needed-in-social-work-training

Le Grand, J. (1991) 'Quasi Markets and Social Policy', *The Economic Journal*, 101(408): 1256–67

Lawton-Smith, S., Dawson, J. and Burns, T. (2008) 'Community Treatment Orders are not a Good Thing', *British Journal of Psychiatry*, 193(2): 96–100

Lemert, E. (1972) *Human Deviance, Social Problems and Social Control*, Englewood Cliffs, NJ: Prentice Hall

Levitas, R. (1998) *The Inclusive Society? Social Exclusion and New Labour*, Macmillan: Basingstoke

Lewis, J. (1992) 'Gender and the Development of Welfare Regimes', *Journal of European Social Policy*, 2(3): 159–73

Lewis, J. (1997) 'Gender and Welfare Regimes: Further Thoughts', *Social Politics,* 4(2): 160–77

Lewis, J. and Campbell, M. (2007) 'Work/Family Balance Policies in the UK since 1997: A New Departure?' *Journal of Social Policy,* 36(3): 365–81

Lewis, J. and Glennerster, H. (1996) *Implementing the New Community Care,* Buckingham: Open University Press

Lewis, J. and West, A. (2014) 'Re-Shaping Social Care Services for Older People in England: Policy Development and the Problem of Achieving "Good Care"', *Journal of Social Policy,* 43(1): 1–18

Lichtenwalter, S. and Baker, P. (2010) 'Teaching about Oppression through Jenga: A Game-based Learning Example for Social Work Educators', *Journal of Social Work Education,* 46(2): 305–13

Lister, R. (2010) *Understanding Theories and Concepts in Social Policy,* Bristol: Policy Press

Living Wage Commission (2014) *Working for Poverty: The Scale of the Problem of Low Pay and Working Poverty in the UK,* http://livingwagecommission.org.uk/wpcontent/uploads/2014/02/Living-Wage-Commission-Report-v2_f-1.pdf

Local Government Association (LGA) (2007) *Putting People First: A Shared Vision and Commitment to the Transformation of Adult Social Care,* London: LGA

Lockwood, D. (1996) 'Civic Integration and Class Formation', *British Journal of Sociology,* 47(3): 531–50

Lombroso, C. and Ferrero, W. (1895) 'The Criminal as a Born Criminal Type' in *The Female Offender,* London: Fisher Unwin

Lonne, B., Parton, N., Thomson, J. and Harrier, M. (2009) *Reforming Child Protection,* London: Routledge

Lorber, J. (2010) *Gender Inequality: Feminist Theorists and Politics,* 4th edition, New York: Oxford University Press

Lorenz, W. (2001) 'Social Work Responses to "New Labour" in Continental European Countries', *British Journal of Social Work,* 31: 595–609

Lorenz, W. (2006) *Perspectives on European Social Work: From the Birth of the Nation State to the Impact of Globalization,* Opladen: Barbara Budrich Publishers

Loseke, D. R. (2010) *Thinking about Social Problems: An Introduction to Constructionist Perspectives,* 2nd edition, New Brunswick, NJ: Transaction Publishers

Lowe, R. (2005) *The Welfare State in Britain since 1945,* 3rd edition, Basingstoke: Palgrave Macmillan

Lowndes, V. and McCaughie, K. (2013) 'Weathering the Perfect Storm? Austerity and Institutional Resilience in Local Government', *Policy and Politics,* 41(4): 533–49

Lukes, S. ([1974] 2005) *Power: A Radical View,* Basingstoke: Palgrave

Lund, B. (2006) 'Distributive Justice and Social Policy' in M. Lavalette and A. Pratt (eds.) *Social Policy: Theories, Concepts and Issues,* 3rd edition, London: Sage

Lupton, R. (with John Hills, Kitty Stewart and Polly Vizard) (2013), *Labour's Social Policy Record: Policy, Spending and Outcomes 1997-2010,* Social Policy in Cold Climate Research Report 1, London: LSE, CASE

Lymbery, M. (2005) *Social Work with Older People,* London: Sage

Lymbery, M. (2010) 'A New Vision for Adult Social Care: Continuities and Change in the Care of Older People', *Critical Social Policy,* 30(1): 5–26

Lymbery, M. and Postle, K. (2010) 'Social Work in the Context of Adult Social Care in England and the Resultant Implications for Social Work Education', *British Journal of Social Work,* 40: 2502–22

Lyons, K. (1999) *International Social Work: Themes and Perspectives,* Aldershot: Ashgate

Lyons, K. (2006) 'Globalization and Social Work: International and Local Implications', *British Journal of Social Work,* 36(3): 365–80

Lyons, K., Manion, K. and Carlsen, M. (2006) *International Perspectives on Social Work: Global Conditions and Local Practice,* Basingstoke: Palgrave Macmillan

Mac an Ghaill, M. (2002) 'Beyond a Black–White Dualism: Racialisation and Racism in the Republic of Ireland and the Irish Diaspora Experience', *Irish Journal of Sociology,* 11(2): 99–122

Macdonald, F. and Midgely, J. (2006) 'Globalization, Social Justice and Social Welfare: A Call for Papers', *Journal of Sociology & Social Welfare,* 33: 1–3

MacDonald, G. and MacDonald, K. (2010) 'Safeguarding: A Case for Intelligent Risk Management', *British Journal of Social Work*, 40: 1174–91

Macdonald, G. and Turner, W. (2005) 'An Experiment in Helping Foster Carers Manage Challenging Behaviour', *British Journal of Social Work*, 35(8): 1265–82

Macey, M. and Moxon, E. (1996) 'An Examination of Anti-Racist and Anti-Oppressive Theory and Practice in Social Work Education', *British Journal of Social Work*, 26(3): 277–314

Macrae, C. N., Bodenhauser, G. V., Milne, A. B. and Jetten, J. (1994) 'Out of Mind but Back in Sight: Stereotypes on the Rebound', *Journal of Personality and Social Psychology*, 67: 808–17

Manning, N. (1987) 'What is a Social Problem?' in M. Loney (ed.) *The State or the Market: Politics and Welfare in Contemporary Society*, London: Sage

Marmot, M. (2010) *Fair Society, Healthy Lives: Strategic Review of Health Inequalities in England Post 2010*, London: Department of Health

Marshall, T. H. (1950) *Citizenship and Social Class*, Cambridge: Cambridge University Press

Martell, L. (2009) 'Global Inequality, Human Rights and Power: A Critique of Ulrich Beck's Cosmopolitanism', *Critical Sociology*, 35(2): 253–72

Martin, G. (2000) 'Social Movements, Welfare and Social Policy: A Critical Analysis', *Critical Social Policy*, 21(3): 361–83

Martin, K., Jeffes, J. and MacLeod, S. (2010) *Safeguarding Children: Literature Review*, Slough: National Foundation for Educational Research

Mayo, M. (2013) 'Providing Access to Justice in Disadvantaged Communities: Commitments to Welfare Revisited in Neo-Liberal Times', *Critical Social Policy*, 33: 679–99

McDonald, A., Postle, K. and Dawson, C. (2008) 'Barriers to Retaining and Using Knowledge in Local Authority Social Work Practice with Adults in the UK', *British Journal of Social Work*, 38: 1370–87

McLaughlin, K. (2005) 'From Ridicule to Institutionalization: Anti-Oppression, the State and Social Work', *Critical Social Policy*, 25(3): 283–305

McLaughlin, K. (2008) *Social Work, Politics and Society: From Radicalism to Orthodoxy*, Bristol: Policy Press

McLaughlin, K. and Cordell, S. (2013) 'Doing What's Best, but Best for Whom? Ethics and the Mental Health Social Worker' in M. Carey and L. Green (eds.) *Practical Social Work Ethics: Complex Dilemmas Within Applied Social Care*, Farnham: Ashgate

Middleton, S. (2011) '"I Wouldn't Change Having the Children – Not at All." Young Women's Narratives of Maternal Timing: What the UK's Teenage Pregnancy Strategy Hasn't Heard', *Sex Research and Social Policy*, 8: 227–38

Midgely, J. (1997) *Social Welfare in Global Context*, Thousand Oaks, CA: Sage

Mill, J. S. ([1859] 1989) *On Liberty and Other Writings*, ed. S. Collini, Cambridge: Cambridge University Press

Mitchell, W., Franklin, A., Greco, V. and Bell, M. (2009) 'Working with Children with Learning Disabilities and/or Who Communicate Non-Verbally: Research Experiences and their Implications for Social Work Education, Increased Participation and Social Inclusion', *Social Work Education*, 28(3): 309–24

Mooney, G. (2006) 'New Labour and the Management of Welfare' in M. Lavalette and A. Pratt (eds.) *Social Policy: Theories, Concepts and Issues*, 3rd edition, London: Sage

Moran, A., Nancarrow, S. and Butler, A. (2005) 'There's No Place like Home: A Pilot Study of Perspectives of International Health and Social Care Professionals Working in the UK', *Australia and New Zealand Health Policy*, 2:25

Morgan, P. (1995) *Farewell to the Family? Public Policy and Family Breakdown in Britain and the USA*, London: Institute of Economic Affairs

Moss, P. and Petrie, P. (2002) *From Children's Services to Children's Spaces*, London: Routledge

Mullen, E., Shlonsky, A., Bledsoe, S. and Bellamy, J. (2005) 'From Concept to Implementation: Challenges Facing Evidence-based Social Work', *Evidence and Policy*, 1(1): 61–84

Munn, M. (2014) 'Plans to Allow Outsourcing of Child Protection Will Put Young People at Risk', *The Guardian*, 2 September

Munro, E. (2010a) *The Munro Review of Child Protection Part One: A Systems Analysis*, London: DfE

Munro, E. (2010b) 'Learning to Reduce Risk in Child Protection', *British Journal of Social Work*, 40: 1135–51

Munro, E. (2011) *The Munro Review of Child Protection: Final Report*, Cm 8062, London: TSO

Murray, C. (1990) *The Emerging British Underclass*, London: Institute of Economic Affairs

Nadan, Y. and Ben-Ari, A. (2013) 'What Can We Learn From Rethinking Multiculturalism in Social Work Education?' *Social Work Education*, 32(8): 1089–102

Narey, M. (2014) *Making the Education of Social Workers Consistently Effective*, London: DfE

Nash, K. (2009) 'Between Citizenship and Human Rights', *Sociology*, 43(6): 1067–83

National Audit Office (2013) *Programmes to Help Families Facing Multiple Challenges*, London: TSO

Needham, C. (2011) 'Personalisation: From Story-line to Practice', *Social Policy and Administration*, 45(1): 54–68

Needham, C. and Glasby, J. (2014) 'Taking Stock of Personalisation' in C. Needham and J. Glasby (eds.) *Debates in Personalisation*, Bristol: Policy Press

Nixon, J. and Parr, S. (2009) 'Family Intervention Projects and the Efficacy of Parenting Interventions' in M. Blyth and E. Solomon (eds.) *Prevention and Youth Crime: Is Early Intervention Working?* Bristol: Policy Press

Nussbaum, M. C. (2011) *Creating Capabilities: The Human Development Approach*, Cambridge, MA: Harvard University Press

O'Brien, M., Bachmann, M., Husbands, C., et al. (2006) 'Integrating Children's Services to Promote Children's Welfare: Early Findings from the Implementation of Children's Trusts', *Child Abuse Review*, 15: 377–95

Office of National Statistics (2006) *Focus on Ethnicity and Religion*, Houndmills: Palgrave Macmillam

Ofsted (2013) *Annual Report 2012–13: Social Care*, Manchester: Ofsted

Ofsted (2015) *Integrated Inspections: Consultation Outcomes, Learning from Pilot Inspections and Next Steps* (Ref: 150031), Manchester: Ofsted

Okitikpi, T. and Aymer, C. (2010) *Key Concepts in Anti-discriminatory Practice*, London: Sage

Open University (2011) 'Social Problems: Who Makes Them?' *Open University, Open Learn*, www. open.edu/openlearn/society/politics-policy-people/sociology/social-problems-who-makes-them/content-section-0

Oppenheim, C. (1997) 'The Growth of Poverty and Inequality' in A. Walker and C. Walker (eds.) *Britain Divided: The Growth of Social Exclusion in the 1990s*, London: CPAG

Osborne, G. (2012) Speech to annual Conservative Party conference, Birmingham, 8 October, www. newstatesman.com/blogs/politics/2012/10/george-osbornes-speech-conservative-conference-full-text

Ottosdottir, G. and Evans, R. (2014) 'Ethics of Care in Supporting Disabled Forced Migrants: interactions with professionals and ethical dilemmas in health and social care in the south east of England', *British Journal of Social Work*, 44 (Supplement 1): i53–i69.

Park, R. E., Burgess, E. W. and McKenzie, R. D. (1967) *The City*, Chicago: University of Chicago Press

Parrott, B., MacIver, A. and Thoburn, J. (2007) *Independent Inquiry into the Circumstances of Child Sexual Abuse by Two Foster Carers in Wakefield*, Wakefield: Wakefield County Council

Parry, N. and Parry, J. (1979) 'Social Work Professionalism and the State' in N. Parry, M. Rustin and C. Satyamurti (eds.) *Social Work, Welfare and the State*, London: Edward Arnold

Parton, C. and Parton, N. (1989) 'Child Protection, the Law and Dangerousness' in O. Stevenson (ed.) *Child Abuse, Public Policy and Professional Practice*, Hemel Hempstead: Harvester Wheatsheaf

Parton, N. (1996) *Social Theory, Social Change and Social Work*, London: Routledge

Parton, N. (2009) 'From Seebohm to Think Family: Reflections on 40 Years of Policy Change of Statutory Children's Social Work in England', *Child and Family Social Work*, 14: 68–78

Parton, N. (2011) 'Child Protection and Safeguarding in England: Changing and Competing Conceptions of Risk and their Implications for Social Work', *British Journal of Social Work*, 41(5): 854–75

Pascall, G. (2008), 'Gender and New Labour: After the Male Breadwinner Model?' in T. Maltby, P. Kennett and K. Rummery (eds.) *Social Policy Review 20*, Bristol: Policy Press

Payne, G. (ed.) (2015) *Social Divisions*, 3rd edition, Basingstoke, Palgrave

Payne, M. (1996) *What is Professional Social Work?* Birmingham: Venture Press

Payne, M. and Askeland, G. A. (2008) *Globalization and International Social Work: Postmodern Change and Challenge*, Aldershot: Ashgate

Pearson, G. (1975) *The Deviant Imagination: Psychiatry, Social Work and Social Change*, London and Basingstoke: Macmillan

Penna, S. (2003) 'Policy Contexts of Social Work in Britain: The Wider Implications of "New" Labour Policy and the "New Legal Regime"', *Social Work and Society*, 1(1): 37–51

Penna, S. and O'Brien, M. (2006) 'What Price Social and Health Care? Commodities, Competition and Consumers', *Social Work and Society*, 4(2): 217–31

Petch, A., Cook, A. and Miller, E. (2013) 'Partnership Working and Outcomes: Do Health and Social Care Partnerships Deliver for Users and Carers?' *Health and Social Care in the Community*, 21(6): 623–33

Pfau-Effinger, B. and Rostgaard, T. (2011) 'Welfare-state Change, the Strengthening of Economic Principles, and New Tensions in Relation to Care', *Nordic Journal of Social Research*, 2, Special Issue, 1–6.

Philp, M. (1979) 'Notes on the Form of Knowlede in Social Work', *The Sociological Review*, 27(1): 83–111

Pierson, J. (2001) *The New Politics of the Welfare State*, Oxford: Oxford University Press

Pincus, A. and Minahan, A. (1973) *Social Work Practice: Mode and Method*, Itasca, IL: Peacock

Pinker, R. (1983) 'Social Work Is Casework' in T. Philpott (ed.) *A New Direction For Social Work? The Barclay Report and Its Implications*, Sutton: Community Care / IPC Business Press

Pinkney, S. (1998) 'The Restructuring of Social Work and Social Care' in G. Hughes and G. Lewis (eds.) *Unsettling Welfare: The Reconstruction of Social Policy*, London: Routledge

Pithouse, A. (1987) *Social Work: The Social Organization of an Invisible Trade*, Aldershot: Avebury

Platt, A. M. (1969) *The Child Savers: The Invention of Delinquency*, Chicago: University of Chicago Press

Ploesser, M. and Mecheril, P. (2011) 'Neglect – Recognition – Deconstruction: Approaches to Otherness in Social Work', *International Social Work*, 55(6): 794–808

Pollitt, C. (2003) 'Joined-up Government: A Survey', *Political Studies Review*, 1: 34–49

Postle, K. (2002) 'Working "Between the Idea and the Reality": Ambiguities and Tensions in Care Managers' Work', *British Journal of Social Work*, 32(3): 335–51

Poulantzas, N. (1975) *Classes in Contemporary Capitalism*, London: New Left Books

Powell, M. (1999) 'Introduction' in M. Powell (ed.) *New Labour, New Welfare State?* Bristol: Policy Press

Powell, M. and Doheny, S. (2006) 'In Search of the Citizen Consumer', paper presented at Conference on Citizenship and Consumption: Agency, Norms, Mediations and Spaces, Trinity Hall, Cambridge, 30 March – 1 April

Powell, J. and Robison, J. (2007) 'The "International Dimension" in Social Work Education: Current Developments In England', *European Journal of Social Work*, 10(3): 383–99

Pratt, A. (2006) 'Neo-liberalism and Social Policy' in M. Lavalette and A. Pratt (eds.) *Social Policy: Theories, Concepts and Issues*, 3rd edition, London: Sage

Preston-Shoot, M. (2011) 'On Administrative Evil-doing within Social Work Policy and Services: Law, Ethics and Practice', *European Journal of Social Work*, 14(2): 177–94

Pugh, R. (1998) 'Attitudes, Stereotypes and Anti-Discriminatory Education: Developing Themes from Sullivan', *British Journal of Social Work*, 28: 939–59

Putnam, R. (2001), *Bowling Alone: The Collapse and Revival of American Community*, London: Touchstone

Quinney, R. (1977) *Class, State and Crime: On the Theory and Practice of Criminal Justice*, New York: David McKay Co.

Rajan-Rankin, S. and Beresford, P. (2011) 'Observations on the Munro Review of Child Protection', *Social Work Action Network*, Newsletter 4, Autumn 2011

Rattansi, D. (1992) 'Changing the Subject: Racism, Culture and Education' in J. Donald and A. Rattansi (eds.) *Race, Culture and Difference*, London: Oxford University Press

Rawls, J. (1971) *A Theory of Justice*, Cambridge, MA: Harvard University Press

Rawls, J. (1999) *The Law of Peoples*, Cambridge, MA: Harvard University Press

Reisch, M. (2013) 'Social Work Education and the Neo-Liberal Challenge: The US Response to Increasing Global Inequality', *Social Work Education*, 32(6): 715–33

Reisch, M. and Jani, S. J. (2012) 'The New Politics of Social Work Practice: Understanding Context to Promote Change', *British Journal of Social Work*, 42: 1132–50

Robinson, K. and Webber, M. (2013) 'Models and Effectiveness of Service User and Carer Involvement in Social Work Education: A Literature Review', *British Journal of Social Work*, 43: 935–44

Robinson, L. (2005) 'Practice Issues: Working with Children of Mixed Parentage' in T. Okitikpi (ed.) *Working with Children of Mixed Parentage*, Lyme Regis: Russell House Publishing

Rogowski, S. (2010) *Social Work: The Rise and Fall of a Profession?* Bristol: Policy Press

Rose, J. (2011) 'Dilemmas of Inter-professional Collaboration: Can They Be Resolved?' *Children & Society*, 25: 151–63

Rosenhan, D. (1973) 'On Being Sane in Insane Places', *Science*, 179(4070): 250–8

Roskill, C. (2011) 'Research in Three Children's Services Authorities' in C. Ashley (ed.) *Working with Risky Fathers: Fathers Matter*, Volume III: *Research Findings on Working with Domestically Abusive Fathers and Their Involvement with Children's Social Care Services*, London: Family Rights Group

Rowlingson, K. and Connor, S. (2011) 'The "Deserving" Rich? Inequality, Morality and Social Policy', *Journal of Social Policy*, 40(3): 437–52

Rowlingson, K. and McKay, S. (2012) *Wealth and the Wealthy: Exploring and Tackling Inequalities between Rich and Poor*, Bristol: Policy Press

Rubington, E. and Weinberg, S. (eds.) (2003) *The Study of Social Problems: Seven Perspectives*, 6th edition, Oxford: Oxford University Press

Rush, M. and Keenan, M. (2014) 'The Social Politics of Social Work: Anti-Oppressive Social Work Dilemmas in Twenty-First-Century Welfare Regimes', *British Journal of Social Work*, 44(6): 1436–53

Rutter, D., Francis, J., Coren, E. and Fisher, M. (2010), *SCIE Systematic Research Reviews: Guidelines*, 2nd edition, SCIE Research Resource 1 www.scie.org.uk/publications/researchresources/rr01.pdf

Ryan, M., Fook, J. and Hawkins, L. (1995) 'From Beginner to Graduate Social Worker: Preliminary Findings from an Australian Longitudinal Study', *British Journal of Social Work*, 25: 17–35

Ryan, W. (1976) *Blaming the Victim* New York: Vintage Books

Sakamoto, I. and Pitner, R. O. (2005) 'Use of Critical Consciousness in Anti-Oppressive Social Work Practice: Disentangling Power Dynamics at Personal and Structural Levels', *British Journal of Social Work*, 35(4): 435–52

Sale, A. U. (2002) 'Workers of the World', *Community Care*, www.communitycare.co.uk/Articles/2002/07/18/37250/workers-of-the-world.html

Saltkjel, T. and Malmberg-Heimonen, I. (2014) 'Social Inequalities, Social Trust and Civic Participation – the Case of Norway', *European Journal of Social Work*, 17(1): 118–34

Sautman, B. (1996) 'Theories of East Asian Intellectual and Behavioral Superiority and Discourses on "Race Differences"', *Positions*, 4(3): 519–67

Scheper-Hughes, N. (1992) *Death without Weeping*, Berkeley: University of California Press

Scheyett, A. and Kim, M. (2004) 'Using Facilitated Dialogue to Positively Change Student Attitudes towards Persons with Mental Illness', *Journal of Teaching in Social Work*, 24(1–2): 39–54

Schraer, R. (2014) 'Academics Criticise Frontline "For a Worrying Lack of Clarity"', *Community Care*, 14 October, www.communitycare.co.uk/2014/10/26/group-academics-criticises-frontline-evaluation-worrying-lack-clarity

SCIE (2013) *Fair Access to Care Services (FACS): Prioritising Eligibility for Care and Support*, Guide 33, London: SCIE

SCIE (2014) 'Care Act Presentation Transcript', www.scie.org.uk/care-act-2014/files/care-act-presentation-transcript.pdf?res=true

Scourfield, J. (2006) 'Gendered Organizational Culture in Child Protection Social Work', *British Journal of Social Work*, 51(1): 80–2

Scourfield, P. (2007) 'Social Care and the Modern Citizen, Consumer, Service User, Manager and Entrepreneur', *British Journal of Social Work*, 37: 107–22

Scourfield, P. (2012) 'Caretelization revisited and the lessons of Southern Cross', *Critical Social Policy*, 32(1): 137–48

Seebohm, F. (1968) *Report of the Committee on Local Authority and Allied Personal Social Services*, London: HMSO

Seed, P. (1973) *The Expansion of Social Work in Britain*, London: Routledge

Seidman, S. (2005) 'From Outsider to Citizen' in E. Bernstein and L. Shaffner (eds.) *Regulating Sex: The Politics of Intimacy and Identity*, New York: Routledge

Sellick, C. (2011) 'Privatising Foster Care: The UK Experience within an International Context', *Social Policy and Administration*, 45(7): 788–805

Sen, A. (2009) *The Idea of Justice*, London: Allen Lane

SEU (Social Exclusion Unit) (2004) *The Social Exclusion Unit*, London: Office of the Deputy Prime Minister

Sewpaul, V. (2006) 'The Global–Local Dialectic: Challenges For African Scholarship and Social Work in a Post-Colonial World', *British Journal of Social Work*, 36(3): 419–34

Sheldon, B. (2001) 'The Validity of Evidence-based Practice in Social Work: A Reply to Steven Webb', *British Journal of Social Work*, 31: 801–09

Simmons, H., Mafile'o, T., Webster, J., Jakobs, J. and Thomas, C. (2007) 'He Wero: The Challenge of Putting your Body on the Line: Teaching and Learning in Anti-Racist Practice', *Social Work Education*, 27(4): 366–79

Simpson, G. and Connor, S. (2011) *Social Policy for Social Welfare Professionals: Tools for Understanding, Analysis and Engagement*, Bristol: Policy Press

Singh, G. and Cowden, C. (2011) 'Multiculturalism's New Fault Lines: Religious Fundamentalism and Public Policy', *Critical Social Policy*, 31(3): 343–64

Singh, G. and Cowden, S. (2013) 'Is Cultural Sensitivity Always a Good Thing? Arguments for a Universalist Social Work', in M. Carey and L. Green (eds.) *Practical Social Work Ethics: Complex Dilemmas Within Applied Social Care*, Farnham: Ashgate

Skegg, A. (2005) 'Brief Note: Human Rights and Social Work: A Western Imposition or Power to the People?' *International Social Work*, 48(5): 667–72

Skills for Care South West (2007) *Manager's Guidebook on Employing Overseas Workers*, Leeds: Skills for Care South West

Small, J. (1991) 'Ethnic and Racial Identity in Adoption within the United Kingdom', *Adoption and Fostering*, 15(4): 9–14

Smith, C. (2001) 'Trust and Confidence: Possibilities for Social Work in "High Modernity"', *British Journal of Social Work*, 31(2): 287–305

Smith, J. R. (2013) 'Students' Role Confusion when Working with Older Adults: The Voices of Foundation Students', *Journal of Social Work Education*, 49(2): 250–64

Social Mobility and Child Poverty Commission (2014) *State of the Nation 2014: Social Mobility and Child Poverty in Great Britain*, London: HMSO, https://www.gov.uk/government/uploads/system/uploads/attachment_data/file/365765/State_of_Nation_2014_Main_Report.pdf

Solas, J. (2008) 'Social Work and Social Justice: What Are We Fighting For?' *Australian Social Work*, 61(2): 124–36

Sowell, T. (2005) *Affirmative Action Around the World: An Empirical Study*, New Haven: Yale University Press

Spandler, H. (2004) 'Friend or Foe? Towards a Critical Assessment of Direct Payments', *Critical Social Policy*, 24(2): 187–209

Spatscheck, C. (2012) 'Creating Capabilities: The Human Development Approach', *European Journal of Social Work*, 15(3): 413–15

Spicker, P. (1993) 'Needs as Claims', *Social Policy and Administration*, 27(1): 7–17

Spicker, P. (2008) *An Introduction to Social Policy*, Aberdeen: The Robert Gordon University

Spicker, P. (2013) 'Personalisation Falls Short', *British Journal of Social Work*, 43(7): 1259–75

Spicker, P. (2014) *Social Policy: Theory and Practice*, Bristol: Policy Press

Stanford, S. (2010) '"Speaking Back" to Fear: Responding to the Moral Dilemmas of Risk in Social Work Practice', *British Journal of Social Work*, 40: 1065–80

Stanley, N., Austerberry, H., Bilson, A., et al. (2012) *Social Work Practices: Report of the National Evaluation Research Report*, DFE-RR233, London: Department for Education

Stanley, N., Manthorpe, J. and Penhale, B. (eds.) (1999) *Institutional Abuse: Perspectives across the Life Course*, London: Routledge

Statham, J., Cameron, C. and Mooney, A. (2006) *The Tasks and Roles of Social Workers: A Focused Overview of Research Evidence*, London: Thomas Coram Research Unit

Steckley, L. (2012) 'Touch, Physical Restraint and Therapeutic Containment in Residential Child Care', *British Journal of Social Work*, 42(3): 537–55

Stevenson, O. (ed.) (1999) *Child Welfare in the UK 1948–1998*, Oxford: Blackwell Science

Stoy, V. (2014) 'Worlds of Welfare Services: From Discovery to Exploration', *Social Policy and Administration*, 48(3): 343–60

Subramanian, S. V. and Kawachi, I. (2006) 'Whose Health is Affected by Income Inequality? A Multilevel Interaction Analysis of Contemporaneous and Lagged Effects of State Income Inequality on Individual Self-rated Health in the United States', *Health Place*, 12(2): 141–56

Sullivan, E. (1998) 'Dip. S.W. Students and Anti-Discriminatory Practice: Questions of Learning Outcomes and Assessments', *British Journal of Social Work*, 28: 745–61

Sutherland, E. H. and Cressey, D. R. (1966) *Principles of Criminology*, 7th edition, Chicago: IL, Lippincott

SWTF (Social Work Task Force) (2009) *Building a Safe, Confident Future: The Final Report of the Social Work Task Force*, London: SWTF

Tanner, D. (2003) 'Older People and Access to Care', *British Journal of Social Work*, 33(4): 499–515

Taylor, I., Walton, P. and Young, J. (1973) *The New Criminology: For a Social Theory of Deviance*, Abingdon: Routledge

Taylor, N. (2008) 'Obstacles and Dilemmas in the Delivery of Direct Payments to Service Users with Poor Mental Health', *Practice: Social Work in Action*, 20(1): 43–55

Taylor-Gooby, P. (2008) *Re-framing Social Citizenship*, Oxford: Oxford University Press

Taylor Gooby, P. (2011) 'Taking Advantage: Informal Social Mechanisms and Equal Opportunity Policies', *International Journal of Sociology and Social Policy*, 31(5/6): 253–71

TCSW (2014) 'Survey Reveals People's Worsening Mental Health as Benefit Cuts, Unemployment and Poor Housing Affect Communities', press release, 5 March, www.tcsw.org.uk/pressrelease.aspx?id=8589947367

Thackrah, D. H. and Thompson, S. C. (2013) 'Refining the Concept of Cultural Competence: Building on Decades of Progress', *The Medical Journal of Australia*, 199(1): 35–8

Thane, P. (1996) *Foundations of the Welfare State*, 2nd edition, London: Longman

Theriot, M. T. and Lodato, G. A. (2012) 'Attitudes about Mental Illness and Professional Danger among New Social Work Students', *Journal of Social Work Education*, 48(3): 403–23

Thoburn, J., Chand, A. and Procter, J. (2005) *Child Welfare Services for Minority Ethnic Families: The Research Reviewed*, London: Jessica Kingsley

Thomas, D. N. (1983) *The Making of Community Work*, Hemel Hempstead: George Allen & Unwin

Thomas, W. I. and Znaniecki, F. (1927) *The Polish Peasant in Europe and America*, New York: Dover Publications

Thompson, N. (2003) *Promoting Equality: Challenging Discrimination and Oppression*, 2nd edition, Basingstoke: Palgrave Macmillan

Timmins, N. (2001) *The Five Giants: A Biography of the Welfare State*, London: Harper Collins

Tizard, B. and Phoenix, A. (1993) *Black, White or Mixed Race? Race and Racism in the Lives of Young People of Mixed Parentage*, London: Routledge

Toynbee, P. and Walker, D. (2010) *The Verdict: Did Labour Change Britain?* London: Granta

Trussell Trust (2015) 'Foodbank Use Tops One Million for First Time Says Trussell Trust', www.trus selltrust.org/resources/documents/Press/Trussell-Trust-foodbank-use-tops-one-million.pdf

Trygged, S. (2010) 'Balancing the Global and Local: Some Normative Reflections on International Social Work', *International Social Work*, 53(5): 644–55

Tsang, A. K. T., Sin, R., Jia, C. and Yan, M. C. (2008) 'Another Snapshot of Social Work in China: Capturing Multiple Positioning and Intersecting Discourses in Rapid Movement', *Australian Social Work*, 61(1): 72–87

Turner, B. S. (1997) 'Citizenship Studies: A General Theory', *Citizenship Studies*, 1(1): 5–18

UNICEF (2007) *Child Poverty in Perspective: An Overview of Child Well-being in Rich Countries*, Innocenti Report Card 7, Florence: UNICEF Innocenti Research Centre

United Nations Committee on the Rights of the Child (UNCRC) (2008) *Consideration of Reports submitted by States Parties under Article 44 of the Convention. United Kingdom of Great Britain and Northern Ireland* CRC/C/GBR/CO/4, www2.ohchr.org/english/bodies/crc/docs/ AdvanceVersions/CRC.C.OPAC.GBR.CO.1.pdf

US Department of State (2014) *Trafficking in Persons Report 2014*, www.state.gov/j/tip/rls/ tiprpt/2014/?utm_source=NEW+RESOURCE:+Trafficking+in+Persons+R

Van Ewijk, H. (2010) *European Social Policy and Social Work: Citizen-Based Social Work*, London: Routledge

Van Zoonen, L. (2013) 'From Identity to Identification: Fixating the Fragmented Self', *Media, Culture and Society*, 35(1): 45–51

Waaldijk, B. (2011) 'Social Work between Oppression and Emancipation: Histories of Discomfort and Inspiration in Europe', *Social Work and Society*, 9(2): 1–16

Wade, L. (2011a) 'The Politics of Acculturation: Female Genital Cutting and the Challenge of Building Multicultural Democracies', *Social Problems*, 58(4): 518–37

Wade, J. (2011b) 'Preparation and Transition Planning for Unaccompanied Asylum-seeking and Refugee Young People: A Review of Evidence in England', *Children and Youth Services Review*, 33(12): 2424–30

Wagner, A. and Yee, J. Y. (2011) 'Anti-Oppression in Higher Education: Implicating Neo-liberalism', *Canadian Social Work Review*, 28(1): 89–105

Walby, S. and Allen, J. (2004) *Domestic Violence, Sexual Assault and Stalking: Findings from the British Crime Survey*, Research Study 276, London: Home Office Research, Development and Statistics Directorate

Walby, S., Armstrong, J. and Strid, S. (2012) 'Intersectionality: Multiple Inequalities in Social Theory', *Sociology*, 46(2): 224–40

Walker, A. and Walker, C. (eds.) (1998) *Britain Divided*, London: Child Poverty Action Group

Walker, M. (2013) 'Difference and Diversity' in P. Dwyer and S. Shaw (eds.) *An Introduction to Social Policy*, London: Sage

Walton, R. G. and Abo El Nasr, M. M. (1988) 'The Indigenization and Authentization of Social Work in Egypt', *Community Development Journal*, 23(3): 148–55

Washington, R. E. (1990) 'Brown Racism and the Formation of a World System of Racial Stratification', *International Journal of Politics, Culture and Society*, 4(2): 209–27

Waters, M. C. and Kasinitz, P. (2010) 'Discrimination, Race Relations and the Second Generation', *Social Research*, 77(1): 101–32

Webb, S. (2001) 'Some Considerations on the Validity of Evidence-based Practice in Social Work', *British Journal of Social Work*, 31: 57–79

Webb, S. (2003) 'Local Orders and Global Chaos in Social Work', *European Journal of Social Work*, 6(2): 191–204

Webb, S. (2006) *Social Work in a Risk Society: Social and Political Perspectives*, Basingstoke: Palgrave Macmillan

Webber, M. and Robinson, J. (2012) 'The Meaningful Involvement of Service Users and Carers in Advanced Level Post-Qualifying Social Work', *British Journal of Social Work*, 42: 1256–75

Weiss, I., Gal, J., Ram, A. C. and Maglajlic, I. (2002) 'Where Does it Begin? A Comparative Perspective on the Professional Preferences of First-year Social Work Students', *British Journal of Social Work*, 32: 598–608

Welbourne, P. (2009) 'Twenty-First Century Social Work: The Influence of Political Context on Public Service Provision in Social Work Education and Service Delivery', *European Journal of Social Work*, 14(3): 403–20

Welshman, J. (1999) 'The Social History of Social Work: The Issue of the "Problem Family", 1940–1970', *British Journal of Social Work*, 29: 457–76

White, S. (2007) *Equality*, Cambridge: Polity

White, S. and Featherstone, B. (2005) 'Communicating Misunderstandings: Multi-agency Work as Social Practice', *Child and Family Social Work*, 10(3): 207–16

White, S., Hall, C. and Peckover, S. (2009) 'The Descriptive Tyranny of the Common Assessment Framework: Technologies of Categorisation and Professional Practice in Child Welfare', *British Journal of Social Work*, 39: 1197–217

White, S., Wastell, D., Broadhurst, K. and Hall, C. (2010) 'When Policy O'erleaps Itself: The "Tragic Tale" of the Integrated Children's System', *Critical Social Policy*, 30(3): 405–29

Whiteside, N. (2012) 'The Liberal Era and the Growth of State Welfare' in P. Alcock, M. May and S. Wright (eds.) *The Student's Companion to Social Policy*, 4th edition, Oxford: Wiley-Blackwell

Wiggan, J. (2012) 'Telling Stories of 21st Century Welfare: The UK Coalition Government and the Neo-liberal Discourse of Worklessness and Dependency', *Critical Social Policy*, 32(3): 383–405

Wilkinson, R. and Pickett, K. (2009) *The Spirit Level: Why More Equal Societies Almost Always Do Better*, London: Allen Lane

Wilkinson, R. and Pickett, K. (2010) *The Impact of Income Inequalities on Sustainable Development in London*, London: Greater London Authority

Willetts, D. (2010) *The Pinch: How the Baby Boomers took their Children's Future and How They Can Give it Back*, London: Atlantic Books

Williams, C. and Graham, M. (2014) '"A World on the Move": Migration, Mobilities and Social Work', *British Journal of Social Work*, 44 (Supplement 1): i1–i17

Williams, F. (1989) *Social Policy: A Critical Introduction*, Chichester: Wiley

Williams, F. (2001) 'In and Beyond New Labour: Towards a New Political Ethics of Care', *Critical Social Policy*, 21(4): 467–93

Williams, F. (2010) 'Migration and Care: Themes, Concepts and Challenges', *Social Policy and Society*, 9(3): 385–96

Wilson, K., Ruch, G., Lymbery, M. and Cooper, A. (2011) *Social Work: An Introduction to Contemporary Practice*, Harlow: Pearson Education

Winkelmann, J., Rodrigues, R. and Leichsenring, K. (2014) *To Make or to Buy Long-term Care II: Lessons from Quasi-markets in Europe*, European Centre Policy Brief, Vienna: European Centre for Social Welfare Policy and Research

Wood, M., Hales, J., Purdon, S., Sejersen, T. and Hayllar, L. (2009) *A Test for Racial Discrimination in Recruitment Practices in British Cities*, Department for Work and Pensions Research Report 607, www.natcen.ac.uk/media/20541/test-for-racial-discrimination.pdf

Woodroffe, K. (1962) *From Charity to Social Work*, London: Routledge

Wooton, B. (1959) *Social Science and Social Pathology*, London: George Allen and Unwin

Wrennall, L. (2010) 'Surveillance and Child Protection: De-mystifying the Trojan Horse', *Surveillance and Society*, 7(3/4): 304–24

Wrennall, L. (2013) 'Where Did We Go Wrong? An Analysis of Conflicts of Interest, Perverse Financial Incentives and NOMBism' in M. Carey and L. Green (eds.) *Practical Social Work Ethics: Complex Dilemmas within Applied Social Care*, Farnham: Ashgate

Wright-Mills, C. (1956) *The Power Elite*, Oxford: Oxford University Press

Yan, M. C. (2005) 'Journey to International Social Work: A Personal and Professional Reflection', *Reflections*, 11(1): 4–16

Yancey, G. (2005) '"Blacks Cannot be Racists": A Look at how European-Americans, African-Americans and Asian-Americans Perceive Minority Racism', *Michigan Sociological Review*, 19: 138–54

Yeates, N. (2009) *Globalizing Care Economies and Migrant Workers*, Basingstoke: Macmillan

Yeates, N. (2012) 'Global Social Policy' in J. Baldock, L. Mitton, N. Manning and S. Vickerstaff (eds.) *Social Policy*, 4th edition, Oxford: Oxford University Press

Yeates, N. (ed.) (2014) *Understanding Global Social Policy*, 2nd edition, Bristol: Policy Press

Yee, J. Y. and Wagner, A. E. (2013) 'Is Anti-Oppression Teaching in Canadian Social Work a Form of Neo-Liberalism?' *Social Work Education*, 32(3): 331–48

Yip, K. S. (2004) 'A Chinese Cultural Critique of the Global Qualifying Standards for Social Work Education', *Social Work Education*, 23(5): 597–612

Young, I. M. (1990) *Justice and the Politics of Difference*, Princeton, NJ: Princeton University Press

Young, J. (1971) *The Drugtakers: The Social Meaning of Drug Use*, London: MacGibbon and Kee

Index

Note: page numbers in italics refer to tables or figures